Bohemian
Decorated
Porcelain

Dr. James D. Henderson

4880 Lower Valley Road, Atglen, PA 19310 USA

DEDICATION

The rapid advance of global communication via electronic mail and the internet's World Wide Web has made collaboration with others possible to an extent that was unheard of only a few years ago. Just such an opportunity occurred when I made contact with Dr. Dagmar Braunová, Curator of Applied Art, West Bohemia Museum in Plzeň (Plisen). I had found a book entitled *Porcelánová tradice* published by Dr. Braunová in 1992. Through my friend Dr. Michael Boubelik in Praha (Prague), I was able to locate Dr. Braunová. Since she did not speak English and I speak no Czech, Michael served as our interpreter. In October of 1996, my wife and I visited Dagmar and Michael and toured the porcelain factories and museums in the Karlovy Vary area. Much of the historical research on the early factories have been described in Dagmar's book which was published in the Czech Republic. She consented to allow me access to numerous photographs and factory documents that otherwise would not have been available.

Dr. Braunová was born in Plzeň and graduated from the School of Applied Art and Ceramics in Karlovy Vary (Karlsbad) where she majored in applied art in ceramics and porcelain production. Her graduate work in Greek and Roman archeology and art history was completed at Charles University in Praha where she was granted a doctoral degree. Dr. Braunová is the author of books on Bohemian porcelain, Renaissance and Baroque glass, and antique vases of the Crimea. She has published several papers in international journals, written many exhibition catalogs, and prepared traveling exhibits to other countries.

This book is dedicated to Dagmar and to her efforts to maintain Bohemia's porcelain tradition.

Library of Congress Cataloging-in-Publication Data

Henderson, James D. (James Drynan), 1941-
 Bohemian Decorated Porcelain / James D. Henderson.
 p. cm.
 Includes bibliographical references.
 ISBN 0-7643-0746-0 (hardcover)
 1. Porcelain, Czech--Collectors and collecting--Czech Republic--Bohemia--Catalogs. I. Title.
NK4541.C92B644 1999
738.1'094371'075--dc21   98-51421
                                                            CIP

Designed by Ian Robertson
Type set in Euroslavic LS/Times

ISBN: 0-7643-0746-0
Printed in China
1,2,3,4

Published by Schiffer Publishing Ltd.
4880 Lower Valley Road
Atglen, PA 19310
Phone: (610) 593-1777; Fax: (610) 593-2002
E-mail: Schifferbk@aol.com
Please visit our web site catalog at www.schifferbooks.com

This book may be purchased from the publisher.
Please include $3.95 for shipping.
Please try your bookstore first.
We are interested in hearing from authors
with book ideas on related subjects.
You may write for a free catalog.

In Europe, Schiffer books are distributed by
Bushwood Books
6 Marksbury Rd.
Kew Gardens
Surrey TW9 4JF England
Phone: 44 (0)181 392-8585; Fax: 44 (0)181 392-9876
E-mail: Bushwd@aol.com

TABLE OF CONTENTS

ACKNOWLEDGMENTS

Many people made this book possible. I'd like to thank my wife and best friend, Marge, for her continued support and encouragement throughout this project. She helped immensely with the photographic arrangements of the porcelain pieces and the review of the photos after they were taken. I am especially indebted to my friend and colleague, Dr. Michael Boubelik, at the Czech Academy of Science, Prague, Czech Republic, who has served as my interpreter and contact with sources in Bohemia. A very special thank you is in order to Robert Röntgen who so graciously allowed me to reproduce many of his factory marks. His book, *Marks on German, Bohemian and Austrian Porcelain–1710 to the Present*, stands as the premier reference on this subject. Alan Reed shared his photographic secrets and provided several porcelain trade catalogs that have been invaluable in determining proper descriptions of pieces. I would like to thank my friend Dorothy Kamm for her support and review of my manuscript, and for graciously agreeing to write the Foreward for this book. I also wish to thank my daughter-in-law, Nancy Henderson, who reviewed the manuscript and provided clarifying comments.

Reference materials were provided by the helpful staff and librarians at the Milwaukee Public Library; Peter Van Tassel at the Dukes County Historical Society, Martha's Vineyard, MA; Chicago Historical Society Research Library; Gail Bard at the Radkow Library, Corning Museum of Glass, Corning, NY; Linda Naru, Center for Research Libraries, Chicago, IL; Julie Gores, Interlibrary Loan Librarian, Medical College of Wisconsin, Milwaukee, WI, who spent numerous hours requesting the loan of microfilm and documents from other libraries; Carol Sandler at the Strong Museum library, Rochester, NY, for copies of trade publications; Richard Downes, General Manager, Ivy House Paper Mills, Stoke-on-Trent, UK, for copies of business addresses and maps of early porcelain factories in the Karlovy Vary area; and Paul Makousky and others at the Czechoslovak Genealogical Society International, St. Paul, MN, for geographical information on western Bohemia.

A special thanks goes to Joan Adler of the Straus Historical Society who provided numerous documents concerning the history of the Straus and Gutherz families and to Dr. Edgar Gordon, his sister Eva Hopwood and cousin Renny Freundlich, all descendents of Oscar Gutherz, for family photos and other information about the Gutherz brothers. I am also indebted to Ron Rapelje who provided information about the Ebling and Reuss import business.

Translation support was provided by Dr. Joseph Baboriak who unselfishly gave of his time, Zuzana Griswold, Ruth Hartmann, and Ondrej Zoltan–without their assistance this project would not have been realized.

Several individuals provided porcelain pieces for photography or supplied photographs. These included Leanne and Dick Carlson at Times Remembered Antiques, Nisswa, MN; Maureen Farmer; Dorothy Kamm; Jim and Vivian Karsnitz; Traci Phillips, Fifth Avenue Antiques, Milwaukee, WI; Alan Reed; Richard Rendall who also loaned me reference books from his collection; and Barbara Wade, Legacies, Ltd., Fox Point, WI.

Many individuals, antique shops and malls permitted the photography of backstamps. These included: The Gas Works Antique Mall, Foley, AL; The Gift Horse Antiques, Foley, AL; Antique America Mall, Davenport, IA; Majestic Lion Antique Center, Des Moines, IA; Betty Knuth's Antiques & Collectables, Story City, IA; Corn Country Antiques, Walnut, IA; Don's Antiques, Walnut, IA; Country Treasures Antique Mall, Walnut, IA; Everybody's Attic Antique Mall, Walnut, IA; E & M Antique Mall, Dixon, IL; General Store Antiques, Galesburg, IL; Heartland Antique Mall, Geneseo, IL; Trinkets & Treasures, Peoria, IL; East State Street Antique Malls I & II, Rockford, IL; River Bend Antique Mall, Bowling Green, KY; Louisville Antique Mall, Louisville, KY; Bittersweet Antiques, Berwick, ME; Peter Engelman, Baltimore, MD; Antiques at Anthony's, Bloomington, MN; Country Side Antique Mall, Cannon Falls, MN; 4th Street Antiques, Cannon Falls, MN; Hallet Antique Emporium, Crosby, MN; Linda's Collectables, Crosby, MN; Antiques Minnesota, Minneapolis/St. Paul, MN; Country Coll'age Antiques, Nisswa, MN; Lake Country Antiques, Nisswa, MN; Times Remembered Antiques, Nisswa, MN; Antiques Oronoco, Oronoco, MN; Old Rooster Antiques, Rochester, MN; Antique Mall on Third St., Rochester, MN; Peoples Antiques, St. Paul, MN; Deborah Mazza, Somersworth, NH; Fox River Antique Mall, Appleton, WI; The Harp Gallery, Appleton, WI; Olde Orchard Antique Mall, Egg Harbor, WI; Legacies, Ltd., Fox Point, WI; Miracle on 58th Street, Kenosha, WI; Lake Geneva Antique Mall, Lake Geneva, WI; Milwaukee Antique Center, Milwaukee, WI; Antique Mall of Portage; Portage, WI; Broadway Antiques Mall, Monona, WI; Janet's Antiques, Madison, WI; and Downtown Antique Shops, Ltd., Stevens Point, WI.

FOREWORD

In 1980, Jim and Marge Henderson received a set of 15 plain white place settings with simple gold bands, along with some other decorative ware, all marked with the "O.&E.G. Royal Austria" backstamp. What started as a simple quest to uncover the history of these porcelain pieces that arrived at the family farm at the turn of the last century resulted in a fascinating international adventure nearly 20 years in the making. The result is *Bohemian Decorated Porcelain*, the definitive text relating to Bohemian porcelain.

After reading this book, you will be able to identify, date, and determine the value of Bohemian porcelain. However, *Bohemian Decorated Porcelain* is more than a basic price guide. Henderson went to great lengths to share the history as it relates to the manufacturers, the methods of decoration employed and the key artists involved, and the American china painting market as well as European decorating studios. As a china painter, a collector, and author of two books on American painted porcelain, this subject is of particular interest to me.

It seems unbelievable that it has taken nearly a century to address this subject given that a hundred years ago Americans created a multi-million dollar demand for Bohemian porcelain. However, it is understandable given the fragmentation of resources, the language barrier, the geographical distance, and the ravages of two world wars.

A veterinarian and researcher by training, Henderson was the ultimate person to tackle this daunting task. His persistent nature has led to the development of a broad base of knowledge of the available resources and the ability to pursue questions until satisfactorily answered. His interest in genealogy and his familiarity with the process of retrieving family documents were necessary to locate people who were privy to data pertaining to the manufacturers and distributors. With the help of the Internet and the information highway, he was able to procure contacts in Bohemia (now the Czech Republic) to get to the source of production and even traveled there to meet these people and tour porcelain factories.

Bohemian Decorated Porcelain provides invaluable scholarship about the porcelain tableware and decorative objects that remain such an important part of our backgrounds. Whether these objects were incorporated into our grandparents' homes or purchased at antique shops or estate sales, here is a reference that provides much of the needed facts.

Until recently, only the giants in the porcelain industry were covered. For too long porcelain literature has focused on Germany, France, England, and the Orient, neglecting important areas of the world whose contributions were just as significant. Considering the amount of porcelain manufactured in other countries and the critical commodity they were for American china painters, *Bohemian Decorated Porcelain* is a unique and significant reference that should be part of every collector's, antique dealer's, and historian's library. It provides essential knowledge for understanding the complete story regarding porcelain production and decoration throughout the world.

Dorothy Kamm

PREFACE

Porcelain collectors have numerous choices when price is considered. Pieces of RS Prussia are currently valued at several hundred dollars and Pickard pieces may sell for several thousand. The more modest collector may develop an interest in Bohemian china since prices generally are less than $100 per piece. Specialty pieces may of course have much higher values. In 1900, most of the porcelain produced in Karlovy Vary was for household use (utility ware) and sold to middle class Americans through importers and distributors on the East Coast.

Great sentimentality is often attached to the ownership of porcelain dinnerware. The people who purchase it set it out to show it off to their neighbors, serve their best friends a tastefully prepared meal on it, carefully wash it, and treasure the memories it evokes when used. Two of the sets of dinnerware that we purchased serve as examples. In one case, the woman at the consignment shop contacted the 75-year-old owner of a set for us. This woman told her she had inherited the porcelain in 1950, from her great aunt who had received it in Germany as a wedding gift. The owner then began to cry as she recounted the event. In another case, the dinnerware was being sold to help pay for the owner's nursing home expenses.

When we first acquired a set of dinnerware from my wife's Aunt Hannah, I checked the backstamp in several china mark books and found little written about the company. Later, I discovered that one of the owners worked in a decorating studio in Limoges, France, and had been granted design patents on porcelain pieces by the United States Patent and Trademark Office. Through Czech contacts, I established the location of the buildings where the porcelain was produced.

As porcelain production expanded throughout Europe in the late 1800s, the area around Karlovy Vary became the center of china export primarily to the United States as well as other European countries. Nearby kaolin, feldspar, and coal deposits made for the easy acquisition of raw materials. Just as Bohemian porcelain manufacturing reached a pinnacle, the controlling Habsburg monarchy was declining. The fate of porcelain production in Karlovy Vary and the rest of Europe was closely linked to the fall of the Austro-Hungarian Empire. With the assassination of Archduke Franz Ferdinand at Sarajevo on June 28, 1914, Europe was plunged into war. By 1916, little to no European manufactured porcelain was reaching North America, and when the war ended a severe depression began. Local porcelain factories were forced to consolidate or go out of business—a trend which continued through the end of World War II and the rise of communism. Today, the Habsburg legacy is found in antique shops scattered across America.

Thus, the collection of porcelain is also a collection of history. I've often wondered when picking up a piece of Bohemian porcelain, tucked away on the dusty shelf of an antique shop, just who were the people that made it possible—from the clay miners to the potters and decorators, to the salesmen, the crews of the ships and trains that carried it to America, the freight haulers and handlers, and finally to the young boy from the village hardware store who brought the wood crate of china to my wife's great-great aunt in central Minnesota. Today, there are no collectors' clubs for Bohemian export porcelain nor books in English devoted to the subject. This book describes and illustrates how porcelain was produced in a small central European country, exported to America, and enjoyed by generations of families across the land.

INTRODUCTION

Snow was gently falling on the clapboard farmhouse just north of the small central Minnesota town. It was November, 1905. The early morning chores had been done, the cows milked, and the farmer's wife was setting the dining room table. She laid out the porcelain dinnerware she had purchased that summer through a china distributor's catalog. She remembered that summer of 1905, how hot it had been, and the young traveling salesman that had come knocking on her door.

He had a small sauce dish in his valise that he had showed her. The lightweight translucent porcelain was beautifully decorated with a deep gold band on the bowl's rim. Although expensive, she had ordered a set of 100 pieces for $15 and was assured it would be delivered in time for Thanksgiving. Just last week, the delivery boy from the village hardware store had brought the large wood crate out to the farm. As the pieces of dinnerware emerged from the straw surrounding each piece, she was pleased that all of it had survived the journey without breaking.

Fourteen people would soon be gathering around the table for a festive Thanksgiving feast. The dinnerware had been manufactured by the Oscar and Edgar Gutherz factory located in Stará Role (Altrohlau), Bohemia, during the previous year and shipped to America. Years passed and the china–hand washed after each holiday meal and carefully stacked in the china cabinet–passed to the farmer's daughter, then to her son, and in 1980 to my wife, Marge.

With this gift began nearly two decades of china collecting and research into the history of Bohemian porcelain factories. Our collecting has taken us to out-of-the-way places from coast to coast, introduced us to numerous people we otherwise would never have met, and provided us with countless hours of entertainment, searching through flea markets, antique shops, and malls. Our collection of Gutherz Royal Austria porcelain has grown from the original set of dinnerware to hundreds of pieces.

In this book, we share our collection with you and describe the history of production and exportation of porcelain from factories around Karlovy Vary (Karlsbad), Bohemia, from the early 1800s to the present.

Nowhere else has a country's government and geographic names been so influenced by its neighbors. Wars, invasions, and occupations over the years have resulted in frequent changes of town and street names, languages spoken, and ownership of land and property. Between 1800 and 1945 the area of western Bohemia, or the Sudetenland as it was later called, was under German influence and control. The porcelain factories were for the most part owned by German Jews. Throughout these difficult times the Czech people have maintained their culture and pride.

Certain conventions are used throughout this book. Since the language of commerce was German, for purposes of clarity the Bohemian town names are written in Czech with the German name in parentheses the first time they are used. Since the original names of factories were in German, these have been translated into English. Owner names have been retained using the original German spelling. In the Photography chapter, factory names are in upper case followed by dates of operation. Artists' names are italicized and decorating studio names are in parentheses. The use of "Schleiger numbers" refers to Haviland & Co. china patterns and shapes compiled and published by Donna Schleiger. The terms "china" and "porcelain" are used synonymously throughout the book.

Values that accompany pieces shown throughout the book reflect dealer prices, published price guides, or actual prices paid. Condition of items, buyer interest, and geographic location have a great impact on values of porcelain. These values only represent the opinion of the author. Neither the author nor publisher assumes any responsibility for any losses that a collector may incur while using this guide.

Peter Nelson home, near Grove City, Minnesota, in 1907. Many rural farm families purchased Bohemian porcelain through mail order catalogs.

BOHEMIAN PORCELAIN PRODUCTION

Overview Of Porcelain Manufacturing

Although primitive fired clay vessels have been found in archeological sites more than 7,000 years old, the invention of porcelain dates back to the Chinese Han period, 206 B.C. to 220 A.D. Iranian and Chinese potters produced earthenware as early as 5500 to 5000 B.C. Portuguese traders first brought the Chinese ware to Europe and called it *porcellana*, a derivation of the Italian word porcella, or cowrie shell, literally "a little pig," referring to the smooth compact texture and whiteness it was thought to resemble. When clay is baked hard, it is called earthenware. When more heat is applied, the clay becomes nonporous and is called stoneware. When a mixture of fine clay, feldspar, and quartz are combined and heated to 1,300 to 1,400 degrees Celsius, the materials fuse together forming a vitrified, translucent substance called "hard paste porcelain." Europeans classified porcelain into two groups: true porcelain — hard paste or *pâte dura* and artificial — soft paste or *pâte tendre*.

The fine grained clay used in porcelain manufacturing is called *kaolin*, a French term taken from the Chinese word *kao-ling*, meaning "high place", and the name of a mountain near Ching-tê-Chên in northern China where this white clay was first discovered. Kaolin, a hydrated aluminum silicate is the result of the decomposition of feldspar. High quality deposits of kaolin are free from iron and turn pure white when fired.

Feldspars are a group of minerals widely distributed around the world. The orthoclase-type of feldspar used in porcelain production is called petuntse or china stone. Petuntse binds the kaolin particles together during the firing process.

As deposits of kaolin and feldspar were discovered in Europe, porcelain factories sprung up around them. Kaolin is found in Sedlec (Zettliz), Karlovy Vary (Karlsbad), Plzeň (Pilsen), and Chodov (Chodau) in western Bohemia; several areas in Germany; Denmark, Italy, Spain, Russia; Cornwall, England; and near Limoges, France. The French, when first attempting to duplicate the Chinese process in the 1600s, developed soft paste porcelain. A mixture of ground glass and clay was heated to 1,100 degrees Celsius, allowed to cool, and then a lead glaze applied and the object reheated or "fired" at a lower temperature. The English mixed calcined bone with kaolin and feldspar around the year 1800 and the result was English bone china.

After the kaolin is taken from the mine, it is washed thoroughly with water in a churning machine, then floated in large ponds where the coarse particles are removed. It is important that all iron particles be removed during this process, since on firing, these deposits create black spots in the porcelain. The kaolin suspension is reduced by extracting water from it in cloth filter presses. Stone crushers, crushing rollers, and drum mills are used to reduce feldspar and quartz to dust.

The mixture of kaolin, quartz, feldspar, and water is known as the body composition or mass. In the early days of porcelain production, the exact composition of the body and glaze was a trade secret. This was known only to the owners and the manufacturing superintendent. Secret charging scales were used so the workers shoveling the raw materials into the weighing box couldn't determine the formula. Those that knew or professed to know the secret of porcelain manufacturing were called "arcanists."

Hard paste porcelain is usually a mixture of 40 to 65 percent kaolin, 12 to 30 percent quartz, and 15 to 35 percent feldspar. Kaolin is pliable and very resistant to heating in a kiln. Feldspar and quartz increase the plasticity of kaolin as shrinkage occurs after firing. The latter two also act as a flux to fuse the components together.

The finished slurry mixture is called "slip." The preparation of the clay mixture is done in a building known as a "slip-house." Large cylinders in the slip-house are used to grind the feldspar and quartz (also called flint). All of these materials are placed in large mixing tanks called "blungers." The blunged body is then passed over fine screens called "lawns." Magnets are then used to remove iron particles from the slurry. Water is removed from the slurry by using a large filter press, which consists of an iron or wood frame containing numerous canvas sheets. The filter-pressed clay is then "pugged" to remove air bubbles and compress the clay into a homogenous mass in a kneading machine. After pugging, the clay may be stored for aging in "clay cellars" to increase its plasticity. Just before use, it is re-pugged.

In Bohemian factories, porcelain pieces were formed using four different techniques. Many of these methods are still in use today. Plates, saucers, bowls, vases, and cups, which had a cylindrical shape, were usually turned on the potter's wheel and shaped by hand or mechanical aids. Later, they were produced in molds by skilled potters known as "jiggermen." Gypsum (plaster of Paris) molds were used for the inside or concave surface of flat articles, such as plates and saucers. The lower part of the flat piece, which was turned bottom-side up in the turning process, was shaped with a metal pattern that was pressed against the rotating mass until the extra paste was removed and the desired thickness achieved. Molds were also used to produce items of the same size and shape such as figurines, non-cylindrical cups, and candlesticks. Vases, teapots, covered vegetable bowls, platters, tureens, serving bowls, hollow ware, and other odd-shaped pieces were made from molds. The procedure involved making a clay model of the object. Plaster of Paris was used to make a mold of the object. Frequently, a number was placed on the bottom of the mold that transferred to the piece. Sometimes several mold sections were required to allow removal of the piece. The kaolin mixture containing some soda was poured into the mold. The plaster cast absorbed water as the mixture or "slip" was drying, causing it to shrink away from the sides of the mold. After a time, the slip was poured off and the mold removed from the formed piece. The longer the slip remained in contact with the mold, the thicker the wall of the piece. Smaller parts could be molded separately and then joined together with the main pieces using a thin slip paste. Individuals performing these tasks were known as "repairers." Handles, most other projecting parts, plastic ornaments, and reliefs of tableware and other objects were also molded. They were then embossed or attached to the main piece by a worker known as a "sticker-up."

After an object was formed, it was placed in a kiln along with other pieces and fired. In Bohemian factories in the early 1900s, women did most of this work. Inside the kiln was a box or ring of firebrick called a "sagger." The function of the sagger was to protect the pieces from coming in contact with ashes and flames and help provide proper stacking in the kiln. None of the pieces could touch each other during the firing process. Porcelain was fired two or more times, depending on the quality and degree of painting and gilding desired. The first firing reached a temperature of 800 to 1,000 degrees Celsius (1,500 to 1,800 degrees Fahrenheit). This "glow burning" eliminated all the moisture and hardened the pieces sufficiently for handling. Porcelain in this state was commonly called "glowpaste" or biscuit and was brittle and porous, which enabled the liquid glaze to be easily absorbed. The glaze was composed of the same material that was used for making porcelain, except that more feldspar and other fluxes were added to promote fusion. In the dipping process, a piece was uniformly covered with a thin layer of the fluid-glaze material. The water in the glaze was soon absorbed by the dry porous piece, which then took on a powdered appearance. After glazing, a second or "sharp" firing was made at 1,400 to

1,450 degrees Celsius (2,500 to 2,700 degrees Fahrenheit) causing the porcelain to attain its distinctive and final state. Now the piece appeared hard, white, fine-textured, translucent, impervious surface, and was low-heat conducting.

Glaze resulting in an opaque yellow or cream matt finish was called ivory ware. This type of glazing was used by several Bohemian factories including the Carl Knoll factory in Rybáře and the Gutherz and "Victoria" Schmidt factories in Stará Role. Porcelain ware was decorated either underglaze after the first firing or overglaze after the second firing. The diagram below illustrates the process.

Sometimes porcelain was not glazed and was called "biscuit ware". In this case, the raw ingredients were more finely ground and more feldspar was added.

Porcelain production was not an exact science in spite of the strict controls placed on the ingredients used. Manufacturing defects during the 1800s and early 1900s were commonplace. Quality control was sometimes lax in determining which pieces to destroy.

Defects were divided into various categories according to a detailed description published in a 1915 United States Department of Foreign and Domestic Commerce report entitled *A Report on the Cost of Production in the Earthenware and China Industry of the United States, England, Germany and Austria.* Common glaze defects included crazing, peeling, pinholes, blistering, dryness, unevenness, running, and spitting out. In spitting out, the glaze was rough and contained little black specks. Defects in clay ware included cracks, crooked ware, hollows or lumps, variable thicknesses, differences in size, and roughness.

Kiln defects could occur during the first firing when biscuit was produced, or during the second firing after the biscuit had been dipped in glaze. Brown or yellow biscuit resulted from incorrect placement and failure to wad the saggers correctly, allowing flame to flash the ware. Wadding involved placing lumps of clay in the open spaces between the blocks of firebrick. Cracked pieces could occur if ware was fired too rapidly when first placed in the kiln. Iron spots resulted from a poorly washed clay body. Pieces which when removed from the kiln during the second firing stuck to the stilts they had been placed upon during firing were known as "plucked ware."

Due to the intense heat used to fire porcelain, pieces frequently warped in the kiln. The early Bohemian factories had to overcome a number of problems when switching over to porcelain manufacturing from stoneware or earthenware production. Large oval dishes were quite difficult to produce. Porcelain had to be left unglazed wherever it touched other pieces in the kiln. Covers for tureens or other oval ware were fired on the body so that warping was controlled and the pieces fit each other. This process prohibited making replacement covers for oval hollow ware. Round covered pieces could be fired separately with the body turned upside down so the foot could be glazed.

Bohemian Porcelain Production

A German alchemist, Johann Friedrich Böttger (1682–1719), developed hard paste porcelain in Europe in 1708. Two years later the first porcelain factory was built in Meissen. The Vienna factory was established in 1718. In 1792, the first Bohemian factory was established in Horní Slavkov (Schlaggenwald).

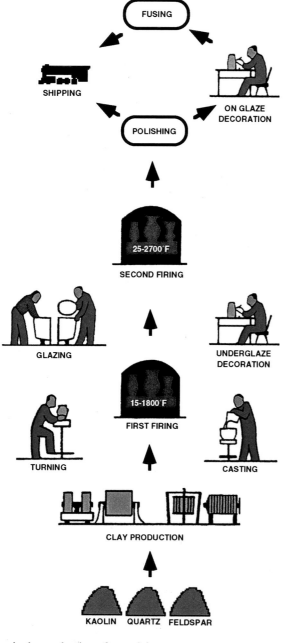

Steps in the production of porcelain.

Raw Material Development

The production of porcelain in western Bohemia was delayed for nearly seventy-five years due to stringent controls exercised by the Imperial-Royal Manufactory in Vienna. The Habsburg monarchy thought that only the state-owned factory could compete with the major factories in Germany.

The government aggressively prosecuted owners of stoneware factories in Bohemia. Those that tried to produce porcelain without gaining approval from the Court Commercial Councillor had their factories destroyed. In 1793, Gottlieb Sontag sought a license from Vienna to produce porcelain in Háje (Rabensgrün). He was denied permission even though he said he was the only one in Bohemia who could make porcelain. A nearby factory owner in Horní Slavkov, Johann Georg Paulus, informed the local government in Loket (Elbogen) that he also could make porcelain. Over the next 19 years, things progressed rather slowly at the Paulus factory. As a result of a special peace treaty signed on September 26, 1811, Austria seceded the kaolin producing area near Passau to Germany. This stimulated the monarchy to mount geological expeditions into northwestern Bohemia in search of raw materials to continue Viennese porcelain production.

The German mineralogist Friedrich Mohs was commissioned to explore the region. Mohs is best known for developing the Scale of Hardness used to identify minerals in the field. The scale which ranges in ascending order of hardness from 1 to 10, places talc (soapstone) as the softest and diamond as the hardest. Mohs was successful in locating deposits of kaolin and feldspar at several sites in western Bohemia.

During the early 1800s, the monarchy encouraged local citizens in the area to construct porcelain factories. Due to the lack of expertise, it was very difficult to get these businesses started. In the beginning, small private undertakings by local people were unsuccessful, but with German assistance the factories developed. The first stoneware factory was established between 1789 and 1793. Later, factories were established in eight towns from 1792 to 1815 (see chapter on Karlovy Vary Area Factories).

Clay mining in Bohemia actually began as early as 1470 in Počerny (Putschirn), a small village about 2 miles west of Karlovy Vary. The Sedlec kaolin mine was opened in 1803 by Christian Nonne (1731–1813) who came from Thuringia, Germany. Sedlec, located one mile northwest of Karlovy Vary, served as the source of kaolin for many of the porcelain factories that later developed in the region.

Early mining was done by hand. The shallow subsurface kaolin deposits made open pit mining feasible in the region.

Kaolin was transported by horse and wagon to a location nearby, where it was ground and floated or washed. This process was done to remove impurities. Western Bohemian kaolin was of such high quality that it was exported to other countries, in addition to being used for local stoneware and porcelain production. Kaolin from these areas was well-known for its freedom from iron and tin impurities, as well as its good plasticity and liquifiablity. Kaolin production is still one of the region's largest industries.

Feldspar, another raw material, was quarried in Andélsá Hora (Engelhaus), a village about 15 miles east of Karlovy Vary, as well as other localities in the region.

The Paulus factory finally received a license to manufacture porcelain in 1812. During the 60 years from 1789 to 1849, 30 potteries were established in Bohemia. Growth of the industry then leveled off until a period of rapid expansion occurred between 1896 and 1912 when 20 new factories were built. This coincided with a large increase in exports of Austrian porcelain to the United States. By 1913, there were 71 factories making earthenware, stoneware, or porcelain in Bohemia. Many of these were located around the Karlovy Vary region due to the availability of kaolin, feldspar, flint, and coal.

Occupational Considerations

The 1915 United States Department of Foreign and Domestic Commerce report described the methods used to manufacture Bohemian porcelain during the late 1800s and early 1900s. These were similar to those employed by the Germans and Austrians.

As in any specialized industry, a whole system of nomenclature was developed over the centuries in earthenware and porcelain factories to describe the functions of the workers. Porcelain manufacturing was very labor intensive, with some 61 different occupations described in Bohemian factories in 1914. About 50 percent of the labor force were women and girls under 16. These workers were paid on average about 40 to 50 percent less than male workers in similar occupations.

Work in these factories was quite physical and demanding. Employees worked 55 to 60 hours a week, generally from 7 A.M. to 6 P.M. In one factory the hours of labor were stated as follows: *From 7 A.M. to noon with a quarter hour intermission from 8:45 A.M. to 9 A.M., and from 1:30 P.M. to 6 P.M. without pause. On Saturday the day shall end at 4 P.M. On the days preceding Easter, Whitsuntide, Christmas, and New Year work shall continue until noon. At 6:45 A.M. a preliminary signal and at 7 A.M. a final signal for beginning work shall be given. Late comers will be fined in accordance with section 15 of the factory regulations (satisfactory excuses for lateness will be taken into consideration). Employees will be permitted to leave their work places 5 minutes before 12 and 5 minutes before 6 for the purpose of cleaning up, and for this purpose a signal will be given. A second signal for leaving the pottery premises shall also be given. Employees are not permitted to leave the pottery premises during the forenoon pause.*

Bohemian earthenware and porcelain workers were exposed to significant hazards in the factories. Over the four year period from 1908 to 1911, 6,200 cases of illness were reported by the China Pottery Workers' Union. Of these cases, 1,250 were

The largest kaolin deposit in Europe is found in this open pit mine at Kaznějov, near Plzeň. 1983 *Glass Review* 38(4): 5.

thought to be due to tuberculosis and 787 were due to other diseases of the respiratory organs. Of the 343 deaths occurring from 1908 to 1912, 192 (56 percent) were diagnosed as TB. The average age at death was 38 to 39 years. In addition, the Union reported 24 cases of lead poisoning in the years between 1908 and 1911. The illnesses were caused by the inhalation of dust from grinding the raw materials, kaolin mixing, and porcelain manufacturing processes. The use of lead oxide in glaze mixtures caused exposure by inhalation and direct contact when hand dipping the ware into liquid glaze.

Workers making plates were called plate jiggermen. A fast worker could make just over 90 dinner plates an hour and earned about $0.11/hour. The batters-out and mold runners were unskilled occupations and assisted the jiggerman. The batters-out was required to produce a piece of clay body in the proper shape for the jiggerman. To do this he would pull off a piece of clay weighing about 1 3/4 pounds, put it in a ball shape on a circular plaster block under the batting machine, and bring the batting profile down on the ball of clay to spread it out into a uniform thickness and smooth the surface of the clay. This was repeated for each plate made by the jiggerman. The mold runner placed the mold containing the finished plate on a drying shelf, returned empty molds to the batters-out, and carried green ware to and from the finisher. In this process, he might lift as much as 5 tons during the day and walk about 5 to 10 miles depending on the plant layout. These workers earned around $0.03/hour. About 40 percent of porcelain factory workers earned less than United States workers in similar occupations. Wages for Bohemian workers averaged about 4 to 5 times less than workers in the United States.

Factory Development

From the beginning in 1792, Bohemian factories had to overcome several economic, developmental, and technical problems. The early factories were influenced by German workers and produced porcelain in late Baroque and Classical styles (see chapter on Porcelain Decoration Methods). The porcelain was of poor quality and a gray or yellowish color and contained numerous impurities which were very obvious after firing. Decorating was of poor quality as well. Designs included birds on a rock or strawflower decoration in cobalt blue or purple (see chapter on Porcelain Decorating Methods).

Bohemian influence in porcelain production began between 1805 and 1820. It was a combination of the German and Viennese forms with a French influence. The quality of the porcelain improved. This was a result of the factories exporting and competing with other countries, as well as improved firing techniques. Early designs and decorations were of mythological, allegorical, and romantic scenes as well as copies from almanac drawings by August Piepenhagen (1791–1868). Piepenhagen, a lithographer, was born in Germany but spent his adult life in Prague. He created many Alpine romantic scenes. Early Bohemian porcelain decorators included J. Ramberg, J. Flasch, J. Ender, and V. Morstadt.

Miniature paintings of almanac scenes from Karlovy Vary were popular, especially from 1815 to 1835. The factory in Horní Slavkov created many of these pieces. Empire cups with raised serpentine handles were frequently decorated with three lines on the bottom or miniature target-like paintings. Decoration of cups and tableware with colored miniatures distinguished Horní Slavkov porcelain from other factories. Bohemian factories had

numerous local painters decorating these wares with copies of Renaissance art and scenic views of Bohemian landscapes and towns.

Hand decoration of Bohemian porcelain flourished between 1840 and 1860. Waltraud Neuwirth lists at least 350 individuals that were employed as porcelain decorators in the Karlovy Vary region. Some artists worked for several different factories during their careers. Many decorators were members of the same family and their artistic skill was commonly passed from father and mother to son or daughter. Artists frequently worked in their own homes and were paid according to the number of pieces they decorated. The table below shows the number of decorators working in Karlovy Vary area towns between 1840 and 1914.

Town	No. of Decorators
Březová (Pirkenhammer)	46
Dalovice (Dallwitz)	6
Horní Slavkov (Schlaggenwald)	69
Karlovy Vary (Karlsbad)	12
Klášterec (Klösterle)	30
Loket (Elbogen)	95
Rybáře (Fischern)	16
Stará Role (Altrohlau)	32

Several of these professional decorators later immigrated to the United States where they were employed by American studios like W.A. Pickard in Chicago. One such individual was John Blažek (1887–?). According to Alan Reed's book, Blažek was trained at the Royal Porcelain Factory in Prague (probably in Smichov, a southwestern suburb) and later was employed in factories in the Karlovy Vary area. He came to the United States in 1905.

A large number of spa cups were produced for visitors traveling to the region's spa towns. These specially designed cups permitted the sipping of hot mineral water through the handle. This practice continues today. In 1828, very large vases were produced principally for export. The Bohemian factories began to compete in expositions and won several prizes for excellence. Prizes were awarded in 1829 and 1831 to the Horní Slavkov factory for exceptional decoration, the Březová factory for originality of form and the Loket factory for perfection of the quality of material.

In time, other factories in Bohemia received permission to produce porcelain. Moving from familiar German ribbed, bellied, or cylindrical shapes in blue underglaze, by the 1830s artists were painting on Classic Revival and Rococo designed cups and vases. Hand painted decoration was slow and costly. In the 1840s, the factories begin using transfer designs on Rococo Revival-styled ware.

The period from 1835 to 1860 was the so-called "plastic phase," named such for the forms used to create new shapes. As the factories expanded, there was a need to consider the tastes of the common person or middle class rather than just the nobility. In a desire to mimic the nobility, the middle class gave preference to some of the older styles. The Rococo style, popular at a time when limited amounts were made just for the privileged class, became popular again. The commercial aspects of production had to be considered as well as the artistic. At this time, several factories changed from stoneware to porcelain production. These included factories in Budov (Buda), Dalovice, Dolní Chodov (Chodau), Doubí (Aich), Rybáře, and Stará Role.

BLEUET ET COQUELICOT

Two shepherdesses dressed as a bluebonnet (bachelor's button) and a corn poppy dance to music played by crickets in this lithograph by J. J. Grandville.

Around the middle of the 1800s small figurines became popular. These were produced in the Karlovy Vary, Loket, and Horní Slavkov factories. Later, the factories began to imitate the German Meissen style, which included idealized children's figures, birds, and idyllic scenes in costumes. Religious figures (especially of Christ and the twelve Apostle's) were produced in this style, which in turn were reproductions of the marble figures in Rome. Personification of flowers were common, with ladies faces on the flowers. Lithographs from J. J. Grandville's *Les fleurs animees* (Animated Flowers) were used as patterns for porcelain designs. Grandville (1803–1847) was a well-known graphic artist in France at the beginning of the Second Empire.

The Klášterec factory produced sets of dinnerware, especially Imperial sets from 1851, Ferdinand's style of coffee sets from 1854, and Thun from 1856. The style names were associated with the nobility who requested them. Imperial sets were produced for the court in Vienna; Thun sets for Count Thun, the owner of the factory; and Ferdinand's style for the Habsburg emperor. These took prizes in Munich, Berlin, London, Paris, and Vienna expositions.

The development of artistic forms peaked in 1860 and then started to decline, largely due to banks and other investors in the factories who wanted greater profitability. This led to mass production with commercial application and less artistic quality. As a result of increased mechanization in all the factories which reduced handwork, the feeling was that the aesthetic aspect also was reduced. During the 1870s, Biedermeier shapes were popular. Some factories tried to return to more hand production during the 1870 to 1885 period of Historicism, which was then called pseudo-Rococo, but this was done only to a limited degree.

Typical Karlovy Vary factory-produced dinnerware, known as "Carlsbad China" in the 1880s and 1890s, had a heavy appearance due to the relative thickness of the plates and hollow ware. By 1900, however, styles had changed to lightweight, thin-walled, translucent pieces which challenged the best Limoges-manufactured ware.

From the late 1890s to 1910, factory owners started to think of developing more original Bohemian designs. The idea failed to gain a foothold since it didn't assure much financial success. Some small versions of these pieces were produced in factories in Březová, Loket, Klášterec, and Ostrov (Schlackenwerth).

During this time, many of the Karlovy Vary area factories were manufacturing similar shapes of household ware for export, including the popular Donetello shape first produced by the Rosenthal factory in Selb, Bavaria, and later trademarked in 1920. The Thomas shape was trademarked in 1922 by the Rosenthal company. Derby, Thomas, Victoria, Iowa, Huyler, and Kermes were all shape names associated with sugar bowls and creamers, salt dips, tea cups, or dresser sets. Several of these shapes were created by the Haviland company in Limoges and copied by Bohemian factories.

In 1910, attempts were made to create a Vienna Work Center to bring together commercial design and aesthetic interests. However, it was difficult to combine functional use with aesthetic design. In Loket, Březová, and Ostrov, the attempt was made and was to some degree successful, though it was largely an attempt at revived styles rather than something new.

After World War I, development continued as before. New Baroque, Rococo, and Empire styles were produced without higher aesthetic consideration. Cubism with typical geometric and asymmetric shapes was also attempted, but not many were interested in it. Art Deco designs were introduced in 1925, but also failed to develop much commercial interest.

In 1930, designs focused on clean shapes and product utility was stressed. This was known as "functionalism." Examples from Praha (Prague) were called *Topic Salon*. Trade schools were developed to teach people how to produce porcelain products. Again, these were only produced in limited series for a small number of people. In 1929, the factories produced a new coffee service in a limited series and decorative porcelain by Jan Lichtac, a teacher from the trade school in Praha. About 99 percent of the porcelain produced, however, was of standard design.

Between 1918 and 1938, factories concentrated on porcelain for hotels. These pieces were thicker and decorated with many different patterns. Wares included coffee, tea, and dinner sets. Decorations varied depending on the price of the wares and the colors of the porcelain, including blue, red, ivory, and whiteware.

In the late 1930s, there were 9,500 people working in Karlovy Vary area porcelain factories and five different companies, twelve large factories and sixteen smaller factories. Capacity was about 1,300 tons of porcelain a month.

On October 1, 1938, historic change began when Germany occupied the region. This resulted in a very negative influence on the industry. Most of the factories were in the Sudetenland of western Bohemia that was seceded to Germany. The factories were incorporated into existing German companies. Numerous problems occurred regarding prices, wages, and legal concerns about factory ownership. The people operating the factories, including the Jewish owners, remained for the most part. Boycott of Bohemian porcelain abroad due to World War II severely affected their exports. This was very serious since 80 percent of their production was exported in 1938. As the war progressed, porcelain products couldn't be shipped and inventory piled up in warehouses. Prices had to be converted from Czech crowns

(Kč) to German reichmarks (RM) with losses due to the currency exchange. With large inventories ready for export when war broke out, prices had to be reduced, resulting in further losses. Wares passing through Germany required additional payments to the Reich. Each factory had to contribute to the war effort. Drinking bottles were produced for the German army, as well as electric heater insulators. Forty percent of porcelain factory production was for the army and hospitals, 30 percent for areas affected by allied bombing, 20 percent for individual orders from other firms, and only 10 percent for export. In addition, porcelain could only be exported to countries friendly with the German government.

Sabotage occurred frequently in the factories. Toward the end of the war, about one-third of the workers were prisoners of war. On May 5, 1944, there were 2,000 people working in Karlovy Vary area factories. Since 1941, no one was investing in porcelain factories due to the war, so exports declined. Factories fell into disrepair; models and equipment were neglected. Rail transportation was affected in late 1944, and after the allies invaded France all exports were cut off. By 1945, customers had to pick up ware at the factory. As the war came to an end, German factory directors fled to Germany leaving no one to run the factories, which resulted in their closure. Conditions improved in late 1945, but the porcelain industry was severely affected and the financial situation was catastrophic.

After the war, new people had to be hired, since ethnic Germans were being deported to Germany. This took some time, however, since 3,980 of the 4,560 people working in the factories in 1945 were Germans.

Czechoslovakian President Edvard Beneš ordered all of the sixteen operating Bohemian porcelain factories to nationalize on October 24, 1945. Fourteen were in the Karlovy Vary area and two in the Teplice area. On March 7, 1946, the nationalized factories were reorganized into six companies.

After the communists took over in 1948, further reorganization occurred in 1950, 1951, 1953, and 1958. The quality and reputation of the Bohemian porcelain industry suffered. The equipment and buildings were old and little money was available for factory improvements since the communist government was supporting heavy industry. New designers and artists had much difficulty getting started in the industry, because it lacked government support. In addition, a certain stigma was associated with the industry as well: The communists suggested that porcelain decorators and designers were lazy because they didn't work in heavy industry. Without investment little production occurred.

Between 1947 and 1957, the Czechoslovakian government instituted design competition in ceramic trade schools for porcelain products, even if the government didn't use the winning designs. The best designer during this time was Jaroslav Ježek. Some of the designs he produced and entered into competition won a prize at the 1958 World Expo in Brussels. Other accomplished designers included Marie Rychliková, Václav Tikal, Otto Eckert, Jindřiška and Provoslav Radovi, Děvana Mírová, and Václav Dolejš. At the 1960 Triennial Exposition in Milan, Václav Serak won a silver metal for design. There was little collaboration, however, between the designer and the artists at this time.

At the 1967 EXPO in Montreal, the designs displayed illustrated the aesthetics and elegance of pieces for use in homes and apartments. This type of superior technical design with its new look satisfied the needs of consumers both at home and abroad. Because many were very functional, it was hoped that they would coordinate the problems of use and decoration. New designs were produced by J. Ježek, R. Rada, L. Švarc, V. Šerák, H. Samohelová, J. Marek, and J. Laštovička.

As a result of the collapse of the Soviet Union and the creation of a democratic government in Czechoslovakia, the porcelain factories there returned to private ownership in 1992. Today, all of the operating factories in the Czech Republic have been privatized and are once again seeking to increase the aesthetic quality of their wares in the hopes of reestablishing themselves worldwide as the prominent exporters of porcelain.

PORCELAIN DECORATION METHODS

Bohemian porcelain factories decorated their ware in several different ways. These included relief patterns in whiteware, transfer or decalcomania designs both under-and overglaze, and hand painted designs under-and overglaze.

Slip-Casting

Bohemian factories created relief forms on the unfired pieces by molding beaded borders, floral designs, and filigrees on plates and bowls. The multi-part plaster of Paris molds contained intaglio designs on their inner surfaces. Slip (liquid kaolin-feldspar mixture) was poured into the mold. The plaster absorbed water from the mixture, leaving a thin film of clay clinging to the mold. The process could be repeated to increase the wall of the piece to the desired thickness. This was called "decoration in the white." Single open molds with intaglio decorations were used to produce ornaments in relief, which were then attached to larger pieces with slip in a process called luting. After these pieces were fired, the sharply detailed reliefs were frequently gold painted and then glazed and fired again.

Since Haviland porcelain was in great demand in America, Bohemian factories produced wares with similar shapes and decoration.

Although some of the Haviland designs, including the popular Ranson (Schleiger #1) dinnerware, were patented, they were copied with slight variation and sold through importers to American china wholesalers, such as Higgins & Seiter in New York and Pitkin & Brooks and Burley & Company in Chicago; directly exported to large retailers, including Marshall Field's, Wanamaker's, Gimbel's, and Bailey, Banks and Biddle; or were sold to mail order firms, like Sears, Roebuck & Co.

The quality of design imitations was touted in an 1891 article in the trade journal *China, Glass & Lamps*. Regarding porcelain sold by L. Straus & Sons, the article stated:

> The lines of vases, etc. called the 'Elite,' are simply perfection. The ware is an imitation of Royal Worcester, but the material is so fine, the colors are so beautiful, the designs and decorations so perfect, that it really takes an expert to distinguish the imitation from the genuine.

In 1900, the W. L. Briggs firm, a New York City importer of Theodore Haviland china, warned dealers that the Haviland designs were patented and not to buy or handle the pirated patterns. Charles Ahrenfeldt & Son issued a similar warning against patent infringement concerning their French china shapes.

Plate, 8.6"d. Coupe, shell-shaped gilded relief, fish with yellow and purple floral hand-decorated transfer, scalloped gold rim, white ground. Unsigned. CHARLES AHRENFELDT & SON, 1886–1917. $20–25.

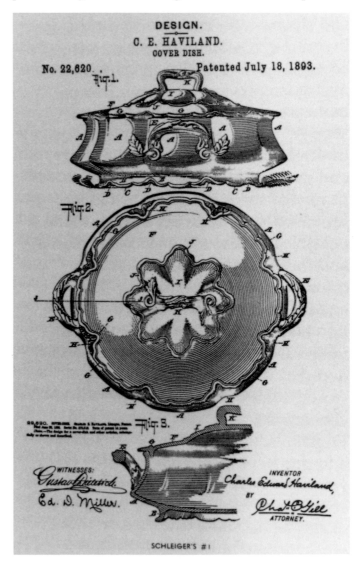

Description of a United States design patent for "Ranson" porcelain ware produced by Charles Haviland, Limoges, France. July 18, 1893. Many Bohemian porcelain factories copied this design.

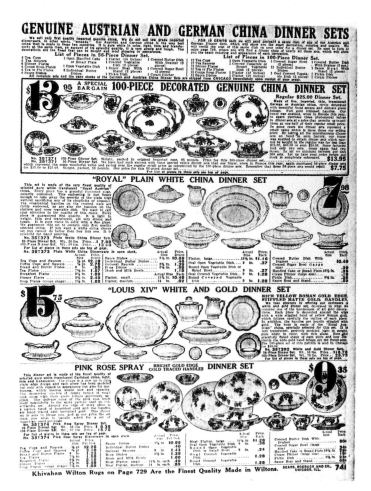

Advertisement. Royal Austria dinner sets. Sears, Roebuck & Co. Catalog, 1914.

Transferware

Bohemian factories produced an extensive variety of transfer decorated porcelain beginning in the late 1800s. Since this method of decoration was so common, the historical development of the process is summarized here.

Prior to 1750, all decorated porcelain was hand painted. Pouncing was a method used to transfer designs to glazed whiteware. Wilder A. Pickard used the process at his Ravenswood studio in Chicago during the early 1900s. It involved making a master design and then numerous pin holes were created along each line. The paper design was placed on the ware and a sand-filled cloth or chamois called a "pounce" was used to pat graphite through the holes, transferring the design to the glazed surface. An alternative method used to transfer the design from the paper to the porcelain required the back of the paper to be coated with graphite and then the lines of the design to be retraced onto the whiteware. Although a slow process, the transferred designs gave good uniformity to the decorated wares. Another method described by John Sadler, a Liverpool printer, involved printing on tissue paper with manganese oxide and white lead in an oily medium. This was then pressed on the ware and the paper removed, leaving a sticky outline of the design on the surface. The outline was dusted with a pounce and the piece was cleaned by blowing air gently across the surface and wiping it carefully with cotton wool. The dusting powder used contained flint glass, which was quite abrasive. By separating the abrasive ingredients from the printing plate, a plate could be used to make several thousand copies. Many individuals had explored the idea of transferring entire designs to porcelain; however, in order for this to be successful, three key obstacles had to be overcome.

Although the intaglio printing process using engraved plates was common, the engraving techniques used in England were such that the depth of the cut in the copper plate was insufficient to hold enough enamel color (a mixture of glass, colored mineral oxides, lavender oil, and turpentine) to make the process work. In addition, the frit (a ground glass composition) and color used in printing were not acceptable for the transfer process. The color had to be more finely ground and the engraved lines needed to be much deeper and harder-wearing so they would not be obliterated after a few impressions by the frit in the color. Initially, the color had to be kept hot and viscid so it would flow into the depressions in the engraving plate. This meant that the entire transfer process, including printing and decorating, had to be performed in sequence at the same location.

A second problem occurred with the paper used in the transfer process. Since it was hand made, it was of variable quality and frequently stuck to the engraved plates during printing. Oils in the color soaked into the paper and left pigment behind that clogged the engraved lines and dots in the plate.

Lastly, after the transfer process was successful and color had been applied to the underglaze or biscuit, the color frequently remained with the paper when applied on a glazed surface or glassware.

Sometime during the middle of the eighteenth century, Simon Francois Ravenet (1721?–1774), a French engraver, is thought to have come to England at the request of the artist and printer William Hogarth (1697–1764). Hogarth admired Ravenet's style of engraving and was interested in using these techniques to further his own work. The Frenchman brought with him new tools and engraving techniques that permitted him to create much deeper cuts in the printing plates. These cuts allowed more color to be transferred to the paper.

In 1752, Ravenet found employment with Stephen Theodore Janssen at the Battersea Enamel Works in London. Here, he met John Brooks (1720–1760), an engraver from Birmingham, who had tried unsuccessfully several times to patent the transfer process from 1751 through 1755. The first enamel transfers were made in 1753 at Battersea. The firm had been in business only a few years when it went bankrupt in 1756.

Working with Brooks and Ravenet at Battersea was engraver and designer Robert Hancock (1730–1817). Hancock took the process to Worcester and by 1756 his engravings were being used as designs at the Royal Worcester Porcelain Company. Thomas Turner, a pupil of Hancock's, began the process at Caughley, England, in 1775. Turner's apprentice, Thomas Minton, took the process to Spode, which Minton founded in 1793.

In Liverpool, John Sadler (1720–1789) and Guy Green (1730–1800) applied for a patent in 1756 to decorate tile using a transfer process. While they likely developed their process independent of Brooks, their application was denied, probably on account of Brooks' earlier attempts at patenting the transfer process. Despite the involvement each of these individuals had in developing the design transfer process, its invention is generally accredited to Robert Hancock.

At first, transfer printing was done over the glaze in red, purple, and black. After 1760, the method was also used for underglaze printing in blue.

15

Intaglio copper plate, onion pattern. BERNARD BLOCH factory, Dubí, 1903. *Courtesy of Dagmar Braunová*.

In 1784, Josiah Spode solved the problem of the wicking action of the paper. He sized the paper by soaking it in a soft soap solution that prevented it from sticking to the hot engraved plate and from absorbing the oils from the color. Later, at Battersea, it was determined that by using a varnish sizing on the paper, designs could be transferred to enamels. This process continued to be used during the next 200 years, even after the discovery of polychrome lithography 100 years later.

The process of producing intaglio transfers, also known as decalcomania or decals, followed the general process described here.

First, a line engraving was made on a copper plate. This was followed by stipple punching the plate. The hot transfer ink called 'color' was applied to the plate with a wooden dabber and rubbed in well. The surplus color was scraped off and a 'boss' or corduroy pad was used to remove the remaining color from the plate. Color remained only in the engraved areas of the plate. Thin tissue paper was sized with a soft soap solution and laid on the engraved plate. The plate was passed through a mangle with a felted top roller to ensure good contact with every line and dot of color. The copper plate was then returned to the hot plate and the tissue removed. The design was trimmed by a worker known as a 'cutter' to the desired shape and the 'transferrer' placed them in position working outward from the center. The tissue was rubbed vigorously with soft soaped flannel to ensure that all color was transferred to the biscuit. Lastly, the tissue paper was washed off under cold running water. The piece was heated slightly to dry the color, and then dipped into a glaze and re-fired. Although the underglaze transfer was considered superior, transfers could also be placed on glazed surfaces as well.

Despite one significant improvement which was made in 1828, the transfer process remained largely unchanged for 100 years. Prior to this, the process used hand made paper of variable quality. In 1827, Henry Fourdrinier (1766–1854), the inventor of the paper machine, joined one of his sons at the Ivy

Production of lithographic transfer prints for use in decorating porcelain in 1827. This process was first used in England and later widely adopted by Bohemian factories. Reprinted from Cyril Williams-Wood, *English Transfer-Printed Pottery and Porcelain*, (Boston: Faber and Faber, 1981) p. 45.

House Paper Mill in Stoke-on-Trent, England, where they installed one of the original machines that Henry and his engineer Brian Donkin had built. The mill was able to produce large amounts of wrapping paper for the local potteries, as well as high quality paper for the design transfer process. Today, the company remains a leading manufacturer of high quality decal papers.

The decorating process described above generally resulted only in monochrome designs. F. & R. Pratt of Fenton produced some polychrome transfers using this process by repeated applications of different colors, but this was very difficult and time-consuming. The company exhibited examples of this at the 1851 London Great Exhibition. In 1855, David Haviland began using transfers in his plant in Limoges. He hired David Cresswell, an Englishman, to supervise this innovation. Later, his son Charles hired Felix Bracquemond (1833–1914), from the Sèvres factory, to develop full color lithographic transfers. Bracquemond was trained as an etcher and later was in charge of the decorating workshops at the Sèvres factory. In 1872, he signed a 10-year contract with Charles Haviland as director of design development at the company's experimental atelier (decorating studio) at Auteuil located outside Paris.

The lithographic printing process, which did not use engraved plates, was discovered between 1796 and 1798 by a Bavarian playwright, Alois Senefelder. He was experimenting with printing in stone in order to find a method for reproducing his plays. Recognizing the importance of his discovery, he spent the remainder of his life developing the lithography process. In 1856, Jablonowski was granted a patent for producing polychrome transfers. This process is still in use today. As a result, the term "lithographs" is the common name for decals in Europe.

In the beginning, a lithographic machine was just a printing press with a flat smooth stone. Different colors were applied in sequence on top of the varnished stone using a dusting technique. This process was adapted from pouncing, a method which had been used to decorate overglaze using paper transfers.

Unlike the engraved copper plate method, lithography could be done at room temperature. Several companies published catalogs of available designs. The J. Bergeon Stempel-Fabrik in Gelnhausen, Germany, produced many of the transfers used by Bohemian factories in the early 1900s.

To fit complex shapes, decorators, however, still wanted to use a thin paper. Since the paper had to pass through the printing operation several times, once for each color, the sheets were lightly stuck to zinc plates during the printing process. The sheets were then cut free for decorating and the plate reused. At the request of Leonard Grimwade, Frederick Haigh at Ivy House Paper Mills produced a duplex paper in 1890 which eliminated the need for the zinc plate. In order for lithography to work in this process, a coated paper had to be used. Paper mills soon developed patented coating machines to make this specialty product.

The lithographic process allowed for the creation of large numbers of designs and were sold by transfer companies to all of the European porcelain manufacturers. Many of the designs were of floral or fruit motifs, gold medallions or filigrees, or portraits of women.

Eventually, in 1892, the method of transferring lithographic designs was described for the amateur china painter by Susan Frackelton, an early American potter and china decorator. After cutting as much paper as possible from around the design, both the printed side of the transfer and the china piece were painted with a thin layer of transfer varnish. When the surfaces became tacky, the coated surface of the transfer was placed in contact with the coated porcelain. A fine damp cloth was used to smooth out the design and a rubber roller was used to press out all the air bubbles. After drying, the porcelain was placed in a container of water to float the transfer paper off.

Many of the transfer designs were further embellished with hand-painting or enamelling to provide additional color or relief. Factories were allowed to affix a "hand painted" mark on these pieces. The Gutherz factory in Stará Role employed at least five decorators for transfer highlighting. In the early years, decorators hand-signed their names directly on the piece. Later, their names were incorporated into the transfer design itself.

American companies also produced decalcomanias for porcelain decorating. Keramic Studio, vol. 10(6), 1900.

Early decorator signature for *Martin*, one of the painters employed by OSCAR & EDGAR GUTHERZ. The fine script in the rose decoration is hand-signed.

Compare the signature for *Martin* next to the oak leaf which appears to be a transfer.

Factory decorated plates were sometimes further embellished by china painters who may or may not have been associated with the factory. It is possible American china painters may have done this secondary decoration as well. The photographs below compare the appearance of two decorative plates one of which has been further decorated by a painter who signed his name as "A. Gunck" on the back of the plate.

By the late 1800s, smaller Bohemian factories had discarded their own lithography presses and purchased colored decals from firms that produced them. The transfer paper was produced by Brittians Ivy House Paper Mills, Stoke-on-Trent, England; Hoffmann & Engelmann, Neustadt, Germany, and a French company. Many of the transfer designs on Bohemian porcelain were similar to Haviland and other Limoges dinnerware patterns.

In 1900, importers like L. Straus & Sons and Bawo & Dotter were advertising their Carlsbad porcelain as equal to French China in "beauty of conception, chasteness of design, depth of color and thinness and texture." In that year alone, Straus imported at least 50 different patterns of transfer-decorated dinnerware. The importer gave names to different shapes of undecorated or whiteware like "Dorothy," "Mabel," or "Marjorie." These were often names of employees or wives of owners.

Decorating techniques used to produce Limoges porcelain were also used by Bohemian factories. This involved a combination of molded whiteware with scalloped borders, scroll work, beading and fancy-shaped handles, knobs, and feet, in addition to transfer designs. The Gutherz factory, for example, used at least 7 different blanks for their dinnerware and decorated them with a variety of floral decals. Transfer designs were used both under and overglaze. Dinnerware transfers were commonly overglaze causing designs to wear off with constant use.

Factory-applied transfer decoration provided added value to the porcelain manufacturer. As much as 50 percent more duty was assessed by the United States Custom inspector on Bohemian decorated china than on whiteware.

Plate, 8.9"d. Coupe, white grapes and multicolored leaves, hand-decorated transfer, ivory ground, gold band. Signed: *Raymond*. OSCAR & EDGAR GUTHERZ, 1899–1918. $40–50.

Plate, 8.75"d. Coupe, white grapes and multicolored leaves, hand-decorated transfer, ivory ground, wide gold band with hand painted apple blossoms. Signed: *Raymond. (A. Gunck, Decorator)*. OSCAR & EDGAR GUTHERZ, 1899–1918. $85–100.

Cup and saucer, 3.75"d. Haviland & Co. "Clover Leaf" (Schleiger #98) pattern, transfer decoration. OSCAR & EDGAR GUTHERZ, 1898–1918. $15–25.

Underglaze Decoration

Between 1738 and 1739, the porcelain factory in Meissen developed a hand painted cobalt underglaze with Chinese influenced floral patterns known as *zweibelmuster* in German. This was widely copied by many factories. The tradition of "onion" decoration on Bohemian porcelain has been described by Dagmar Braunová (see illustration of intaglio plate on page 16). The main design was the aster blossom (*Callistrephus chinensis*) on a stalk with a bud or the strawflower (*Helichrysum bracteatum*) and a peony (*Paeonia officinalis*) winding around a bamboo rod. The edges of the pieces were trimmed with peaches and pomegranates. This appearance reminded Europeans of onions, hence the origin of the name. A more abstract version of the pattern on Rococo-style porcelain can be attributed to Meissen painter Johann David Kretschmar, who worked in the factory from 1726 to 1752. Initially, all fruits were oriented along the edge of the porcelain with their bottoms pointing inward. Later, individual fruits were alternated inwards and outwards. Production of Bohemian "onion" underglaze decoration began in 1885 at the C. Teichert factory in Dubí (Eichwald). The popular method of decoration spread to other factories at Klášterec, Nová Role, and Rybáře.

Overglaze Decoration

After the porcelain was fired, glazed, and refired, different mineral colors were applied by hand. The process required firing a third time in a kiln at a lower temperature (750 to 900 degrees Celsius). These kilns were known as muffle kilns and the process was called muffle kiln decoration.

Different metallic oxides were used as colorants. These included: uranium, copper, iridium, iron, tin, zinc, lead, manganese, chromium, and cobalt. These were mixed with a flux to combine and fix the colors to the glaze and add a shine to the surface. Flux consisted of a mixture containing quartz, fire stone, red lead, bismuth oxide, saltpeter, borax, natron, and calcium carbonate. All of these substances were finely ground, added to lavender oil and filtered, and thickened with turpentine.

Another popular overglaze technique was luster decoration. It is frequently found on Bohemian whiteware pieces decorated by individuals or studios in the United States. The process involved the reduction to a thin metal coating from oxide containing pigments. Copper, gold, platinum, or silver oxide was painted on the glazed surface of the porcelain and fired in a smoke-filled kiln. The resultant luster ware had an iridescent appearance. Mother-of-pearl was the most commonly used luster, but other

Plates, 9.75"d. *Right*, beaded relief border, scalloped edge, red and white roses. *Left*, floral relief, scalloped edge, red and white roses, transfer decoration. Unsigned. OSCAR & EDGAR GUTHERZ, 1898–1918. $15–20.

colors such as blue, copper, green, purple, red, and yellow were also popular. This technique was frequently used in Art Nouveau and Art Deco styles of decorated porcelain.

European Decorative Styles

Ornamentation of porcelain followed the artistic styles popular at the time of production. Changes in style were heavily French driven. The table below summarizes the styles that influenced both the shape of and decoration on porcelain. The Rococo Revival style was very popular in early Bohemian porcelain. The term Rococo was derived from the French words *rocaille-coquill*, meaning rock and shellwork.

Artistic styles did not necessarily follow a progressive order. Instead, much overlapping occurred with respect to porcelain decoration. In general, Bohemian factories followed the styles created by the larger French and German factories of the time.

Decorative Style	Period	Description*
Baroque	mid 1600s–early 1700s	Highly sculptured; heavy plastic shapes including scrollwork, volutes, banderoles, grotesques, human figures, intricate strapwork; symmetrical shapes
Rococo	early 1700s–mid 1700s	Lightly sculptured scrollwork; natural forms including rocks, shells, flowers, foliage, fruit; asymmetric shapes
Classic Revival		
Louis XV	mid 1700s–1800	Light and graceful; Greek and Roman asymmetrical designs
Empire	1804–1820s	Cold, exact, formal; antique Greek and Roman shape including foliage, wreaths, palm leaves, gods and goddesses; pronounced symmetry
Biedermeir	early 1800s–mid 1800s	A lighter Germanic version of Empire style
Rococo Revival	mid 1800s–late 1800s	Swirling, sinuous outlines, relief gilded decoration; floral designs, asymmetrical shapes
Gothic Revival	late 1820s–1890s	Recreation of Gothic leaf shapes
Art Nouveau	late 1800s–early 1900s	Combination of above styles as well as Middle Eastern and Oriental elements; sinuous whiplash curves, Gothic flame-like and leaf-like tracery; asymmetrical shapes
Art Deco	1915–1930s	Rectilinear; broken or interrupted contours; Egyptian and Aztec symmetrical designs

*Louise Ade Boger, *The Dictionary of World Pottery and Porcelain*. Charles Scribner's Sons, New York, 1971.

KARLOVY VARY (KARLSBAD) AREA PORCELAIN FACTORIES

The first porcelain factory in Bohemia was located in Háje (Rabensgrün), about 8 miles south of Karlovy Vary. For several years, it had been known that deposits of kaolin, feldspar, and coal were plentiful in western Bohemia. Thuringian factories across the German border were producing cheap porcelain which traveling salesmen brought to Bohemia, often in baskets on their back. Tales of money made in these factories stimulated the development of factories in Bohemia. The Háje factory founded by Franz A. Habertitzel was in business from 1789 to 1793, but it failed to become fully operational and closed.

Porcelain had been produced in Vienna by Claudius du Paquier since 1718. He was granted a 25-year monopoly by the Habsburg monarchy. Due to du Paquier's poor financial situation, his factory was purchased in 1744 by the monarchy who suppressed the development of other porcelain factories. Although pottery and porcelain production began as early as 1792 in the Karlovy Vary area, many of these factories did not survive through 1900. Most of them produced porcelain for local or regional sale. After the Treaty of Schrönbrunn, following the war of 1809, Austria seceded land to Bavaria, losing its main source of kaolin around the Passau area. The Austrian government then promoted the discovery of new deposits of raw materials and the development of factories in western Bohemia.

To provide a complete overview, all Karlovy Vary area factories exporting porcelain to the United States are described. In 1900, within a 20-mile radius of Karlovy Vary (then called Karlsbad, Austria) were 27 factories producing porcelain in 16 small villages and towns. In addition, there were seven factories in six other towns manufacturing porcelain that may or may not

Emperor Franz Josef I, (1830–1916) Emperor of Austria-Hungary. Ruler during the peak of Bohemian porcelain production before World War I. The Habsburg monarchy restricted the production of porcelain in Bohemia in the early 1800s due largely to their interest in maintaining the state-owned monopoly in Vienna. *Courtesy of the Bridgeman Art Library.*

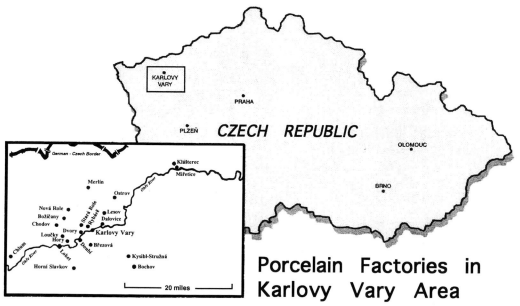

Porcelain Factories in Karlovy Vary Area

Map showing towns with porcelain factories within a 20-mile radius of Karlovy Vary, Bohemia, around 1900.

have exported ware to the United States. Today, there are nine different branches of Karlovarský Porcelán in the area, as well as 10 other privately operated factories.

Several firms produced household, table, and decorative porcelain for export, mainly to the United States. Factories located in Bochov, Božičany, Doubí, Dvory, Horní Slavkov, Hory, Chodov, Klášterec, Loket, Loučky, Merklín, Nová Role, Ostrov, Rybáře, and Stará Role are known to have produced whiteware for the American china decorating market. Factory owners and names are indicated in bold type. Over the years, factories changed ownership several times. Frequently, managers or partners of one factory would sell their interest and move to a neighboring town and establish another porcelain factory. Rarely did a single business remain under the same ownership for more than 20 years. Many did not survive the economic hardship brought on by World War I. Appendix 3 lists the dates the factories were in operation.

Several of the Bohemian factory marks can be found on porcelain pieces at estate sales, in antique shops and malls, and at flea markets across the United States. As early as 1793, the Austrian government required that factories producing earthenware and stoneware identify their goods with a factory mark. Porcelain companies in western Bohemia were required by the monarchy to register their marks at the Chamber of Trade and Commerce in Cheb (Eger). In this way, the government hoped to control the production of earthenware, stoneware, and later porcelain.

A description of the factories in each town along with their marks is presented. Towns are listed by the date their first porcelain factory was established. Populations of towns in 1869 and 1910 are included, where available, to provide a sense of the importance of this industry for employment in the region. When factories were sold, the currency at the time was the Austrian gulden or guilder. For purposes of comparison, the 1914 exchange rate was estimated at one gulden to 40 cents. Dollar values are shown in parentheses.

Horní Slavkov - 1792

Horní Slavkov Town Emblem.

Horní Slavkov (Schlaggenwald) was founded around 1322 and in 1489 was designated as a small city by the monarchy. This identification was accompanied by certain privileges and benefits to its residents. In 1547, Ferdinand I designated it a royal city and gave it a town emblem. Horní Slavkov is situated in a

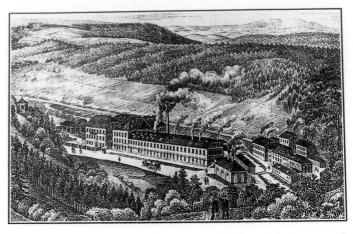

Lithograph illustrating Horní Slavkov factory circa 1870. *Courtesy of Dagmar Braunová.*

deep valley in the heart of the Slavkovský forest and mountains of western Bohemia, about 10 miles south of Karlovy Vary. According to the 1869 census, the town had a population of 4,571. In 1910, its population was 3,701. It is not known why the population decreased so significantly over this 40 year period; however, war and disease may have contributed to it. Many of the inhabitants were employed in the porcelain manufacturing business. Today, a rail line through the town brings tank cars filled with liquid kaolin and other raw materials to the porcelain factory.

It was here that porcelain production first began in Bohemia. In 1792, burgher and retired mining expert **Johann Georg Paulus, Johann Pöschl**, and the Thuringian arcanist **Johann Georg Reumann** established a factory in Horní Slavkov, but failed to obtain a permit to manufacture porcelain. The Austrian monarchy was concerned the factory would compete with the Imperial-Royal Manufactory in Vienna. Paulus turned to making pipe bowls, earthenware, and flints for the army. The owners attempted to begin making simple and rather crude porcelain, but were not financially successful. Faced with continued failure, they lost interest and sold the factory in 1800 to **Louise Sophie Greiner**. She had some previous experience in porcelain production, since her deceased husband had been a co-owner of a factory in Gera, Thuringia. Her son, Moritz, served as the production manager, but lacked the necessary experience. The factory produced coffee sets and mugs. The strawflower pattern with blue and purple underglaze was used beginning around 1800. Greiner also was not successful in making the business profitable and around 1808 left the management to her son-in-law, physician, and mining physicist **Johann Georg Lippert**, who had joined the firm in 1803. After her death in 1808, Lippert gained ownership and took on mining expert Wenzel Haas as a partner and named the factory **Lippert & Haas.** Ten family members were employed in the factory.

Early experiments to produce porcelain were carried out in secret. The owners feared that once the regional governor found out he would order the closure of the factory. This fear proved to be unfounded and the factory was granted the privilege to produce porcelain in 1812. Their success drew the attention of Emperor Franz I, Grand Duke Ferdinand of Würzburg, and the Emperor's daughter, French Empress Marie Louise. Later that year, the royalty visited the factory during their stay in Karlovy Vary for spa treatments. Within a few years, porcelain from this factory became widely known. The factory produced mainly

Lidded jug, Thuringian style with extended shoulders, ear-shaped handle, cobalt blue underglaze decoration, 8.5"h. Both the porcelain and yellowish glaze are of poor quality. LIPPERT & HAAS factory, Horní Slavkov, before 1800. *Courtesy of Dagmar Braunová.*

Decorative cup, late Empire style with impressed teardrop ribbed ornamented base and gilded elevated handle with lily design, 4.7"h. Central panel is a miniature painting of a courtship scene. LIPPERT & HAAS factory, Horní Slavkov, circa 1830. *Courtesy of Dagmar Braunová.*

Baroque style coffee and tea sets, decorative porcelain, and pipe bowls. After 1828, tableware was produced in increasing volume. Porcelain from this factory began to rival that produced by the Vienna factory. In a similar manner, Lippert & Haas in 1819 began marking the date of manufacture by impressing the last three numbers of the year on its porcelain. After Wenzel Haas' death, his son, Eusebius August, joined the company in 1830. The factory produced lithophanes, including lamp shades and cups with lithophane bottoms, between 1830 and 1843. These were light screens of biscuit exploiting the transparency of thin porcelain plates into which relief molds were pressed. After firing, the decoration was visible when a light source was held behind the porcelain. The thicker parts made up the shadows, while the thinner parts supplied the light in the pictures. Generally, the image formed the decoration on the bottom of cups and plates.

The factory also produced large Vienna style decorative plaques painted with theatrical scenes, including Othello (see Godden's Guide, p. 162). Decorators were Lang and Krause.

The factory began figurine production in 1835. When Lippert died in 1843, he left his share of the business to his son-in-law, Johann Möhling. A variety of porcelain was produced including very high quality pieces which were awarded gold medals in Vienna in 1845. The company received several international recognitions. Well-known decorators included L. Gerlach–1814, Hürrer–1834 and Kiesling–1839, and the modeler Karl Fritsch.

Lithophane bottom on decorative cup is a small girl playing with a dog. *Courtesy of Dagmar Braunová.*

Möhling had several disputes with his partner. This finally resulted in selling his shares to **August Haas** in 1847 for 140,000 guldens ($56,000). The factory at this time consisted of 10 buildings, 3 kilns, and 43 potter's wheels. Möhling then opened his own factory in Doubí (Aich). For twenty years, the Haas family operated the factory until 1867 when nephew Johann Cžjžek became a partner. It was then operated as **Haas & Cžjžek** until 1945.

Decorative vase, late Empire style in Medici form, bell-shaped on embellished gilded relief crater pedestal with square base, 8.7"h. Miniature motif is a view of "Das Mühlbad" (the Mill Spring) in Karlovy Vary. LIPPERT & HAAS factory, Horní Slavkov, 1841. *Courtesy of Dagmar Braunová.*

In 1872, the partners acquired the Portheim & Sons porcelain factory in Chodov. The business became a joint stock company in 1931. Over the years, the firm provided increased employment in the town. Starting in 1806 with 10 workers, the factory employed 65 workers in 1818, about 200 workers in 1835, 250 workers in 1846, 513 workers in 1900, and 700 workers in 1937. The company was the first in Bohemia to introduce pensions for invalids, widows, and orphans. In 1899, both owners were knighted by the Austrian monarchy. After World War II, the factory was nationalized by the Czechoslovakian government. The factory has been privately owned since 1992 and is operated as a production plant by **Haas & Cžjžek**. It is unknown just when the factory began exporting porcelain to the United States. Several different plate designs and patterns that were used for American export were found in the factory's archives. These have been reproduced just as they appeared in the pattern notebooks in Appendix 2. The factory continues exporting porcelain to the United States.

A second porcelain factory was founded in Horní Slavkov in 1901 by **Anton Waldmann**. Along with Josef Spinner, who had established a porcelain factory in Krásno (Schönfeld) around 1899, and Alfred Schindler, Waldmann purchased building No. 537, which had been the Rathgeber & Hölzl spinning mill. The

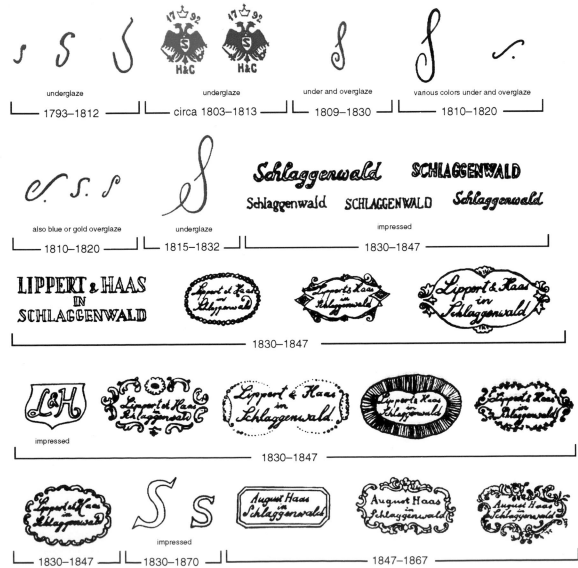

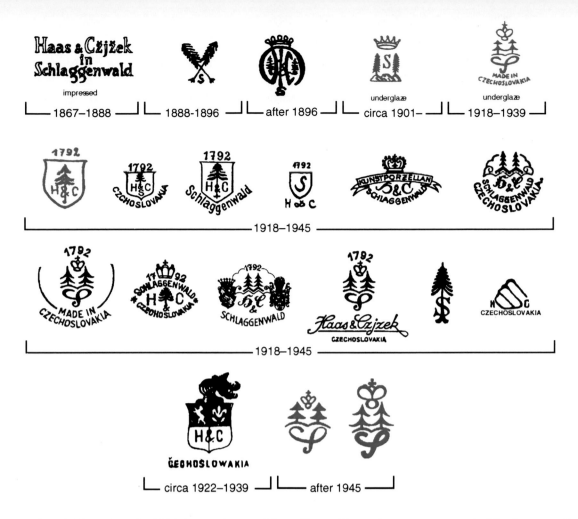

Haas & Cžjžek
in
Schlaggenwald

impressed

└── 1867–1888 ──┘ └── 1888-1896 ──┘ └── after 1896 ──┘ └── underglaze circa 1901– ──┘ └── underglaze 1918–1939 ──┘

└──────────────────────── 1918–1945 ────────────────────────┘

└──────────────────────── 1918–1945 ────────────────────────┘

└── circa 1922–1939 ──┘ └── after 1945 ──┘

small factory employed 80 workers in 1904, increasing to 120 by 1937. The firm employed excellent modelers and talented decorators.

In April of 1904, the factory was sold to Springer & Co. in Elbogen and then to Karl Sommer and Ernst Matschak in September of 1904. The firm was known as **Sommer & Matschak** and produced household and hotel porcelain and dessert, coffee, and tea sets. Ernst Matschak died in 1915 and his share was assumed by his wife, Henriette. Karl Sommer died in 1924. The factory then was owned by Engineer Friedrich Sommer and Anna Pulz until it closed in 1945. The factory exported wares to the United States as well as other European countries.

S. M.

└──1901–1945 ──┘

A third factory was established in 1919 by Josef Grosse, the factory director in Teplicka (Toppeles) and his father-in-law,

Eugen Hanusch, estate manager in Chodov, as well as Heinrich Bernhart and Georg Winterstein in Karlovy Vary. Winterstein had worked at the Vienna firm, Brüder Wetzler. Each owned a quarter share of the firm. It was located in building No. 500, a former spinning mill of a carpet factory in Horní Slavkov and was known as "Unger'sche Teppichfabrik auf der Hub" (carpet factory on the hill). It contained a small porcelain factory called **Schlaggenwald Porcelain Industry Bernhart & Co**. The factory produced porcelain dinnerware, a portion of which was exported to the United States. Even after the area officially became known as Czechoslovakia in 1918, the factory continued to use a backstamp with "Austria" as the country of origin.

In 1922, Bernhart owned three-quarters of the factory and Winterstein one-quarter. In 1925, **Panzer & Co.** was a leaseholder. The owners of this business were Rudolf Vigl from Nürnberg and Emil Krahl, a businessman in Bohosudov (Mariaschein). In 1925, owners of the Haas & Cžjžek and Sommer & Matschak factories protested against Panzer & Co. for using the name Schlaggenwald Porcelain Industry. In 1927, the building was owned by Bernhart, Winterstein, and Krahl. The factory closed in 1928.

HUB

underglaze

└──1919–1928 ──┘

25

Klášterec - 1794

Klášterec Town Emblem.

Klášterec is located in the Ohře river valley between the Krušne and Doupov Mountains. *Courtesy of Úřad Města, Klášterec.*

Klášterec (Klösterle) was founded around 1352 according to earliest known documents and may even date back to 1150 when a Benedictine monastery was established there. Before the sixteenth century, it was designated as a small city by the monarchy. The town's emblem dates back to this time. From 1620, the town was the estate of the Thun family. It is located 20 miles northeast of Karlovy Vary along the Ohře river near the German border. The city had 1,914 inhabitants according to the 1869 census. In 1910, its population was 2,943.

Kaolin deposits were discovered in nearby Černovice (Tschernitz) in 1793. **Johann Nikolaus Weber** established an earthenware factory here in 1794, along with Johann Gotlieb Sontag. Sontag had some training by working in the factory in Háje near Horní Slavkov. He had also worked in a porcelain factory in Grossbreitenbach, Thuringia. The local nobleman, Count Franz Josef von Thun, financed it. Weber was from Lützelstein, Saxony, and was 60 years old when he attempted to produce porcelain from local kaolin. He had been a forestry superintendent on the Count's estate. Weber enlisted the help of arcanist Johann Heinrich Vollrath of Potůčky (Breitenbach) and Johann Nikolaus Fetzer of Ilmenau, Thuringia, as a "glazing expert." The owners built a kiln in the Count's garden in 1793, but it failed to result in the production of porcelain and fell apart due to the poor quality of fire brick used. It soon became apparent that Vollrath knew little about the secrets of porcelain composition since he had only worked as a blue decorator in the Potůčky factory. Fetzer also lacked knowledge of glaze preparation, since he had only worked as a potter at Ilmenau.

Another kiln was built the following year and it was able to reach a high enough temperature to produce some porcelain. The result was a cup and saucer with a purple glaze with a festooned decoration and the inscription "Vivat Böhmen." Thirty workers in Weber's factory produced coffee and chocolate sets, jugs, tureens, mugs, teapots, plates, salad bowls, toilet sets, fruit baskets, butter dishes, pipe bowls, and custom-made dinnerware. Weber's failures far outnumbered his successes in porcelain production. He just couldn't manufacture consistent ware. In addition, his application for a government privilege to produce porcelain was refused in 1795. Since the business was not successful, Weber decided to lease it to **Christian Nonne** who produced coffee and tea sets, table, and decorative porcelain from 1797 to 1803. Along with his son-in-law, Karl Rösch, and nine other Thuringian workers, Nonne improved the quality of the porcelain along with its decoration. He also began to export his wares to Poland, Saxony, and Holland.

After Weber's death in 1801, the landlord, Count Josef Matthias von Thun, raised the rent so high that Nonne was forced to give up his lease. He moved to Kysibl-Stružná (Gießhübel) and began his own business. The Count continued to operate the factory from 1803 to 1805 using the same marks as Weber and Nonne. He then leased it to **Josef Melzer,** the estate tax collector, and **Josef Andreas Rafael Habertitzel**, son of Franz A. Habertitzel and founder of the first porcelain factory at Háje. The two successfully ran the factory until 1819 when the Thun family did not renew the lease. Despite this, Habertitzel continued to serve as its director.

Lithograph illustrating Klášterec factory circa 1870. *Courtesy of Dagmar Braunová.*

Lidded jug, Dresden style with vertical ribbing and channels, 8.25"h. Strawflower decoration in cobalt blue underglaze. Both the porcelain and glaze are rather poor quality. JOHANN WEBER factory, Klášterec, 1794–1800. *Courtesy of Dagmar Braunová.*

From 1819 until 1945, the business was run as **Count Thun's Porcelain Factory** and produced tobacco pipes, household, table and decorative porcelain, coffee and tea sets, and figurines. Decoration included scenes of battles, mythological and allegorical figures, portraits, botanical paintings, and geometrical designs in blue, brown, red, or natural colors. In 1822, the factory had 100 workers and at that time received government approval as a national factory. Rafael Habertitzel continued to manage the factory until 1835.

Johann Hillardt, the next director and a graduate of the Praha School of Engineering, improved the quality of the porcelain and glaze. He also added a third kiln and used dried turf as a source of fuel. Additionally, gold relief decoration was used. During Habertitzel's management, the factory developed copper plate and lithographic technology for transfer printing in 1843.

From 1848 to 1872, the factory was directed by Karl Venier, a graduate of the polytechnical school in Praha. He modernized production and improved the quality of the porcelain as well as its decoration. Under Venier, the factory employed 179 workers, including 13 modellers and 55 decorators. The factory's kilns were fired with gas and hard coal.

During the 1840s and 1850s, the factory won several awards at exhibitions in Praha and Vienna. The firm produced the "Imperial" dinner set for the Imperial Court in Vienna and its variant, the "Thun" set, during this time. These designs were rated very high from a technical and artistic standpoint and were probably some of the best porcelain produced in the region at the time. Early decorators included Vollrath, Santvoort (from Brussels), Schlott (from Ilmenau), and Rösch (from Thuringia). The factory produced an 'onion pattern,' and an Ilmenauer strawflower pattern, as well as bird and rockery patterns.

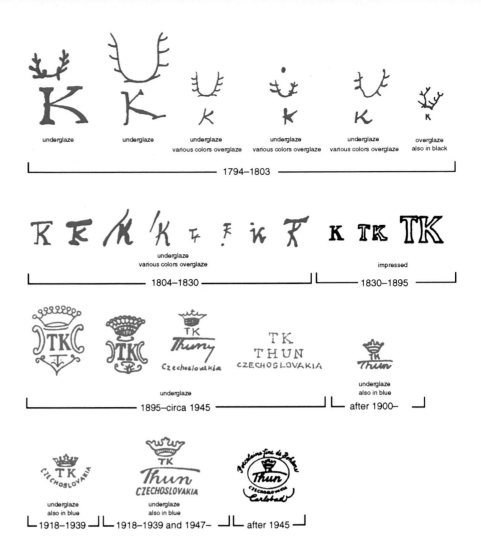

underglaze | underglaze | underglaze various colors overglaze | underglaze various colors overglaze | underglaze various colors overglaze | overglaze also in black

—————— 1794–1803 ——————

underglaze various colors overglaze

—————— 1804–1830 —————— | —————— 1830–1895 ——————

underglaze

—————— 1895–circa 1945 —————— | underglaze also in blue after 1900–

underglaze also in blue 1918–1939 | underglaze also in blue 1918–1939 and 1947– | after 1945

Figurines in painted biscuit. Allegorical design of yearly seasons. From the *left*: "Spring," 7.5"h., "Summer," 7.1"h., "Winter," 7.7"h. COUNT THUN'S PORCELAIN FACTORY, Klášterec, 1857–1861. *Courtesy of Dagmar Braunová.*

As porcelain which was formerly produced in small volume and hand-decorated became accessible to lower class families, the demand increased. By 1870, the factory was producing 189 tons of porcelain a year. Hand decoration was laborious, time consuming, and unprofitable. As the mass production of porcelain and its decoration using transfer designs was employed in 1892, the artistic level of the factory's porcelain declined.

The numbers of workers employed in the factory were 550 in 1887, 650 in 1904, and 600 in 1937. Wares were exported to the United States beginning in the late 1800s. Production included household, tableware, coffee, tea, and wash sets. The factory produced the well-known "Vienna" brand of porcelain, which was imported by P.H. Leonard and later Bawo & Dotter (see chapter on Marketing and Sales of Bohemian Porcelain). In 1883, production of Karlsbad coffee and Vienna tea machines (awarded a seven-year patent in 1878) began and production continued through 1904. In 1905, the New York City importer Bawo & Dotter advertised artist-signed "hand painted" floral designs. At the end of World War II, the factory was nationalized by the Czechoslovakian government and in 1947 became part of a state-owned enterprise called **Duchcovsky Porcelain in Dux**. In 1978, the factory fired 3,630 tons of porcelain. In 1988, it became part of **Karlovarský Porcelán**. At present, the factory is a production plant operated by **Karlovarský Porcelán A.S. Závod Klášterec**.

A second firm was founded in 1921 in Miřetice (Meretitz), which is near Klášterec. It was called **Porcelain Union, United**

Porcelain Factories AG. The business was established from the merger of two smaller factories by the Anglo-Czechoslovakian Bank. The factories closed in 1934.

The first of these was known as **Venier & Co., Ceramic Factory Products**, which was founded in 1900 by Franz Venier. His brother, Christian, joined him in 1901. The factory employed 70 workers. Josef Koch was the owner in 1914. In 1921, Anton Gottfried and Oskar Vielgut owned the factory which was called **Gottfried and Vielgut**. By this time, the factory had 160 workers.

The second small factory was an earthen and stoneware business established by August Wolf in 1910, known as **August Wolf & Co**. Wenzel Tuma owned the factory in 1913 and employed 60 workers. In 1921, the firm was called **W. Tuma & O. Vielgut Porcelain Factory**.

Oscar Gutherz was employed as Porcelain Union's director and his brother, Edgar, the technical director after the Gutherz factory in Stará Role was sold to OEPIAG on June 1, 1918. Their offices were in Karlovy Vary. In 1927, Porcelain Union also joined the EPIAG group in Karlvoy Vary. The firm exported porcelain from its factories in Turn and Miřetice to the United States. The business ceased in 1939.

A third firm, located by the train station and near the Venier & Company, was called the **Julius Neuman Porcelain Factory**. Little is known concerning the history of this factory.

Březová - 1803

Březová (Pirkenhammer) was founded in 1543. It is a small suburban town located about 5 miles southeast of Karlovy Vary in the Lomnický river valley. The town had 1,128 inhabitants in 1869. Today, it is part of the Karlovy Vary city district.

Production began when the **Höcke & List** factory was founded between 1802 and 1803 by the potter Johann Gottlob List and financial backer Friedrich Höcke who was a tradesman from Bullstedt, Saxony-Weimar. Höcke was a relative of the owner of the porcelain factory in Horní Slavkov. The factory produced household stoneware and pipe bowls.

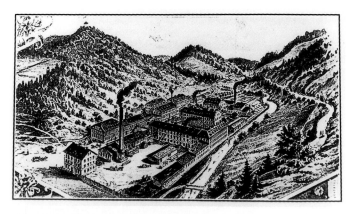

Lithograph illustrating Březová factory circa 1870. *Courtesy of Dagmar Braunová.*

Breakfast set, Empire style with cylindrical shape and curved handles. Coffee pot, 7.5"h., milk pitcher, 5.3"h., sugar, 3.9"h., cup, 2.6"h., bowl, 5.2"d. Idyllic country scenes with gold borders and grain stem ornamentation. Low quality porcelain and glaze. FRIEDRICH HÖCKE factory, Březová, 1803–1810. *Courtesy of Dagmar Braunová.*

The factory changed hands seven times before the end of World War II. Höcke established the factory with the aid of the Greiner family, who were well-known porcelain manufacturers from Thuringia. List developed financial problems so they tried to sell the factory in 1803 to others in nearby Loket. However, the sale was not authorized by the courts. The firm name was **Friedrich Höcke**. The appointed representative for the factory in 1804 was Johann Tennemann. On April 1, 1805, Höcke leased the factory to Ferdinand Kranz, who was the factory's accountant, and Gottlob Winkel. A secondary lease was granted to Friedrich Brothäuser. Kranz died in 1807 and by 1809 Winkel was in debt. Höcke then sold the nearly bankrupt factory in 1811 to local potter Christopher Reichenbach and to Christian Nonne, who had previously owned factories in Klášterec and Stružná. Nonne persuaded his former teacher and businessman Johann Martin Fischer from Erfurt, Germany, to become a strong financial partner in the factory. They purchased the firm for 6,000 guldens ($2,400) on December 21, 1810.

The factory, then known as **Fischer & Reichenbach**, produced table and decorative porcelain, coffee and tea sets, and, in the 1840s, figurines, doll heads, and busts. On June 21, 1822, the firm was licensed by the government as a national porcelain

Decorative cup, late Empire style, bell-like shape on heavy base, elevated handle with holly design, 4.7"h. Central motif is a miniature portrait of a young woman wearing a fur stole and reading a book. JOHANN MARTIN FISCHER AND CHRISTOPHER REICHENBACH factory, Březová, circa 1830. *Courtesy of Dagmar Braunová.*

Coffee set, late Empire style, egg-shaped body with elevated handles and gilded pedestal base, coffee pot, 6.5"h. Floral motifs in miniature decoration. JOHANN MARTIN FISCHER AND CHRISTOPHER REICHENBACH factory, Březová, circa 1830. *Courtesy of Dagmar Braunová.*

factory. In 1829, they received government permission to print decals from copper plates for use as both under and overglaze decoration for 5 years. Even in these early times, the application had to be reviewed by the Vienna Faculty of Medicine to insure that they had no objections to the process from a sanitary standpoint. As early as 1824, porcelain from this factory was praised for its high quality and especially its translucency. The source of kaolin was from Seldec.

After Fischer died in 1816, his wife, Sophie, inherited his share in the factory. In 1824, their eldest son, Christian, took over the business, along with Reichenbach. In 1833, Christian married Emma Karolina von Meig after receiving his mother's shares of the business in 1831. He trained at the National Manufactory in Sèvres, France.

Christian is credited as being the technical and aesthetic founder of the Březová factory. He changed the production designs from Saxony and Thuringia to new Bohemian shapes and styles using local craftsmen. During Fischer and Reichenbach's ownership, production competed with the best French porcelain.

Decorative amphora style vase in Medici form, 16.5"h. Miniature floral decoration painted by Ferdinand Quast. JOHANN MARTIN FISCHER AND CHRISTOPHER REICHENBACH factory, Březová, circa 1835. *Courtesy of Dagmar Braunová.*

Reichenbach served as the technical director. In 1846, he retired and in 1852 sold his shares for 110,000 guldens ($44,000) to Fischer. At that time, the firm employed 230 workers. The factory was then known as **Christian Fischer**. In 1852, Fischer's daughter, Wilhelmine, married her cousin, Ludwig von Mieg, who later became a joint-owner in the factory. In 1853, Fisher took his son-in-law into the business.

Von Mieg was an expert when it came to marketing porcelain. He had a sense for demand and recognized the need for expensive high-quality decorated articles. Under his management, the factory achieved world-wide recognition.

In 1859, Fischer sold the factory to his son, Rudolf Karl Fischer, and son-in-law, Ludwig von Mieg. It was then known as **Fischer & Mieg**.

Porcelain dinnerware and other products were exported to the United States perhaps as early as 1860. Ownership changed several times after this. In 1885, Rudolf Karl Fischer and Wilhelmine Mieg were owners. Fischer's son Rudolf was an owner in 1897. Unfortunately, the son drove the factory into bankruptcy. After 1897, Otto Seiferheld, Wilhelmine Mieg, and Arthur and Walter Mieg were owners. The factory was finally sold at auction in 1908 to Wilhelm and Victor Maier. The factory name remained Fischer & Mieg even after the owners died, but merged into **OEPIAG** in 1918. It was then operated as Branch Pirkenhammer. In 1920, the name was changed to **EPIAG** and it maintained this name until 1945 when the factory was nationalized by the Czechoslovakian government and became part of the state-owned **Karlovarský Porcelán** enterprise.

After 1990, the business was privatized. Part of the factory is presently operated as the China Research Institute plant by **Karlovarský Porcelán A.S. Závod Vújk.** The Institute was established following World War II when several factory laboratories were merged together to form a central porcelain research center. The remainder of the factory is called **Artporcel, s.r.o. Manufaktura Pirkenhammer.**

During its early history, the factory competed for and received numerous awards and medals in several porcelain exhibitions, beginning with the first award at an exhibition in Praha in 1828. Other medals were awarded in Praha in 1829; Vienna in 1835, 1839, and 1845; Paris in 1855, 1867, 1878, 1900, 1925, and 1937; Rio de Janerio in 1922; Bruxelles in 1958; and Brno in 1981. The Vienna Gold Medal Award in 1839 described the porcelain "as a good taste in shapes, clean body, a smooth glaze, and high quality of painting." The outstanding decorator at the time was 26-year-old Johann Zacharis Quast (1814–1891). His father, Ferdinand Quast (1789–1845), was also employed as a decorator in the factory, as well as in other factories in Loket, Dalovice, and Kysibl-Stružná. The well-known Praha sculptor Thomas Seidan created models for figurines produced by the factory in 1857. André Carriére, a famous French painter, was employed by the factory from 1868 to about 1901. The firm established a decorating studio for him in Paris in 1874 where he worked exclusively for the Březová factory.

Carriére had a great influence on several artists. He was well-known for his floral and scenic paintings. The two vases illustrated here were produced and decorated by the Fisher & Meig factory and represent an example of eighteenth-century artwork copied on nineteenth-century porcelain. The reverse scenes are believed to be of local Bohemian origin.

Decorative vase, Vienna style, ivory glaze panels, cobalt ground, raised paste gilding, 17"h. Double portrait, playful figural scene "Blindman's Buff," on reverse a pastoral scene "Maiden with Lamb." Unsigned. FISCHER & MEIG, circa 1875. *Courtesy of Richard Rendall.* $2,500–3,000.

Decorative vase detail, pastoral scene "Maiden with Lamb." *Courtesy of Richard Rendall.*

Decorative vase detail, playful figural scene "Blindman's Buff." Copy of original painting (1750–1752) by Jean-Honoré Fragonard. *Courtesy of Richard Rendall.*

Decorative vase, Vienna style, ivory glaze panels, cobalt ground, raised paste gilding, 17"h. Double portrait, pastoral scene "Bohemian Bagpiper," on reverse a playful figural scene "The See-saw." Unsigned. FISCHER & MEIG, circa 1875. *Courtesy of Richard Rendall.* $2,500–3,000.

Decorative vase detail, pastoral scene "Bohemian Bagpiper." *Courtesy of Richard Rendall.*

Decorative vase detail, playful figural scene "The See-saw." Copy of original painting (1750–1752) by Jean-Honoré Fragonard. *Courtesy of Richard Rendall.*

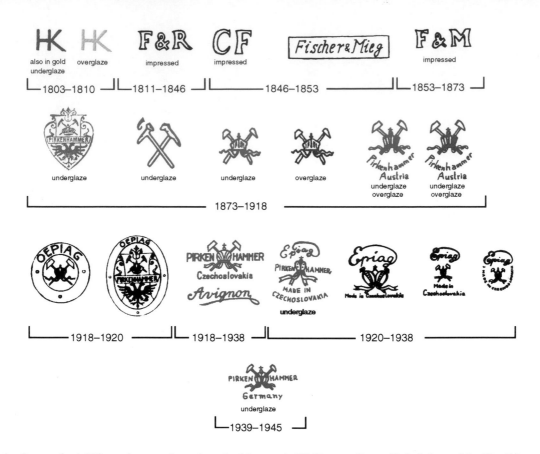

HK	HK	F&R	CF	Fischer & Mieg	F&M
also in gold underglaze	overglaze	impressed	impressed		impressed

└─1803–1810─┘ └─1811–1846─┘ └──────1846–1853──────┘ └─1853–1873─┘

underglaze · underglaze · underglaze · overglaze · *Pirkenhammer Austria* underglaze overglaze · *Pirkenhammer Austria* underglaze overglaze

└──────────────────────────1873–1918──────────────────────────┘

OEPIAG · OEPIAG · PIRKEN HAMMER Czechoslovakia *Avignon* · Epiag PIRKEN HAMMER MADE IN CZECHOSLOVAKIA underglaze · Epiag Made in Czechoslovakia · Epiag Made in Czechoslovakia · Epiag

└──1918–1920──┘ └──1918–1938──┘ └──────────1920–1938──────────┘

PIRKEN HAMMER Germany underglaze

└──1939–1945──┘

By 1904, the factory had 500 workers and produced table, coffee, wash and hotel services, pharmaceutical articles, bath tubs, luxury, and a variety of craft and art objects. Between 1908 and 1915, the factory produced lithophanes. In 1937, the number of factory workers had dropped to 350. Despite this drop and poor economic conditions, the business built a new building to accommodate their pottery production. The firm also produced porcelain art objects, special luxury services, vases, and colored figurines.

Kysibl-Stružná - 1803

Stružná (Gießhübel) was founded in 1378. It is located 7 miles southeast of Karlovy Vary in the Slavkovský forest. In 1869, its population was 688.

The German porcelain manufacturer Christian Nonne established a stoneware factory here in 1803 after he lost his lease in Klášterec. Count H. J. Stibar of the Kysibl estate allowed him to establish the factory on his land. Owners in 1803 were Christian Nonne and his son-in-law, Ernst Karl Rösch. The factory was called **Nonne & Rösch**. Their porcelain was of poor quality. Thuringian workers included August and Hans Friedrich Kühn, modeler Gabriel Klein, turner Adam Trost, and decorators H. Ch. Meissinger and Ch. Eilers. The color of the porcelain was gray, brown, or yellow and the glaze was flawed. Decoration included bird and rock patterns in blue underglaze, floral

Decorative cup with underplate, late Empire style with pedestal base. Cup 4.75"h., underplate 5.5"h. Central motif is a country scene. Gold painted floral design on underplate. FRANZ LEHNERT factory, Stružná, 1830–1840. *Courtesy of Dagmar Braunová.*

Lithograph illustrating Stružná factory circa 1870. *Courtesy of Dagmar Braunová.*

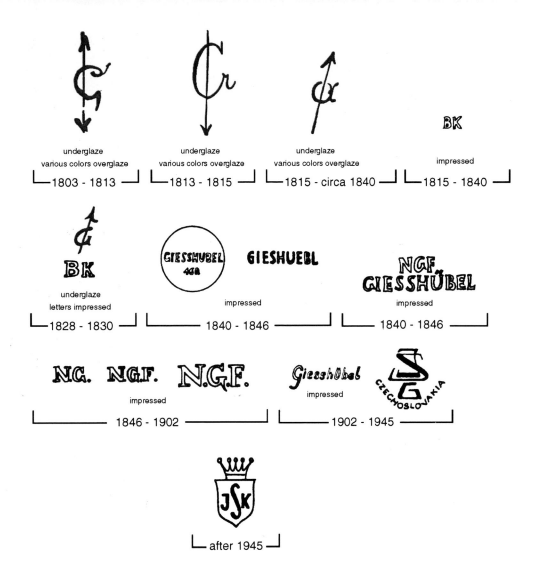

<table>
<tr><td>underglaze
various colors overglaze
1803 - 1813</td><td>underglaze
various colors overglaze
1813 - 1815</td><td>underglaze
various colors overglaze
1815 - circa 1840</td><td>impressed
1815 - 1840</td></tr>
</table>

underglaze
various colors overglaze

└─1803 - 1813─┘

underglaze
various colors overglaze

└─1813 - 1815─┘

underglaze
various colors overglaze

└─1815 - circa 1840─┘

impressed

└─1815 - 1840─┘

underglaze
letters impressed

└─1828 - 1830─┘

impressed

└─1840 - 1846─┘

impressed

└─1840 - 1846─┘

impressed

└─1846 - 1902─┘

impressed

└─1902 - 1945─┘

└─after 1945─┘

designs, and geometrical shapes in blue or red overglaze. The strawflower pattern was used. Following his death in 1813, the factory was purchased by **Johann Anton Hladik**, the new estate owner, who operated it until 1815 when he leased it to **Benedikt Knaute and Josef Schmellowski**. The factory began producing coffee and tea sets and decorative porcelain about 1825.

Josef Müller was the factory decorator in the 1820s. He produced scenic views of Karlovy Vary, as well as mythological scenes with finely detailed leaves and gilding. The factory switched from its production of Late Baroque Thuringian forms to Empire shapes in 1833. In 1840, **Franz Lehnert** continued the lease. He had been a partner and the manager of the factory since 1835. Six years later, he lost the lease and founded a new factory in Lubenec (Lubenz), which in 1842 had 55 workers. Production included utility and luxury ware, much of which was exported to other continental countries.

Over the next four decades, the factory and estate was owned by various noblemen in the area. Wilhelm G. Ritter von Neuberg and his wife, Antonie (born Hladik), owned the factory in 1829, Johann Ritter von Neuberg in 1855, and Count Hermann von Czernin in 1868. The factory was known as **K.k. Privileged Count Czernin's Porcelain Factory** in 1892. In 1902, Johann Schuldes, who owned the factory, called it **Porcelain Factory Gießhübel Johann Schuldes**. Hugo Schuldes and Frieda Schindler (born Schuldes) from Vienna were owners in 1923 and Irma Eckl and Frieda Schindler from 1940 to 1945. Several individuals leased the factory over the years of its operation. Lessees were J. Kratochwill (1865), Josef Wallisch (1879), and Adolf Schuldes from 1892 to 1902. The factory produced good quality tableware, and decorative porcelain, coffee and tea sets, and figurines in Meissen and Vienna styles.

Later, the business was operated as a branch of the Dalovice factory. The factory produced household and decorative porcelain for export until it closed in 1945.

A porcelain decorating shop operated here from 1890 to around 1930. It was owned by **Josef Riedl.** The firm exported decorated plates to the United States.

underglaze

└─circa 1890 - circa 1945─┘

underglaze

└─circa 1890 - 1918─┘

underglaze

└─circa 1890 –┘

Josef Riedl Factory Marks.

Dalovice - 1804

Church of the Virgin Mary in Dalovice built in 1929. *Courtesy of Úřad Města, Karlovy Vary.*

Dalovice (Dallwitz) was founded in 1502. The village is located on the east bank of the Ohře River 3 miles north of Karlovy Vary. In 1869, its population was 1,194. By 1910, it had grown to 1,986. Today, it is a part of the Karlovy Vary city district.

Johann and Wenzel Ritter von Schönau (noblemen and owners of the Dalovice estate) established a stoneware factory here between 1802 and 1804 along with Benedikt Haßlacher, a potter from Praha. From 1804 to 1818, Haßlacher was the director until he began his own pottery in Stará Role. The firm was known as **Ritter von Schönau Brothers and Hasslacher**. The factory was granted official permission to produce stoneware in 1807.

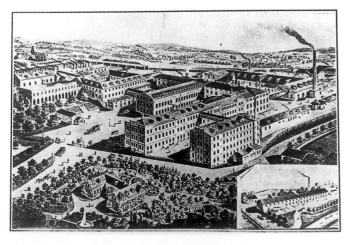

Lithograph illustrating Dalovice factory circa 1870. *Courtesy of Dagmar Braunová.*

Jug, egg-shaped body, elevated handle and double spout, 8"h. Central motif is an allegorical mythological scene entitled "Der Friede" (Peace) with gold border and grain stem ornamentation. RITTER VON SCHÖNAU & HASSLACHER factory, Dalovice, after 1820. *Courtesy of Dagmar Braunová.*

After Johann's death in 1821, his son, Wolfgang Julius, continued to produce stoneware from 1822 to 1832. In 1830, he was granted permission to produce porcelain. A year later, he installed a printing press for transfer designs. He sold the factory and estate to **Wilhelm Wenzel Lorenz** in 1832, who produced pottery and household porcelain and decorative ware as well as figurines.

Decorative cup, late Empire style, bell-like shape resting on impressed teardrop base, elevated serpentine handle, 3.9"h. Central panel is a Greek mythological scene in miniature of a blind Homer and guide on the seashore. RITTER VON SCHÖNAU BROTHERS AND HASSLACHER factory, Dalovice, circa 1830. *Courtesy of Dagmar Braunová.*

Lidded bonbon with oval handles, parrot figurine in biscuit on cover, 10.2"h. Glazed porcelain bowl is decorated with gilded leaves in relief. WILHELM WENZEL LORENZ factory, Dalovice, before 1850. *Courtesy of Dagmar Braunová.*

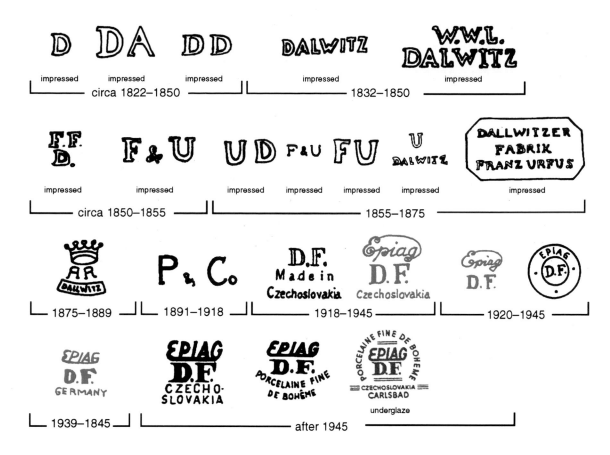

D	DA	DD	DALWITZ	W.W.L. DALWITZ
impressed	impressed	impressed	impressed	impressed

circa 1822–1850 — 1832–1850

F.F. D.	F&U	UD	F&U	FU	U DALWITZ	DALLWITZER FABRIK FRANZ URFUS
impressed	impressed	impressed	impressed	impressed	impressed	impressed

circa 1850–1855 — 1855–1875

AR DALWITZ	P & Co	D.F. Made in Czechoslovakia	Epiag D.F. Czechoslovakia	Epiag D.F.	EPIAG D.F.
1875–1889	1891–1918	1918–1945		1920–1945	

EPIAG D.F. GERMANY	EPIAG D.F. CZECHO-SLOVAKIA	EPIAG D.F. PORCELAINE FINE DE BOHÈME	PORCELAINE FINE DE BOHEME EPIAG D.F. CZECHOSLOVAKIA CARLSBAD underglaze
1939–1845	after 1945		

Lorenz, a gentleman farmer and lawyer, expanded the factory. In 1844, he began using transfer printing, employed over 100 workmen, and had a rather extensive production program. The factory produced Late Empire shapes and high-quality painting. Ferdinand Quast was the chief decorator. The factory produced plaited fruit baskets which were well-known. In 1850, he sold the business to his chief accountant, **Franz Fischer**, who in turn sold it to a local businessman, **Franz Urfuss**, in 1855. The factory began producing Rococo Revival pieces at this time including figurines. **Franz and Julie Urfuss** owned the factory from 1860 to 1861. The factory was operated by the Thuringer Bank from 1861 to 1871.

The factory was then sold to **David and Friedrich Reidel von Riedenstein** in 1871 for 600,000 guldens ($240,000). It produced porcelain household ware and luxury articles, earthenware wash sets and tableware with lead-free glaze, and majolica in a variety of shapes. It was sold to **Baron von Springer** from Loket in 1889. The Baron sold the factory to **Ludwig Pröeschold & Co.** in 1891. Co-owners were Rudolf Gottl, Donath Zebisch, Pfeiffer, and later Pauline Köstler, all were heirs to the business. The factory exported ware to the United States. After 1891, only porcelain was produced. It is known that the factory employed 500 workers in 1904. In 1918, it became a part of the **OEPIAG** merger and then in 1920 part of **EPIAG**.

Following World War I, the factory was modernized. The old circular kilns were replaced by tunnel kilns. Household ware was produced in 1940. In 1945, EPIAG was nationalized by the Czechoslovakian government. The factory is presently operated as a production plant by **EPIAG D.F. Porcelán Dalovice**.

Dolni Chodov - 1811

Chodov Town Emblem.

Chodov Town Photo. The town hall is in the background. *Courtesy of Úřad Města, Chodov.*

Decorative cup and saucer, Sévres style, Vienna adaptation, cup 3.1"h., saucer 5.7"d. Clam-like form with cobalt blue ribbing. JOHANN HÜTTNER & COMPANY factory, Chodov, circa 1840. *Courtesy of Dagmar Braunová.*

Chodov (Chodau) was founded in 1195. It was designated a small city by the monarchy in 1869 and given a town emblem in 1895. It is located about 5 miles west of Karlovy Vary. In 1869, its population was 1,532, which grew to 5,603 by 1910.

Franz Mießl, a coal businessman and owner of the Chodov estate, founded a stoneware factory in Chodov in 1811. Porcelain production began in 1830 using kaolin from Mießl's estate. From 1812 to 1814, Benedikt Haßlacher was a partner and in 1820 Christian Traugott Kreißl became a partner in the business. Several individuals leased the factory from Mießl. These included Franz Lang (1822 to 1824), Wenzel Peter (1830), Wolfgang Julius Freiherr von Schönau (1830 to 1832) from Dalovice, and Franz Weiß (1832 to 1834). Weiß had been the chief decorator at the Kysibl factory. On July 1, 1834, Mießl sold the factory to Johann Dietl, also a coal mine owner, and his partners Johann Hüttner and Johann Schreyer. Hüttner had been a decorator at the Horní Slavkov factory. **Johann Hüttner & Co.** gained the regional license to manufacture porcelain in 1835. They produced table, household and decorative porcelain, and coffee and tea sets.

Shapes were mainly in the Empire style. Biscuit busts of nobility were produced, including Empress Maria Anna and Archbishop A. Schreutz von Notzing. Decorations also encompassed landscapes or flowers.

From 1835 to 1840, the factory produced lithophanes for lamp shades. In 1843, the factory was taken over by Dr. Ernst August Geitner and his partners Johann Stirba and Christian Friedrich Wesenberg. **Geitner & Stirba** operated it until 1845. Alois Peter Porges, a nobleman from Portheim, owned the business from 1845 to 1847. From 1847 to 1870, the factory was owned by Moses Porges, a Praha textile industrialist. Later, his sons Ignaz and Gustav joined him. The factory was expanded and renamed **Portheim & Sons.** Production included hand-decorated household porcelain, painted cups, figurines, candlesticks, vases, writing implements, and drinking glasses. The Rococo Revival style of shapes was produced with extensive gilding.

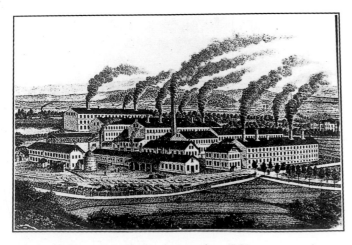

Lithograph illustrating Chodov factory circa 1870. *Courtesy of Dagmar Braunová.*

Figurine of Greek goddess Eris with clam sitting on a dolphin, 5.7"h. Detailed sculpted statue in biscuit with glazed porcelain base has functional use. GEITNER & STIRBA factory, Chodov, 1845–1850. *Courtesy of Dagmar Braunová.*

Large decorative amphora style vase, curved handles with pedestal stand, and swivel square base, 26.8"h. Confluent floral composition with gilded ornamentation. GEITNER & STIRBA factory, Chodov, circa 1850. *Courtesy of Dagmar Braunová.*

Double-sided bowl, clam-shaped with crayfish handle and two small sauce dishes, 13.8"d. Decorative gilded grill work on bowl ribbing. PORTHEIM & SONS factory, Chodov, mid 1800s. *Courtesy of Dagmar Braunová.*

Biscuit porcelain was also produced. Members of the Portheim family continued to operate the business until October of 1872 when **Haas & Cžjžek** in Horní Slavkov acquired the factory. The business grew over the next 50 years, and by 1928 there were 25 people in administration and 500 to 600 workers. At this time, the factory produced household, hotel, and restaurant porcelain. The business exported ware throughout Europe, European colonies, Asia, and the United States. The owners were Olga Baroness Haas von Hasenfels and Felix Cžjžek von Smidaich. In 1945, the factory was nationalized by the Czechoslovakian government. The factory is presently operated as a production plant of **Karlovarský Porcelán A.S. Závod Chodov.**

Another factory in Chodov was operated by Albert Richter, Karl Fenkl, and Alois Hahn from 1883 to 1945 and produced household and table porcelain, coffee and tea sets, and decorative porcelain. In 1882, Karl Fenkl and Alois Hahn from Haas & Cžjžek in Chodov, along with manufacturer Albert Richter in Bärenstein, Saxony, who had previously built a porcelain factory, purchased land to build a factory. It was called the 'New Factory,' in contrast to the Haas & Cžjžek factory, which had been established earlier. The firm name was **Richter, Fenkl &**

Hahn. Fenkl was the technical director. In 1885, Hahn died and his share was transferred to his son-in-law, businessman Anton Langner, who became the factory director.

By 1890, they owned one of the largest porcelain factories in the Karlovy Vary area. At that time it was called **Fenkl & Langner.** Alois Hahn's widow, Anna, was given 4,000 guldens ($1,600) for her interest in the business, which was paid by 1891. In that year, the firm borrowed 80,000 guldens ($32,000) from the Loket bank and expanded the land and buildings. The company was quite profitable and was able to repay the loan by 1896. They produced household ware that was exported to the Netherlands and its colonies, England, and the United States. The company maintained several warehouses overseas.

In 1904, the factory had 800 workers and by 1928 there were 40 administrative staff and up to 8,000 workers. Family members and descendants continued to operate the factory. However, times changed. A lack of skilled labor following World War II (due to the expulsion or deaths of German workers) and the lack of interest in such operations by the communist government forced the factory to close between 1947 and 1948 (*see marks p. 38*).

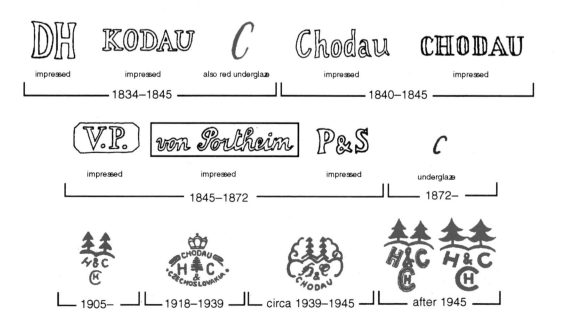

DH	KODAU	C	Chodau	CHODAU
impressed	impressed	also red underglaze	impressed	impressed

└──────── 1834–1845 ────────┘ └──────── 1840–1845 ────────┘

V.P.	von Portheim	P&S	C
impressed	impressed	impressed	underglaze

└──────── 1845–1872 ────────┘ └── 1872– ──┘

└─ 1905– ─┘ └─ 1918–1939 ─┘ └─ circa 1939–1945 ─┘ └─ after 1945 ─┘

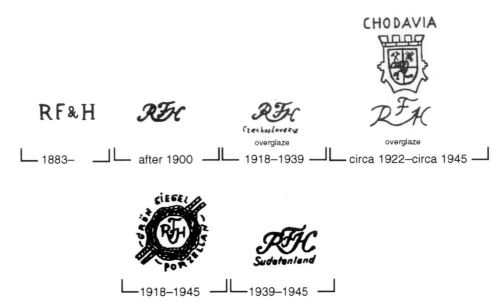

CHODAVIA

RF&H *RFH* *RFH* Czechoslovakia overglaze *RFH* overglaze

└─ 1883– ─┘└─ after 1900 ─┘└─ 1918–1939 ─┘└─ circa 1922–circa 1945 ─┘

└─ 1918–1945 ─┘└─ 1939–1945 ─┘

Stará Role - 1811

Stará Role (Altrohlau) was founded in 1422. It is located 2 miles west of Karlovy Vary across the Ohře river and approximately 25 miles east of the German border. The town takes its name from the Rolava river which runs through it. In 1854, the population was 525. In 1869, it was 1,331, and by 1900 it had grown to 5,358. Stará Role is now part of the Karlovy Vary city district.

In 1900, there were three porcelain factories and three decorating studios in Stará Role. The factories employed 1,624 workers in porcelain manufacturing including throwers, repairers, and decorators.

The oldest factory in Stará Role was established in 1811 by **Benedikt Haßlacher** when he founded the Faience and Earthenware Factory. He built a mill, a round kiln, a stoneware factory, and a residence on the left bank of the Rolva river. Although he had gained permission from the monarchy to produce stoneware, he attempted to produce some porcelain, but was not successful.

Haßlacher (1778–1835) was the former director of a stoneware factory in Dalovice. He produced several kinds of plain and painted pottery. Although an experienced potter, the business in Stará Role was not profitable. As a result, he leased part of the factory to Jan Nódherné in 1820, sold part of it to Ondřej Schwengsbier, sold the administrative part of the business to his son, and then moved to Praha. Later, he was employed by the Vienna Porcelain Factory and explored the mountains around Zagreb, Croatia, finding excellent deposits of kaolin. He became director of the stoneware factory in Nová Ves, a suburb of Zagreb.

After the lease expired in 1823, Haßlacher sold the factory to Praha businessman **August Franz Nowotny** who continued to produce only faience (a French term for lead glazed earthenware) and pottery. These included a variety of products - tea or coffee sets, doll sets, and household ware including jars, flower pots, ink wells, and sinks. Export limits of pottery into Saxony, Prussia, and other German states along with the cheap imports of English stoneware, created economic hardship on the factory (although not as much as on other Stará Role factories). As a result of a petition he sent to the Austrian king, complaining about the English imports damaging his business, he received permission from the monarchy in 1838 to produce household, table, and decorative porcelain.

Nowotny and other family members renovated the factory and expanded the business. In 1842, he installed a printer and introduced transfer printing, which was used on pottery until the factory began porcelain production. He also received permission to establish stores for his products in Praha, Vienna, and

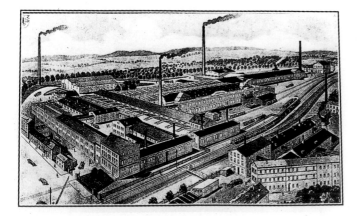

Lithograph illustrating Altrohlau Porcelain Factories circa 1920. *Courtesy of Dagmar Braunová.*

Individual tea set, Historical style with purple violet decoration and gilded ornamentation, teapot 6.7"h. AUGUST NOWOTONY factory, Stará Role, 1880s. *Courtesy of Dagmar Braunová.*

Budapest. Nowotny paid more attention to quality and design than the founder. Not only did he copy popular English styles of the time, he also developed new designs and shapes by working with Praha painter and designer Jiří Dobler. Models for several pieces were created by the Praha sculptor Thomas Seidan (also see Březová factory). The 'little flower' decoration of tulips and roses was frequently used in the middle of plates and dishes. The process was used to transfer the monochrome (blue, green, brown, or red) outline of the design, which was then hand painted in color.

Nowotny was a good businessman. He satisfied his customers and followed the changing fashions. In the 1840s, it was Chinese patterns, later romantic countrysides, castles, fortresses, popular tourist places, and Rococo Revival style. He also mass produced small figural pieces. These were sold to people of middle-class means who wanted something impressive looking to display in their homes. Other items that were popular included multi-purpose pieces such as figures serving as flower holders, match cases, bonbon dishes, and candle holders. A specialty of Stará Role were ink wells with figures having dinner. These were usually not marked. The business employed more than 100 people. A new factory was built between 1866 and 1871 on the right bank of the Rolva river and the old factory was torn down except for two buildings, which were retained for living quarters. At this time, the factory consisted of eight round kilns, a cobalt kiln, a printing facility, ninety turning wheels, a modern warehouse, and shipping area and a new rail connection to Karlovy Vary. New steam powered machines were also installed. Nowotny owned and operated the factory for twenty-five years. In 1868, it was taken over by his nephew, Emanuel Nowotny. In 1870, the factory employed 800 workers including 116 potters and 40 apprentices, 83 decorators with 40 apprentices, 16 printers, 176 raw material workers, 36 machinists, and 120 warehousemen and packers, who each worked ten hours a day. The firm maintained a kindergarten for the children. In 1873, the country suffered an economic crisis which started in Vienna. This lead to a decrease in sales for the porcelain industry.

In 1884, the business was sold at auction and was purchased by **Moritz Zdekauer**, a Praha banker, who continued the same mass production, much of it for American export. Zdekauer had loaned the business money in prior years, so the purchase was most likely made in an attempt to recover some of the bad debt. The factory sold porcelain under the Habsburg China mark as well as its own mark, and manufactured porcelain for United States importers such as Lazarus Straus & Sons and Burley & Tyrell Company. As the economy failed to improve after the acquisition, Zdekauer was forced to lay off hundreds of workers. In 1887, the factory employed 320 workers.

In 1886, the Association of Austrian Porcelain Manufacturers was formed to promote the marketing and sale of porcelain. Alexander Schäferling, the factory director at the time, was named to the Association's council. During this time the social conditions in the industry improved due to the establishment of life and health insurance programs for workers. Several strikes by workers occurred in attempt to improve salaries and to shorten the work day.

The factory experienced significant growth in the early 1900s. Electricity was installed in 1904. In 1900, the firm had 430 workers and by 1907 employed 1,100. Wares were exported to North and South America, Holland, and the Dutch colonies.

A United States bank failure in 1908 caused another reduction in sales for the factory. This lead to another change in own-

ership. In 1909, **C. M. Hutschenreuther** in Hohenberg, Bavaria, purchased the factory and operated it as **Altrohlau Porcelain Factories**. The Praha banking firm retained some small ownership in the business until 1921 when it became a joint stock company. At this time, the factory covered 13.3 acres of which 10 acres were buildings. The firm also gained control of a kaolin mine in Otovice and a 1,900 square foot store in Praha. German money infused into the business increased its capitalization from 1.8 million German marks to 2.3 million marks. In 1911, the factory was modernized and the first tunnel kiln in the country was installed. This allowed the factory to continuously fire their ware and make major improvements in productivity. The company was one of the leaders in establishing recovery after World War I. By 1922, the firm employed 1,260 workers. In 1928, the factory had 3 tunnel kilns which produced 25 carloads of household porcelain. After the depression of the 1930s, the business quickly recovered and by 1937 employed 1,200 workers. During World War II, the factory's main customer was the German war economy. Porcelain ware was produced for the German army, hospitals, prisoner canteens, and supplies for bombed areas. Only ten percent of wares could be exported and only then to countries doing business with the German Third Reich (see chapter on Marketing and Sales of Bohemian Porcelain).

The director in August of 1945 was Engineer Cerný. The factory wasn't damaged much due to the war so its equipment could be used again. In late 1945, following World War II, it was nationalized by the government of Czechoslovakia and was known as **Starorolský Porcelán**. The factory produced household porcelain. During the 1950s, the business was supposed to be an example of a model factory; however, over 20 percent of its wares were discarded due to defects in production. Several reorganizations ensued; but until workers could be properly trained, little improvement occurred. In 1958, when the national state corporation **Karlovarský Porcelán** was created, it was incorporated as a part of this business and was called Stará Role I. It presently is operated as the joint stock company **Starorolský Porcelán Moritz Zdekauer A.S.** The chairman is Engineer Antonin Salva. It is located at Závodu miru 93.

Starorolsky Porcelain factory, Stará Role, Bohemia. It was founded in 1810 as an earthenware factory and in 1884 was acquired by Moritz Zdekauer, a Praha banker. The MZ logo on the building has been in use since that time.

William Pistor founded the **Crown-Porcelain Works William Pistor & Co.** in 1870 as a decorating studio. Josef Dutz bought the shop in 1908 and began manufacturing porcelain. The firm was called **Porcelain Industry Dutz & Co.** in 1923. The owners from 1925 to 1930 were Franz Dutz and Franz Holdschik. Ownership transferred again in 1932 and the factory was renamed **Holdschick & Co.** In 1936, Franz Manka from Telnice (Tellnitz) bought the factory and named it **Porcelain Factory Franz Manka**. He expanded the business producing household, hotel, and decorative porcelain and electrical insulators and fireproof cookware. Luxury porcelain was also produced

Starorolsky Porcelain factory, Stará Role, Bohemia. Factory store at Závodu míru 93. Although the sign indicates the factory was established in 1810, it did not receive permission from the Habsburg monarchy to produce porcelain until 1838.

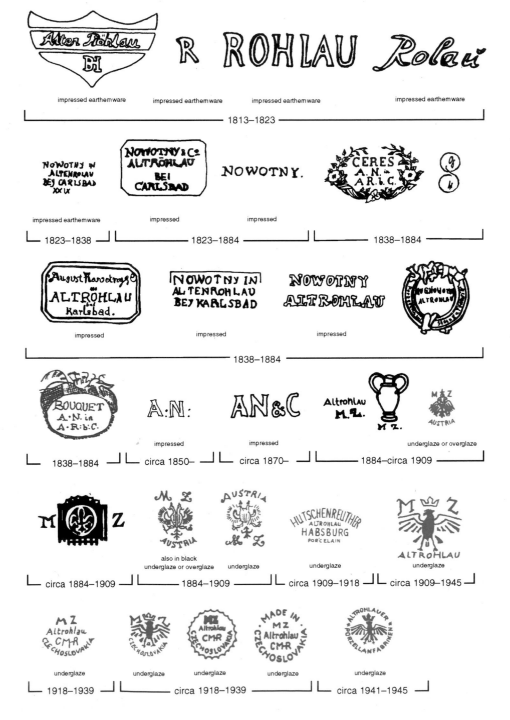

in 1944. The business continued through 1945. It was confiscated by the Czechoslovakian government in 1946 and merged with other factories in the area. The factory closed in 1951. The firm employed 40 workers in 1920, 100 workers in 1927, and 150 workers in 1937.

1936–1945

Maximilian Marx (1852–1898) and **Oscar Gutherz** (1856–1938) established a porcelain decorating factory along the Rolava (Rohlau) creek in Stará Role around 1884. Marx was born in Otterburg, Germany, which also was the hometown of Lazarus Straus (see chapter on Marketing and Sales of Bohemian Porcelain). Following the Franco-Prussian war, he emigrated to the United States and settled in Georgia. Later, he joined the Straus firm in New York City and ultimately became their foreign buyer around 1879. The business was financed by Lazarus Straus, who was Gutherz's father-in-law. The partners were distant cousins-in-law through members of the Straus family. Their business was the predecessor of the Oscar and Edgar Gutherz factory. The firm initially decorated porcelain purchased from other factories but later expanded to produce porcelain with the impressed LS&S (Lazarus Straus & Sons) mark as well as their own mark. In 1893, Marx was taken ill and confined to his home so that the factory was managed solely by Oscar Gutherz. At that time, the firm employed 350 workers in the decorating department and shipped over 5,000 large casks of ware to the United States. In 1898, Oscar Gutherz' brother, Edgar, purchased Marx's share of the business following his death. Edgar had been vice-president of the Straus-owned porcelain factory in Rudolstadt, Germany. The brothers added five new kilns and enlarged the buildings. In the 1890s, the factory produced household and decorative porcelain. The Gutherz factory's motto was: "French Taste, French Quality at Carlsbad Prices." Prior to 1899, the Marx &

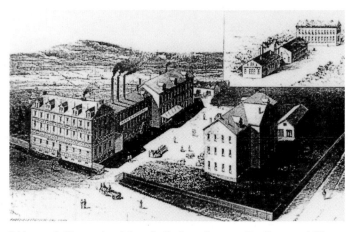

Lithograph illustrating Marx & Gutherz factory. *Crockery and Glass Journal* 37(2): 26 (1893).

Gutherz factory had an exclusive agreement with L. Straus & Sons to market their porcelain both under the LS&S as well as their own factory mark. After the Gutherz brothers took over the factory, the exclusive agreement was changed to permit them to sell to other importers. The factory was identified as No. 888, Carlsbad, by L. Straus & Sons. The year 1899 was an excellent year for porcelain export to the United States. In an advertisement in the December 1899 *Crockery and Glass Journal,* the Gutherz brothers attributed their success to low prices, superior quality, tasteful shapes, attractive patterns, immense assortment, and variety of lines.

The firm was located in two factories. The smaller of the two was devoted to underglaze decoration and special work that required "hard firing." It also was used to produce ware for LS&S (see chapter on Marketing and Sales of Bohemian Porcelain). The larger buildings served as the main porcelain manufacturing area.

On April 1, 1918, toward the end of World War I, a corporation was formed that acquired the Gutherz factory for 800,000 krones ($80,000) and it became part of the Austrian Porcelain Industry AG (Österreichische Porzellan-Industrie AG) known as **OEPIAG**.

According to the sales contract, assets included the surrounding property, some residences, manufacturing buildings, packing halls, kilns, a courtyard, a melting oven, and a mechanic shop. Several items were not included in the sale. These were: the manufactured goods, all accounts receivable, all supplies present on April 1, 1918 of porcelain ware finished and unfinished, packaged and unpackaged, samples, raw materials especially the supplies of clay, gravel, kaolin processed or unprocessed, glazing material, coloring material, printing material, paints, gold supplies, special tones processed or unprocessed, grinding stones, and special minerals.

In 1920, the name of the corporation was changed to First Bohemian Porcelain Industry (Erste Porzellan-Industrie AG) known as **EPIAG**. After World War II, the company was nationalized by the communist government of Czechoslovakia. The original Gutherz factory is presently used as a decalcomania plant by Karlovarský Porcelán and is known as **Karlovarský Porcelán A.S. Závod Sitotisk**. The director is Engineer Jan Toufar. It is located at Závodu miru 90, between the Moritz Zedkauer factory owned by Starorolský Porcelán and the old 'Victoria' Schmidt & Co. factory, which also is part of Karlovarský Porcelán.

Oscar and Edgar Gutherz family taken in 1896. *Left standing,* Edgar, age 37; *left seated,* Oscar, age 40; *infant,* Emmi; Oscar's wife, Jeannie, age 25; *right standing,* Edgar's wife, Lina, age 24; *standing on chair,* Edgar's son, Oscar, age 2.

Karlovarský Porcelán A.S. Závod Sitotisk factory, Stará Role, Bohemia. The factory was the original site of the Marx & Gutherz factory in 1885 and later the Oscar & Edgar Gutherz factory. It now produces decalcomania (transfers or decals) used for porcelain decoration.

Types of Wares

During the 20 years the Gutherz factory existed, it manufactured an extensive variety of porcelain ware. The table below lists several of the wares the factory produced.

Items

Ash Trays	Jardinieres
Berry Bowls	Muffineers
Bonbons	Napkin Rings
Bouillon Cups and Saucers	Nut Bowls
Bowls	Nut Dips
Boxes	Olive Dishes
Bread Trays	Pancake Bowls
Cake Sets	Perfume Bottles
Cake Plates	Pin Trays
Candle Sticks	Pitchers
Celery Trays	Platters
Chop Plates	Puff Boxes
Chocolate Pots	Punch Cups
Coffee Pots	Rim Plates
Collar Button Boxes	Salad Bowls
Condensed Milk Jars	Salt Dips
Coupe Plates	Salts and Peppers
Cream Soups	Shaving Mugs
Creamer and Sugars	Stick Pin Holders
Cups and Saucers	Stud Boxes
Dinnerware	Talcum Shakers
Dresser Sets	Teapots
Dresser Trays	Tea Sets
Fish and Game Sets	Tea Tiles
Hair Receivers	Toothpick Holders
Hatpin Holders	Tumblers
Ice Cream Sets	Tumbler Stands
Jelly Jars	Trays
Jugs	Vases

Many of these items are illustrated in Chapter 5. Hollow ware such as vases, salt and pepper shakers, salt dips, and perfume bottles were frequently identified with a mold number.

Impressed mold number with factory backstamp on the underside of a vase. OSCAR & EDGAR GUTHERZ, 1898–1918.

The Gutherz factory used lithographic transfers extensively for decoration. Many of these were highlighted by hand painting in selected areas. The technique is known as *mixtion* from the French meaning "a mixture." This process allowed the manufacturer to apply a 'hand painted' stamp on the back of the ware. Early in the production, the decorator individually signed his name and later it appeared to be incorporated into the transfer itself. At least five decorators were employed. They were known only by their first names. They were Fann, George, Laporte, Martin, and Raymond. The hand-decorated transfers were given several different pattern names including *Rose du Barry*, which, according to Ludwig Danckert, is a misapplied use of the name *Rose Pompadour* which also was used. This name was taken from the rose colored glaze of Sèvres porcelain. Other pattern names included *Boule de Neige* or "snow ball" for the hydrangia flower, and *Gloire de Dijon*, a famous French rose. These names aren't surprising given Oscar Gutherz's early training in Limoges. Much of the whiteware exported by the factory to the United States was hand painted by American decorating studios and individual artists.

In addition to decorated porcelain, the Gutherz factory sold whiteware to other factories in the area, and for export to America. One such business was the Carl Friedrich Boseck & Co. factory (1880–1934) in Nový bor (Haida). The city is located about 50 miles north of Praha. In the 1890s, Edgar Gutherz had worked in the Straus-owned glass factory in Kamenický Šenov (Steinschöngau), which is located about 4 miles east of Nový bor, and he probably knew Carl Boseck from that time. The factory used a red overglaze mark.

overglaze
circa 1882–after 1934

Gutherz produced dinnerware in several popular designs. In 1899, the factory produced the "Washington" line with patterns 3214, 3239, 3248, 3306, 3413, 3508, and 3604. This line consisted of eight different decorations including sprays and flowers, wild roses, and foliage clusters. Border patterns included forget-me-nots and a laurel wreath intertwined with tiny roses. Other lines included "Virginia" patterns 2761 and 2771; "Duchesse" patterns 81, 3040, 3064 and 3136; "Festoon" patterns 25 and 46; "Canada" pattern 3277; and "Savoy" pattern 2835. These were all open stock patterns exported to L. Straus & Sons in New York City. The Haviland "Ranson" blank was called "Louis XIV" in the 1914 Sears, Roebuck and Co. catalog. A similar pattern produced by Hutschenreuther, a well-known German firm in Selb, Bavaria, was called "Racine." Other Haviland style blanks produced in the Gutherz factory included: "St. Cloud" (Schleiger no. 116) with a beaded relief border added; a floral modification of the "Shantilly" pattern (Schleiger no. 7); "Marseille" (Schleiger no. 9); and "Portia" (Schleiger no. 12). Hundreds of Haviland patterns have been identified since 1950 by Arlene and Donna Schleiger. Each pattern has been assigned a unique "Schleiger number." Gutherz also produced several pieces using the "Donatello" shape popularized by Philip Rosenthal & Co. AG, Selb, Bavaria. Some of the patterns continued to be produced and exported to the United States after the Gutherz factory became part of EPIAG.

A number of Haviland-like cup shapes were produced. These included styles similar to Schleiger Smooth Blank Cup Shapes B, D, F, and J.

Dinnerware (see Chapter 5) included several serving and accessory pieces, in addition to different plate sizes. The composition of a popular Gutherz dinnerware set is shown in the table below.

O.&E.G. Royal Austria Dinnerware
Louis XIV Pattern No. 1779 (Similar to Haviland "Ranson")

Sauce Boat, oval, attached plate
Sauce Boat, oval, mayonnaise, 7 3/4"l
Bowl, Cereal, 6 5/8"d
Bowl, oval, baker, 9 1/2"l
Saucer, fruit, 5 1/4"d
Soup Plate, coupe, 7 3/4"d
Vegetable bowl, oval, covered, 11 1/4"l
Cup, tea, 3 1/4"d
Saucer, coupe, tea, 5 3/8"d
Plate, coupe, cake, 11 1/2"d

Plate, rim, dinner, 9 5/8"d
Plate, rim, breakfast, 8 3/4"d
Plate, rim, dessert, 7 3/4"d
Plate, rim, bread & butter, 6 1/4"d
Plate, rim, butter, 3 5/8"d
Platter, oval, 15 5/8"l
Platter, oval, 12"l
Pickle Dish, oval, 8 1/4"l
Butter Dish, drainer, 7 1/2"d

The largest factory in Stará Role was **"Victoria" Schmidt & Co.**, begun in 1883. The factory was founded by Lazarus and Rosenfeld, Ltd., an import and commission firm in London, with showrooms in New York City, Australia, and South Africa. In March of 1885, they sold the factory to Franz Schmidt. Proprietors in 1904 were Abraham and Benedikt Rosenfeld, London. In addition to pottery, the factory produced household, hotel and decorative porcelain, coffee and tea sets, keepsakes, souvenir cups and tumblers, and ivory ware, much of it for United States export.

Marshall Field's department store was a large account. Both the factory mark and department store name are found on pieces of dinnerware. The factory's main goal was commercial production and did not strive for artistic value. In addition, they produced inexpensive stoneware items such as soup bowls which were called "Porelite." These were produced for individuals who couldn't afford the more expensive porcelain ware. The company also manufactured high quality gold-decorated Rococo porcelain miniature dining room sets including pianos, chairs, tables, sofas, and cabinets with mirrors.

By 1900, the factory employed 975 workers. It became a joint stock company around 1927. By 1937, 1,400 were employed there. During World War II, the factory produced porcelain for the German Waffen SS. The factory was nationalized by the Czechoslovakian government in 1945 and merged with EPIAG (the old Gutherz factory) to become part of **Starorolský Porcelán**. In 1958, during another reorganization of the porcelain industry in Bohemia, it was incorporated as part of **Karlovarský Porcelán** and called Stará Role II. In 1970, the factory became a training facility for apprentices. Presently, it serves as the machine plant for Karlovarský Porcelán and is located at Závodu miru 70. The director is Engineer Jirí Stocek.

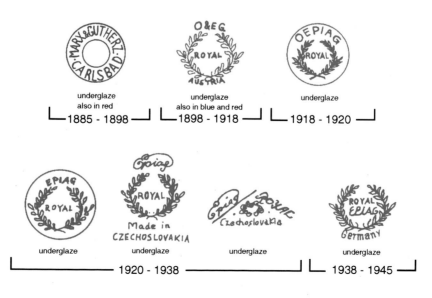

underglaze
also in red
└── 1885 - 1898 ──┘

underglaze
also in blue and red
└── 1898 - 1918 ──┘

underglaze
└── 1918 - 1920 ──┘

underglaze   underglaze
Made in CZECHOSLOVAKIA
underglaze
└────── 1920 - 1938 ──────┘

underglaze
└── 1938 - 1945 ──┘

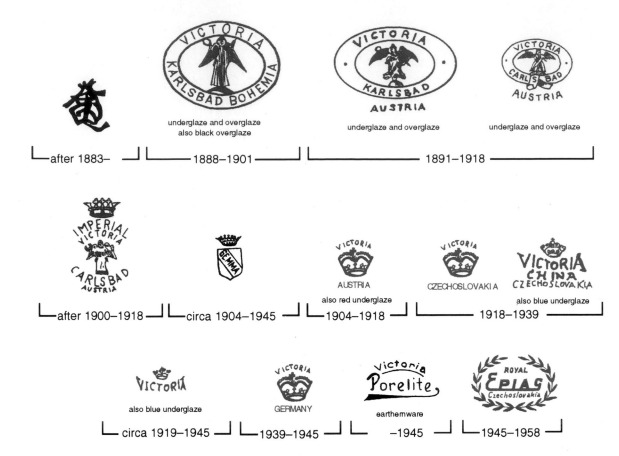

underglaze and overglaze
also black overglaze

after 1883–

1888–1901

underglaze and overglaze

underglaze and overglaze

1891–1918

after 1900–1918

circa 1904–1945

also red underglaze

1904–1918

also blue underglaze

1918–1939

also blue underglaze

circa 1919–1945

GERMANY

1939–1945

earthenware

–1945

1945–1958

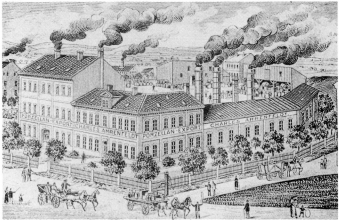

Charles Ahrenfeldt & Son decorating factory in Stará Role. *Crockery and Glass Journal* 53(6): 23 (1904).

Charles Ahrenfeldt & Son (see Chapter on Marketing and Sales of Bohemian Porcelain), operated a factory and decorating studio in Stará Role from 1886 to 1910. The factory was renovated and enlarged in 1896. Richard Linke and Carl Sulzer were factory directors. In 1899, production included table and household ware. Much of its output was exported to the United States.

The firm was purchased by **Bosshard & Co.** who operated it until 1920. From 1920 to 1925, it was known as **Eberl, Möschl & Co.** Owners in 1925 were Alfred Möschl and Ferdinand Hein. In 1929, the factory was known as **"Gloria" Porcelain Manufacturing Factory.** Anton Weidl was the owner and operated it along with Ernst Weidl.

The firm produced mocha and coffee sets and mocha cups. After 1926, the factory was only involved in decorating souvenir ware. In 1927, the factory employed 100 workers. The factory closed in 1949 when it was merged along with other Stará Role factories into the national corporation known as **Starorolský Porcelán**.

overglaze

overglaze

also in red overglaze

1886–1910

1886–1917

44

J. Schneider & Co. manufactured household porcelain and utility ware from 1904 to 1945. The factory was founded by F. Anton Schneider and Johann Geier. Later, they were joined by Josef Lenhart. In 1910, the firm produced coffee and cooking pots. By 1927, there were 150 workers producing household ware with underglaze decoration. In 1926, the factory was purchased by **Josef Lenhart** and later operated by his descendants, Anton Lenhart, Otto Lenhart, and Berta Lippert from 1943 to 1945. The Schneider & Co. name was used through 1937. It closed in 1949. The company exported dinnerware to the United States.

Between 1919 and 1920, **Engineer Julius Fritsch** and **Karl**

also in blue

└─ 1904–1945 ─┘

Weidermann began a small factory, which they operated until 1945. The business had its origin as a porcelain decorating studio founded by Carl Weidermann in 1876. It is not known when the business first began the production of household porcelain.

In the ensuing years, there were several changes in ownership and lessors. In 1925, the owners were Karl Weidermann, Engineer Julius Fritsch, and Alosia Lippmann; in 1930, Karl Weidermann, Engineer Julius Fritsch, and Albertine Fritsch (From 1936 to 1939, the factory was under compulsory management by the bank); in 1940, the Volksbank Altrohlau; and **Herbert Manka** about 1943. In 1938, the factory was leased to Franz Manka. From 1942 to 1944, the firm Schützler & Company operated the business, then Herbert Manka again from 1944 to 1945. The factory produced bottle stoppers and electrical insulators in 1944. The firm employed 60 workers in 1924 and 29 workers in 1944. The factory closed in 1946.

└─ 1921-1939 ─┘ └─ 1939-1945 ─┘

Josef Plaß operated a porcelain decorating studio in Stará Role from 1870 to around 1920.

also in black overglaze

└─ circa 1897–circa 1920 ─┘

Loket - 1815

Loket Town Emblem.

The arched concrete bridge leads to the Loket town square. The church of St. Wenceslaus (1734) is just to the right of the castle. *Courtesy of Úřad Města, Loket.*

Loket (Elbogen) was founded perhaps as early as 1170 when parts of the existing castle were built. Between 1308 and 1352, it was designated a small city by the monarchy and given a town emblem. It is located in the Slavkovský forest about 10 miles southwest of Karlovy Vary in a bend of the Ohře river, hence its name which means elbow. In 1869, its population was 3,257 and in 1910 it was 3,968. Today, the town is a well-known tourist destination. Three porcelain factories and a decorating studio were located in Loket.

Two brothers, **Rudolf K.** and **Eugen K. Haidinger** from Vienna founded a branch factory in 1815 and three years later called it the **Haidinger Brothers Porcelain Factory in Elbogen**. It also was known as **Vienna Porcelain and Earthenware Factory of Haidinger Brothers**.

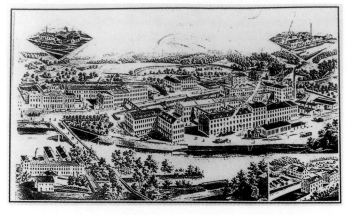

Lithograph illustrating Spring & Company factory circa 1885.
Courtesy of Dagmar Braunová.

Figurines, Meissen style, girl with bird and boy with dog in historical costumes, 4.7"h. RUDOLF AND EUGEN HAIDINGER factory, Loket, 1840. *Courtesy of Dagmar Braunová.*

Decorative cup, Meissen style with elevated gold banded handle, 3.1"h. Central miniature painting is a scene from Loket. RUDOLF AND EUGEN HAIDINGER factory, Loket, circa 1820. *Courtesy of Dagmar Braunová.*

The Haidinger brothers had served a three-year apprenticeship at the Vienna factory and made several visits to potteries in Germany, France, and England. They were the first to use local coal for firing instead of wood and English methods of slip casting in making their ware. Johann Josef Niedermeyer, master modeller in Vienna, helped establish the factory. They used kaolin from Seldec. In its early days, the Loket factory only produced porcelain that had a grayish color. As they improved the kaolin washing process, the color improved as well. Wares were sold to Viennese porcelain decorating studios. In 1820, as the Vienna factory's financial condition worsened, the Haidinger Brothers were forced to separate the Loket business from it. In 1828, their brother, Karl Wilhelm, a mineralogist, became a partner. They produced table and decorative porcelain, coffee and tea sets, laboratory porcelain, and figurines.

After Karl Wilhelm joined the firm, the factory made several improvements. They hired experienced workers to improve productivity, installed new clay mixing equipment, and began blue underglaze decoration.

Next to some of the factory marks they impressed three numbers. These indicated the last three digits of the year it was produced. During the 1830s, the factory won several gold and silver medals at porcelain exhibitions in Praha and Vienna. Their

Decorative cup and saucer, Rococo Revival style, gilded relief with floral design and scalloped edges, cup 2"h., saucer 5.7"d. RUDOLF AND EUGEN HAIDINGER factory, Loket, 1835. *Courtesy of Dagmar Braunová.*

Coffee set, thin-walled porcelain in Secession style (Austrian version of Art Nouveau), coffee pot 8.7"h. Tulip decoration, mold no. 2770, decoration no. 1889. SPRINGER & CO. factory, Loket, circa 1900. *Courtesy of Dagmar Braunová.*

production of Meissen style figurines and Rococo Revival shapes during this time was well-known. The company exported dinnerware to the United States as early as the 1860s. Following the death of the Haidinger Brothers, the business was sold in 1873 to Springer & Oppenheimer and named **First Elbogen Porcelain and Coal Industry.**

Johann Walenda (1867–1886), Ludwig Pröscholdt (1887–1890) and Max Roesler (1890–1894) were the factory directors. In 1884, the factory produced luxury articles and faience.

Oppenheimer left the factory in 1885 and the business became a joint-stock company. The factory name was changed to **Springer & Co.** In 1896, the factory exported white and decorated porcelain, sanitary goods, druggist's sundries, and fancy specialties to the United States through the import firm Loewe

& Dierckx. In 1900, the firm produced a variety of religious figurines. The factory director, Ludwig Pröscholdt, was a co-owner in 1904. Rudolf Wesel directed the factory from 1908 to 1921. Dinnerware patterns during that time included "Meteor," "Aria," and "Asmanit." In 1918, following World War I, the firm became part of the **OEPIAG** operation and in 1920 the name was changed to **EPIAG.** Gustav Lenter was the factory director from 1922 to 1939. During this time, the factory produced ivory porcelain and the dinnerware pattern "Rosee," as well as hotel porcelain. The factory is presently operated as a production plant by **Karlovarský Porcelán A.S. Závod Loket.**

A second factory was established in Loket by Johann Kempf, a potter, and his wife, Margarethe, who operated a kiln at Zechtalstraße 8 from 1872 to 1880. Between 1886 and 1887,

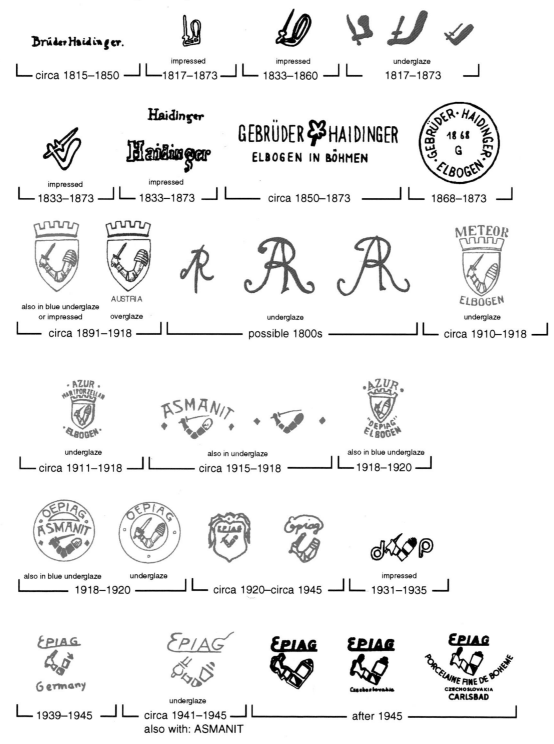

they hired Klement Winter, a porcelain decorator, and his wife, Julie, a restaurant owner, to manage the factory which was then called **Winter & Co**. At first, they produced pottery and then in 1888 both earthenware and porcelain. In 1888, Winter married Margarethe Kempf. Records are not available, but it appears that the two couples must have divorced with Winter marrying Kempf's wife. In 1890, Johann Kempf sold his share in the factory to restaurant owner Andreas Maschauer and the factory cashier, Hermann Lochschmidt, who lived in Loket (see below). Kempf then built a new pottery in Hory (Horn). After Kempf left, the firm built a larger factory at Zechtalstraße 32. They employed Friedrich Schmid, a porcelain decorator from Horní Slavkov, and his wife, Emilie.

The factory produced children's cups, coffee and milk pots in several sizes, mocha cups, cooking pots, egg cups, Turkish cups, religious keepsakes, figurines, and vases. Much of the production was exported.

In 1891, the firm sold their small factory at Zechtalstraße 8 to Heinrich Kretschmann and Franz Wurda for 8,000 guldens ($3,200). Kretschmann had been a factory officer, and Wurda, who was from Loket, provided the financial backing. In 1892, the factory was sold to Georg Friedrich from Hřebeny (Hartenberg) for 9,650 guldens ($3,860). The factory's financial situation declined, and in 1893 workers took over the business under the name **Lippert, Much & Co**. The factory was sold at auction in 1894 for 13,005 guldens ($5,202) to Ernst Schlesinger in Neudek, Bavaria, the brother-in-law of Georg Friedrich. Schlesinger bought the factory for his sister, Anna, who had a previous financial interest in it. They leased the factory to Heinrich Kretschmann who purchased it in 1898 for 14,500 guldens ($5,800). It was then called **Kretschmann & Co**. Adalbert Hofmann, owner of a porcelain decorating studio in Stará Role, was a co-owner. In 1899, Kretschmann purchased Hofmann's share for 8,100 guldens ($3,240) and became sole owner. In 1900, the business employed 26 workers. After making improvements and expanding the factory in 1891, 1898, 1905, and 1907, he leased the factory to Albert Stark in 1910. Stark had formerly been with Rokyta Decorators which was located at Zechtalstraße 17. The firm was known as **Stark & Co**.

From 1894 to 1910, the factory had no modellers or decorators. Kretschmann sent his whiteware and cooking pots to independent decorators in Stará Role, Krásno (Schönfeld), Doubí (Aich), Nový bor, Děčín (Varnsdorf), Plzeň, Praha, Budapest, and Loket. The modeller Franz Wolf in Hory and Rudolf Glaser in Loket and porcelain decorators Rudolf Harnischdörfer and Albert Stark did occasional work for him. His figurines of Faust, Gretchen, baptismal fountains, the Madonna, and Christ were painted during the 1890s by the Horní Slavkov decorator Franz Langhammer. Loket artist Johann Thomaier decorated figurines and vases.

In 1912, shares were sold to Heinrich Fieler in Karlovy Vary and the Bohemian Escomptebank. In 1916, Kretschmann sold his remaining shares to Fieler who merged the porcelain decorating business with his factory. During World War I, the factory was closed from November of 1914 to February of 1916. Fieler's daughter, Ernestine Rokyta, sold her shares in the factory in 1919 for 278,315 Czech krones (Kč) and the accompanying furnishings for 250,000Kč. The factory employed 85 workers in 1922. Heinrich Rokyta, Ernestine's husband, continued to direct the factory until he died in 1935. During this time, the world-wide depression had caused severe economic setbacks for the Czechoslovakian porcelain industry. In 1935, it was taken

over by the Karlsbader Vereinsbank. After Rokyta's death, the factory was directed by Rudolf Lippert until it closed in 1938. About 1940, it was used for porcelain decorating by Johann Hoffman. It was closed from 1942 to 1945. The factory was under government operation from 1945 to 1949. At that time, Johann's brothers, Franz and Ernst, were lumber dealers and used the building in their business.

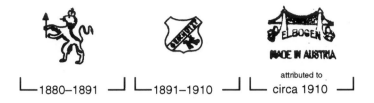

| 1880–1891 | 1891–1910 | attributed to circa 1910 |

A third porcelain factory began operation in 1890 and was called **Winter, Lochschmidt & Co**. The owners were Klement and Julie Winter, Andreas Maschauer, and Herman Lochschmidt. Friedrich Schmied, an owner of a porcelain decorating factory in Horní Slavkov, helped them plan the factory. His wife, Emilie, was also a partner in the firm. During the first quarter of 1891, the main building, including the kiln house and turning room, the clay mill and machine and boiler house, were constructed. Lochschmidt, tired of the business, sold his shares to businessman Ernst Renz in Vienna in September of 1891. During 1892, they added decoration and packing rooms. The factory employed 163 workers at that time. By 1895, the Winter & Company firm (see above) was in financial trouble. It was sold to Carl Speck for 130,000 guldens ($52,000). Speck was a brother-in-law of Hajniště (Hegewald) porcelain factory owner Adolf Persch who served as a guarantor of the loan. The factory name was **Austria**. Benjamin Hunt purchased an interest in the business in 1896 and in 1897 it was called **Benjamin F. Hunt & Son**.

They leased the factory for 4,000 guldens ($1,600) per year. This permitted them to use Speck's decorating, storage, and packing rooms, and the building was enlarged. Under the agreement, Hunt could only produce the 1998 and 2004/2 patterns. The contract allowed them to become owners within 10 years; but in 1901 Speck went bankrupt and the factory was sold to the **Adolf Persch** factory in Hajniště. The Loket factory was operated by his sons Adolf and Rudolf. Hajniště is located about 120 miles

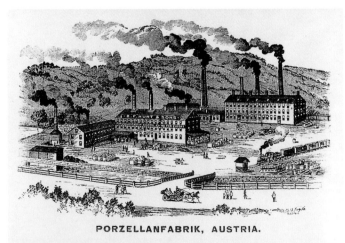

PORZELLANFABRIK, AUSTRIA.

New China Factory, Elbogen, Carlsbad.

Lithograph illustrating Hunt factory. *Crockery and Glass Journal* 45(9): 15 (1897).

northeast of Karlovy Vary near Frýdlant (Friedland). Persch founded a factory there in 1850. Household ware with a straw-flower pattern was produced. Tableware and decorative plates were exported to the United States.

In the early 1900s, the factory expanded and more land was acquired. Unable to make loan payments to the Karlovy Vary bank, the firm declared bankruptcy and the factory was sold at auction. It was leased to Julius Dietl in Jalový Dvůr (Kaltenhof) in 1934. Jalový Dvůr is a small village near Loučky (Grünlas). Until 1939, it was known as **Julius Dietl Porcelain Factory in Elbogen and Kaltenhof**. At the beginning of 1940, it was leased to the R. Kämpf factory in Loučky. In 1941, by official government approval, it was leased to the firm **Porag**. In 1943, Porag bought the factory from Karl and Rudolf Persch, Adolf Persch in Nové Město (Neustadt), and the widow of Max Persch. Max had died in Loket in 1938. Grete and Julius Groß operated the factory through 1945.

In 1940, the Porag firm, also known as Porag, Porcelain Radiator GmbH was part of the German Economic Industry, Berlin, along with the R. Kämpf factory in Loučky. Josef Dengler, a Karlovy Vary ceramist, and Arthur Dieterle, director of the glass factory in Nové Sedlo (Neusattl), were business directors until 1945 when it closed.

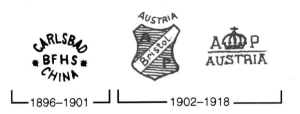

1896–1901	1902–1918	

Johann Hoffman operated a decorating studio in Loket from around 1927 to 1945.

underglaze

1926–1945

Rybáře - 1848

Rybáře Town Emblem.

Rybáře (Fischern) is located 1 mile north of Karlovy Vary on the opposite side of the Ohře river and today has been incorporated into the city district. The town gets its name from the fish that were caught in the river. It was founded in 1511. In 1869, it had a population of 1,479 and by 1910 it was 10,374.

The **Karlsbad Porcelain Factory Carl Knoll** was established in Rybáře in 1848. Carl Josef Knoll initially started it in 1842 as a kaolin processing factory. After Knoll's death in 1868, his sons, Adolf, Karl and Ludwig, expanded the factory and produced household, table, and decorative porcelain and gift and collector articles. Knoll's son, Gustav, built a kiln factory between 1872 and 1876. In 1877, decorated blue porcelain was produced. Factory ware included ice cream, coffee, tea and wash sets, display plates, and artistic and luxury articles in 1895; hotel dinnerware, mugs, decorative vessels, jardinieres, luxury services, wall tiles, and doll heads in 1904; and fireproof cookware from 1937 to 1944. The factory was owned by Anton Weber from Hohengrund, and Wilhelm Lorenz, Alfred Lorenz, and Karl Knoll in 1903; Rudolf Weber, Wilhelm Lorenz, and Alfred Lorenz in 1925; Rudolf Weber, Wilhelm Lorenz, and Heinrich Endres; then Ernst Mayer and Heinrich Endres in 1935; and Ernst Mayer and Mathilde Endres in 1944. The factory name was continued until 1945. In 1887, the factory employed 423 workers; in 1895, there were 350 workers and in 1937 there were 450 workers. The reduction in workers in 1895 may have been due to the rapid expansion of porcelain manufacturing in the area at this time and the demand for skilled labor to operate them.

Wares were exported to the United States. In 1920, the 'onion pattern' was added to its stock of decoration. At least thirteen different marks were used by the company. They used the banded escutcheon or 'beehive' mark beginning in 1883. Carl Rädler of Vienna objected to the factory using this mark and the company had to withdraw it later that same year. However, it continued to be used on export porcelain.

In 1885, the firm constructed the Japanese Porcelain Pavilion in the middle of a small artificial island in a fish pond across from the factory. It was designed by Adolf Mießner and decorators were Wilhelm Jeßl and Hermann Zimmermann. The angular-shaped building with tri-level roofs was capped with three towers reminiscent of a pagoda. The porcelain roof tiles were decorated with oriental dragon designs. The walls were constructed of Parian porcelain containing four small and eight large paintings on porcelain plates. These depicted different types of

Lithographic illustration of the Japanese Porcelain Pavilion built in 1885 by the Carl Knoll factory in Rybáře to demonstrate the firm's ability to decorate using Japanese designs. *Courtesy of Státí okresní archiv Karlovy Vary.*

larger-than-life Japanese birds, complimented by country scenes in the background. Additional paintings provided a balanced and aesthetic feeling to the building. This effect was enhanced by the different materials that were incorporated including faience, Parian, and hard paste porcelain. A cafe inside the pavilion served the visitors of the Knoll factory. From the pavilion, tourists could view the beautifully landscaped grounds as white swans idyllically swam through water lilies bobbing on the surface. A small boat could be rented for fishing. The island was reached by a 140-foot long bridge. The Japanese Porcelain Pavilion was well-known throughout Europe and many Karlovy Vary spa guests came to see it.

The pavilion was destroyed by Soviet soldiers in 1945. Today, the pond serves as the Rolavé swimming pool.

Photo of the Japanese Porcelain Pavilion showing construction details. *Courtesy of Anna Gnirs and the Sudetendeutsches Archiv, München.*

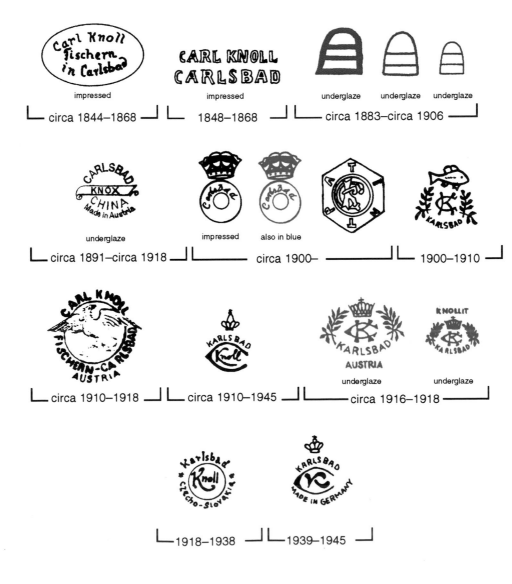

50

Bawo & Dotter Carlsbad factory in Rybáře. *Crockery and Glass Journal* 23(14): 15 (1886).

In 1883, **Bawo & Dotter** established a decorating studio here.

Between 1883 and 1884, they began producing decorative porcelain in Vienna and Sèvres styles, coffee and tea sets, dinnerware, toilet sets, and gift and collector articles in addition to porcelain decorating.

The firm's main import office was in New York City (see chapter on Marketing and Sales of Bohemian Porcelain). By 1897, the factory employed 250 workers. The factory closed in 1913. Later, it operated in 1930–1933 under the same name as porcelain enamel decorators. The main European office of the company was located in Kötzchenbroda (a Dresden suburb), Saxony. In 1910, the factory exported porcelain ware that ranged in price from 25 cents to 2 dollars. These prices were similar to those of other factories at the time.

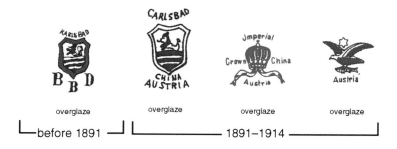

Doubí - 1849

Doubí (Aich) is located 2 miles southwest of Karlovy Vary. The town was founded in 1365. In 1869, it had a population of 916 and by 1910 the population was 2,031.

In 1849, **Johann Möhling** started a factory here after dissolving his partnership with August Haas in Horní Slavkov. He produced household and decorative porcelain and figurines. Möhling also manufactured porcelain coins that were used instead of metal coins in times of economic crises. Later, he produced both household and luxury ware which were exported to the United States. In 1862, he sold the factory to **Baron Franz Freiherr von Ziegler** from Würzburg who operated the business for only two years, selling it to **C. V. Anger** in 1863 with

A. **Carl Anger** joining in 1864. Anger continued to produce similar items as his predecessors, as well as coffee and tea sets and portraits painted on porcelain. Anger's heirs operated the factory in 1899. There were 310 workers in 1900.

In 1902, the factory was sold to **Ludwig Engel & Son**, who operated the business until 1918. Under Engel's ownership, it also manufactured hard porcelain rollers and drums. The factory then became a branch of **Josef Thomas Menzl & Co.** Leo Hähnl and Edward Wolf were also partners in the business. The factory was called **Porcelain Factory Aich, Menzl & Co.** and its products included household and oven proof porcelain. In 1922, the factory was acquired by **EPIAG** and converted for the mass production of household and hotel porcelain and coffee and tea sets. It closed in 1933.

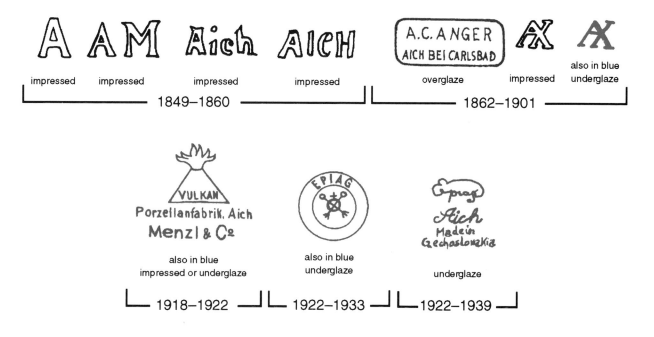

Duchcov - 1853

Duchcov (Dux) is located 50 miles northeast of Karlovy Vary. It was founded in 1207 and by 1869 had a population of 3,352 and 12,164 by 1910.

Edward Eichler established an earthenware factory here in 1853 which became the **Dux Porcelain Manufactory** in 1860. The factory produced figurines and decorative and table porcelain in Baroque, Rococo, Empire, and Art Nouveau styles. The firm became well-known for its production of human and ani-mal figurines. By 1905, the factory had 400 workers, operated on steam, and produced its own electricity. After 1945, the factory merged with the Eichwald Porcelain, Stove and Tile Factory, Dr. Widera & Co. in Dubí, and Count Thun's Porcelain Factory in Klášterec to form a state-owned business called **Porcelánova Manufaktura Royal Dux Bohemia A.S**. Now, it is privately owned since the establishment of a democratic government in the Czech Republic. The company produces household, decorative and table porcelain and coffee and tea sets. It continues to export ware to the United States.

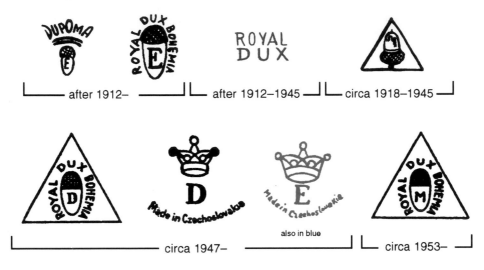

after 1912–   after 1912–1945   circa 1918–1945

circa 1947–   also in blue   circa 1953–

For a short time, beginning in 1883, **C. Riese Porcelain, Terra Cotta and Majolica Factory** produced decorative porcelain and earthenware.

1883–

Merklín - 1868

Merklín Town Emblem.

Merklín(Merkelsgrün) is located 7 miles north of Karlovy Vary along the Bystřice river. The town was founded in 1273. In 1869, it had a population of 134.

Lithograph illustrating Camill Schwalb factory in Merklín. *China, Glass and Lamps* 3(12): 3 (1892).

The **Becher & Stark** porcelain factory was established here in 1868 by Alfred and Malvine Becher. It produced earthenware and household and decorative porcelain. In 1871, it was owned by Fanni Becher and Anna Stark. Ten years later, the factory was taken over by the Karlsbad Savings Bank. The firm exported large amounts of household porcelain to the United States in the 1880s, including ice cream, coffee, tea, and chocolate sets.

In 1882, the factory was known as **Schwalb Brothers**. Advertisements in the *Crockery and Glass Journal* of 1886 stated that the New York City import firm of Benedikt & Friedman were United States agents for the factory. The Schwalb Brothers also purchased a small porcelain factory in 1882 from Heckmann & Company (established in 1878) in Rybáře (Fischern). This factory was damaged by fire in 1883 and closed.

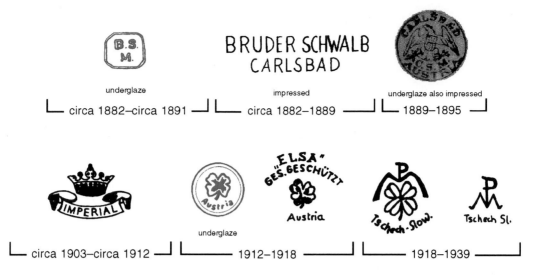

BRUDER SCHWALB
CARLSBAD

underglaze

circa 1882–circa 1891

impressed

circa 1882–1889

underglaze also impressed

1889–1895

IMPERIAL

Austria

"ELSA"
GES. GESCHÜTZT
Austria

Tschech. Slow.

Tschech Sl.

circa 1903–circa 1912

underglaze

1912–1918

1918–1939

By 1889, the owner was **Camill Schwalb**. George Borgfeldt & Co., a New York City commission merchant (see chapter on Marketing and Sales of Bohemian Porcelain), was the sole United States and Canadian agent for the factory in the 1890s. In addition to household porcelain, the factory also produced electrical insulators.

In 1895, the business was known as **Karlsbad Kaolin Industry Co**. The factory employed 426 workers in 1900, which grew to 500 by 1904. At that time, the factory was producing technical porcelain ware, in addition to household ware and electrical insulators. In 1912, the business merged with **Zettliz Kaolin Works Department Porcelain Factory Merkelsgrün**, operating until 1945. After 1926, the factory mostly produced electrical porcelain insulators. In 1937, production included laboratory porcelain as well, and in 1944 the factory was producing porcelain bottle stoppers, electrical insulators, and candlesticks. The firm also served as a laboratory for low voltage, high frequency electrical testing.

Ostrov - 1873

Ostrov Town Emblem.

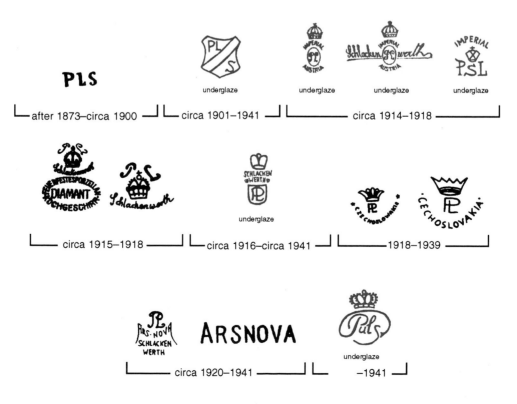

PLS

after 1873–circa 1900

underglaze

circa 1901–1941

underglaze

underglaze

underglaze

circa 1914–1918

circa 1915–1918

underglaze

circa 1916–circa 1941

1918–1939

ARSNOVA

circa 1920–1941

underglaze

–1941

Ostrov (Schlackenwerth) is located 7 miles northeast of Karlovy Vary. It was founded in 1207. In 1869, it had a population of 1,774.

Josef Pfeiffer (?–1912) from Rybáře and Ludwig Löwenstein established a factory here in 1873. Josef Pfeiffer, Jr. (?–1942) managed the factory around 1900. At that time, they employed 132 workers. **Pfeiffer & Löwenstein** produced household, hotel and decorative porcelain, coffee and tea sets, and gift articles. The factory exported porcelain to the United States. In 1937, the factory had 280 workers. Luise Löwenstein who followed Ludwig Löwenstein lost his shares in 1938. In 1941, it was renamed **Porcelain Factory Schlackenwerth Josef Pfeiffer**. In 1944, the owners were Louise Pfeiffer, Engineer George von Hoffman, and Dr. Wilhelm Pfeiffer. The factory closed in 1949.

Dvory - 1883

Dvory (Meierhöfen) is located 7 miles southwest of Karlovy Vary. It was founded in 1653. In 1869, it had a population of 124 and 2,335 by 1910.

Between 1883 and 1885, Veit and Philipp Benedikt founded the **Benedikt Brothers Porcelain Factory**. The business exported porcelain to the United States (see chapter on Marketing and Sales of Bohemian Porcelain). In 1907, Veit Benedikt was the owner, followed by Leo and Otto Benedikt in 1910. In 1923, the firm was known as **Benedikt Brothers AG** and in 1925 it was called **United Porcelain Factory Meierhöfen**. The owners around 1928 were Leo Benedikt and Berthold Moser-Benedikt. From 1929 to 1945, the factory was part of **EPIAG**. Berthold Moser-Benedikt was born in 1901 in Dvory and served as director general of EPIAG in 1931. He was the vice-president of "Kaolina" and an executive director of Porcelain Factory and Kaolin Wash "Alp," located in Hlubany (Lubau). This firm also merged into EPIAG in 1939. Berthold moved to England in 1938 just before the outbreak of World War II. From 1899 to 1911, the factory employed 400 workers. This increased to 550 by 1937.

A second factory known as the **Moser Brothers Britannia-Porcelain Works** was established in 1898 by Otto, Felix, and Hugo Moser. It produced household, table, luxury and decorative porcelain, which it exported to the United States (see chapter on Marketing and Sales of Bohemian Porcelain). In the early 1900s, the business was called **Porcelain Factory Meierhöfen**. In addition to its earlier wares, the factory produced ivory porcelain vases. In 1899, the factory had 150 employees and 237 in 1900. By 1904, the number of workers had dropped to 150. It was purchased in 1912 by Stará Role factory cashier Ludwig Eberhardt. It was then known as **Eberhardt & Co.** until 1918 when it merged with Benedikt Brothers. The new business was known as **United Porcelain Factories Meierhöfen**. In 1928, there were 1000 workers employed in the combined factories. In 1937, the factory produced whiteware and decorative porcelain and in 1944 household ware. The factory is presently operated as a production plant by **Hotelovy Porcelán A.S.**

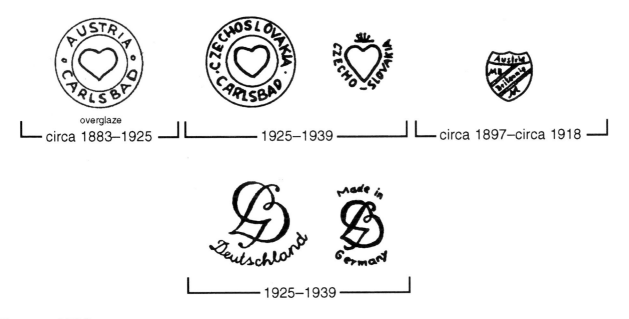

overglaze
└─ circa 1883–1925 ─┘ └─ 1925–1939 ─┘ └─ circa 1897–circa 1918 ─┘

└─ 1925–1939 ─┘

Božičany - 1890

Božičany (Poshetzau) is located 4 miles northwest of Karlovy Vary. The town was founded in 1379 and by 1869 had a population 370. In 1910, the population was 1,175.

In the castle on March 31, 1890, Philipp Schreyer, the accountant from Haas & Čžjžek in Chodov, established a formal contract with Israel S. Maier from Karlovy Vary and Nathan Ehrlich from Chodov to produce porcelain in Božičany. The factory was known as **I. S. Maier & Co., Poschetzau Porcelain Factory**. In 1900, it was owned by I. S. Maier and Philipp Schreyer and employed 400 workers. Maier's widow, Berta, took over her husband's shares following his death in 1909. In 1924, the owners were his daughter, Bertha Heinzmann, and later Gertrud Kastl in Chodov. In 1928, Nathan Ehrlich's share was transferred to his sons, Engineer Karl and Otto. In 1911, I. S. Maier's share went to his son Arthur. In 1937, the factory employed about 500 workers and produced household porcelain including wash services, coffee, tea and chocolate sets, plates, and white and decorative bowls for export to England, France, the Orient, and North and South America. In 1938, Otto and Josef Ehrlich as well as Arthur Maier lost their shares to the German Reich. The factory was taken over by Dr. Engineer Hugo Apfelbeck in Karlovy Vary. Dr. Heinrich Langl of Chodov took over Gertrud Kastl's share. From 1945 to 1967, the factory remained closed. The business was dissolved in 1968.

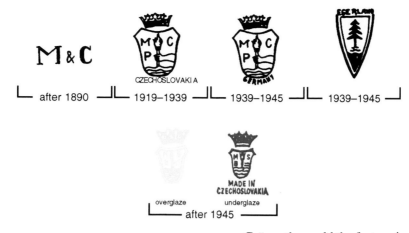

Hory - 1897

Hory (Horn) is located near Loket and 4 miles southwest of Karlovy Vary. The town was founded in 1350. In 1869, it had a population of 268 and by 1910 the population was 906.

In 1897, **Louise Klier** purchased an earthenware factory from **Johann Kempf** who had established it in 1890 (see Loket factory). Two years later, she converted it to both a porcelain and an earthenware factory. Her husband, Alois Klier, was the decorating supervisor in the porcelain decorating factory owned by B.F. Hunt & Sons in Loket. In 1899, the small factory was sold to **Wenzl Grünes**, a porcelain factory manager in Stará Role, and his brother, Franz, who was a kaolin and grain handler in Ostrov. In 1902, Wenzl bought out his brother. In 1903, the firm was known as the **Grünes & Co. Porcelain Factory and Decorating Studio**. In 1904, the factory produced white and decorated ware including cups, coffee pots, goblets, children's cups, coffee and tea services, fruit bowls, trays, candlesticks, and vases.

Grünes then sold the factory in 1905 to his friend, Heinrich Wehinger, who was director of the Doubí porcelain factory, and to Rudolf Wagner. It was known as **H. Wehinger & Co**. The new owners enlarged the factory. In 1907, the factory employed 150 workers and produced household ware, including thin cups, tableware, tea sets, trinkets, miniatures, vases, and soft porcelain coffee pots. By 1913, the factory employed 230 workers which grew to 350 by 1920. The employees of the Schamott brickworks, also owned by Rudolf Wagner, and the porcelain factory were combined in 1920. The factory produced household and electrotechnical porcelain. The company exported ware to the United States.

In 1921, the factory was incorporated and called **H. Wehinger & Co. AG**. Drs. Berthold Knopflmacher and Oswald Kochler in Litoměřice (Leitmeritz) were investors. After 1922, the factory was threatened with closure, but continued producing household ware and pottery until the economic crises that affected the Czechoslovakian porcelain industry in 1928. Unable to pay their electric bill of approximately 88Kč to the Loket government, the factory was forced to close. The firm was dissolved in 1930.

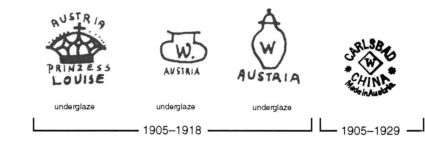

Karlovy Vary - 1900

Karlovy Vary (Karlsbad) was founded by the Czech and Roman Emperor Charles IV in 1358. The town emblem dates to this time. The twelve mineral hot springs located in the central part of the city gush out of the ground at temperatures between 30 and 72 degrees Celsius. Individuals from all over Europe and Asia come to this spa town for the restorative cures the thermal waters are thought to bring. In 1869, its population was 7,887 and by 1910 it was 15,000. Today, the city has 58,000 inhabitants. It is surrounded by the Slavkovský forest and overlooks the Sokolov plateau and the Krušné mountains to the west.

The city was the center of the Bohemian porcelain industry. Several factories were not actually located in the city, but included the name in their marks. Following World War I, it served as the headquarters of **OEPIAG** and in 1920, **EPIAG** (see chap-

Karlovy Vary Town Emblem.

55

The city of Karlovy Vary is nestled in a valley at the confluence of the Teplá and Ohře rivers. In the distance is the Imperial Spa Hotel, a well-known luxury hotel in the 1920s and 1930s. *Courtesy of Úřad Města, Karlovy Vary.*

ter on Marketing and Sales of Bohemian Porcelain). Today, several porcelain producing towns are within the boundaries of the city district, including Březová, Doubí, Hory, Rybáře, and Stará Role.

Karlovy Vary also served as the headquarters of **Porcelain Union, United Porcelain Factories AG** from 1922 to 1927. This was a consolidation of factories in Klášterec and Turn. In 1927, this organization also became part of **EPIAG**. Many of the EPIAG marks retain some connection with the original towns where the factories were located. After the sale of the Gutherz factory in Stará Role in 1918, Oscar Gutherz became the director of Porcelain Union. Edgar Gutherz served as the technical director.

L—1920–1945—J

The **Porcelain Manufactory Josef Kuba** produced household and decorative porcelain and gift articles, and operated a decorating studio here from 1900 to 1945. After World War II, the factory moved to Wiesau, Bavaria. The firm exported decorative ware to the United States.

L—1900–1945—J

Friedrich Simon had a decorating studio here from 1920 to 1931. The firm exported decorative ware to the United States. Blanks were purchased from local factories including the "Bohemian" Ceramic Works AG. in Nová Role.

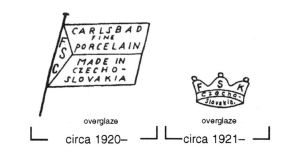

overglaze   overglaze
L—circa 1920—J   L—circa 1921—J

Bochov - 1902

Bochov Town Emblem.

Bochov (Buchau) is located along the Střela river 11 miles east of Karlovy Vary in the Slavkovský forest. It was founded in 1349 and by 1869 had a population of 1,803.

Alfred Pollak began producing porcelain doll heads here in 1902 and attached them to dolls in his factory in Rybáře. In 1904, Pollak and Hoffman were owners. They sold the business to Josef Plaß in 1907, who later took in Paul Roesner as a partner in 1912 and enlarged the factory. Plaß also operated a decorating studio in Stará Role. The business was then known as **Buchau Porcelain Factory Plaß & Roesner**. Biscuit doll heads with hairstyles were produced in addition to vases, bowls, and religious items. In 1927, the factory changed production to fine household porcelain and in 1944 added tableware. In 1924, owners were Paul Roesner, Therese Roesner, Franziska Ullmann, Anna Schramm, Amalie Plaß, and Auguste Plaß. Although the

factory was closed from 1933 to 1937, it opened again producing household porcelain mainly for export. Paul Roesner was the sole owner from 1938 until the factory closed in 1945.

Loučky - 1907

Loučky (Grünlas) is located 4 miles southwest of Karlovy Vary. The town was founded in 1397. In 1869, it had a population of 309 and by 1910 the population had grown to 1,908.

Benjamin F. Hunt & Sons in Boston established a factory here in 1907. It was known as **Egerland Porcelain Factory**, which was still under construction when it went bankrupt a year later due to a United States bank failure. The firm advertised a location in Nový bor but may only have had an office there. Hunt, located in Boston and New York City, was an importer of souvenir china in addition to several lines of dinnerware. The name "Imperial Austria" was used on some lines. In 1908, the business was taken over by **Ludwig Engel & Son** located in Doubí. They used the factory to decorate finished whiteware produced in Doubí. By 1911, the unfinished factory had been sold to Richard Kämpf and was known as **Porcelain Factory Richard Kämpf**; it produced table and household porcelain and coffee and tea sets until 1945. Kämpf's wealthy friend Richard Dieterle, director of the glass factory in Nové Sedlo, became a partner in 1911. The firm was then known as **R. Dieterle & R. Kämpf GmbH**. Kämpf's shares in the firm were inherited by his widow, Josefine, and later his son, Hans, and daughter, Antonie Kümmelmann. The heirs to Dieterle's shares were his son, Arthur, and his sisters, Gertrude Schuberth, Doris Langhans, and Elfriede Dieterle. The factory was enlarged several times between 1920 and 1943. Wares were exported to the United States. Today, the firm is known as **Leander 1946 s.r.o.** It is located at U porcelány 143.

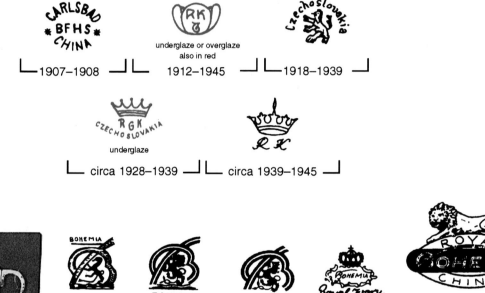

Nová Role - 1921

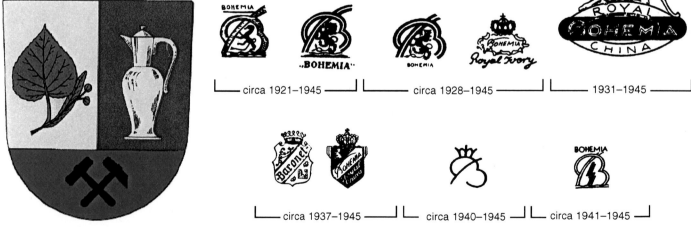

Nová Role Town Emblem.

Nová Role (Neurohlau) is located 5 miles northwest of Karlovy Vary. The town was founded in 1293. In 1869, it had a population of 377 and by 1910 the population was 869.

The **"Bohemian" Ceramic Works AG** was founded here in 1921 and produced household and hotel porcelain, and coffee and tea sets. Wares were exported to many countries, including the United States. Beginning in 1922, the Phillip Rosenthal AG porcelain factory in Selb, Bavaria, was a partner. In 1937, the factory employed 600 workers. Following World War II, it was nationalized by the Czechoslovakian government. In 1976, the factory used the "onion" pattern on their ware. The business is presently operated as **Karlovarský Porcelán A.S. Závod Nová Role**. A refractory plant is also located in Nová Role and is called **Karlovarský Porcelán A.S. Závod Karborundovna**. The factory produces firebrick for lining furnaces.

Other Regional Factories

At present it is not known if the following Karlovy Vary area factories exported porcelain to United States.

Budov (Buda) is located 16 miles east of Karlovy Vary. **Franz Lang** founded an earthenware factory here in 1825. In 1831, he began manufacturing porcelain coffee and tea sets. In 1860, his son, **Anton Lang**, took over the business and began producing decorative porcelain. By 1870, the factory was only producing porcelain. The factory was closed from 1883 to 1891. It then operated again under Anton Lang until 1904. It was owned by **Kasseker & Reiger** in 1908 and then **A. Eichler** through 1914. From 1914 to 1938, it was owned by the brothers **Josef and Franz Spitzl**. The factory produced household ware. It closed on April 1, 1938.

impressed	underglaze	impressed	impressed
circa 1825–circa 1860	1831–1860	1860–1880	1860–1880

Chlum (Klum) is located 17 miles southwest of Karlovy Vary. **Anton Burgemeister** established a factory here in 1819. He leased it in 1821 to Adelbert Lauda and Josef Köchler as an earthenware factory. Following Lauda's death in 1828, the business was operated by his widow through 1831. It was then leased by **Anton Walz** from Leipzig who later purchased it. Under his ownership the business declined. It was auctioned to **Johann Feresch** in 1835 and he operated it through 1853. It produced household and decorative earthenware and porcelain.

impressed	impressed	impressed
	1800–1850	

Jakubov (Jokes-Wickwitz) is located 10 miles northeast of Karlovy Vary. **Ernst Mader** from Lesov purchased a farm and built a small porcelain and decorating factory here between 1895 and 1896. Ownership changed several times: In 1895, Emanuel Gareis and Ernst Mader were the owners. The factory was known as **Gareis & Mader**. Ernst Mader was the owner in 1898, Leo Höhnl in 1906 and **Emil Schürer & Co.** in 1908. Josef Thomas Menzl was a partner about 1911 and then ownership transferred to **Anton Renz** from Chodov about 1913. From 1916 to 1945, it was owned by **Menzl & Co.** and produced household porcelain.

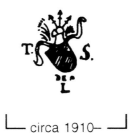

1914–1945

Jeleny (Hirschen), a small village near Lubenec, is located 23 miles east of Karlovy Vary. Franz Lehnert from Kysibl-Stružná founded a factory here in 1846. Lehnert died in 1881, but the firm name **Franz Lehnert** continued until 1883. It was closed for a time and then was reopened in 1898 by the brothers Josef and Kleophas Kasseker from Horní Slavkov. In 1912 it was owned by **Heinrich Reinl**. By 1933 the factory was operated as a branch of the factory in Teplička (Töppeles). In 1943 owners were Heinrich, Rosa and Dr. Anton Reinl. The factory produced household porcelain and tiles from 1846 to 1945. The company also had a branch factory in Lubenec.

circa 1912–circa 1945	–circa 1945	after 1914–

Lesov (Lessau) is located 4 miles northeast of Karlovy Vary. There were two factories in this town. At one time they were owned by the same individual. Malvine and Alfred Becher from Karlovy Vary founded a factory here in 1883 (also see Merklín). Alfred Becher died in 1885 and Franz Schmidt from Stará Role became the owner (see "Victoria" Schmidt factory). Several owners then followed: Emil Schüer and Franz Schmidt were owners in 1890, Gareis & Kasseker Company in 1893, Ernst Mader in 1898, Tichy & Schönfeld in 1904, Schönfeld & Dötz in 1910, Wilhelm Paris from Oberködiitz, Thuringia, around 1914, and Schneider & Company in Stará Role in 1917. The factory produced household ware. In 1937, dinnerware with the blue "onion" pattern was manufactured. The factory employed 39 workers in 1900, 100 workers in 1927, and 60 workers in 1937. It is presently operated as **Atelier Lesov A. S.**

circa 1910–

A second factory was founded here in 1888 by Ernst Mader with permission from the provincial authority. **Kühnel & Co.** purchased it in 1904. The partners were Ernst Mader, Josef Kühnel, and Anton Salomon. At that time the firm employed 140 workers. The factory produced coffee and milk pots, mugs, children's cups, plates, cookware, and jugs.

Following bankruptcy of the company in 1919, the new owners were the Löw Brothers. The factory name was **K.k. Porcelain Factory 'Concordia.'** Josef and Adolf Löw also owned a kaolin washing plant in Lesov from 1904 to 1945. From 1923 to 1930, the factory produced lithophanes. J. A. Wolff was a modeller here and also in Březová during that time. The products included utility and luxury ware, figurines, decorative porcelain lamps with animal figures, vases, lamp stands, clock cases, and knick-knacks.

Winterling & Co. in Oberköditz became leaseholders of the porcelain factory in 1933. They produced Turkish coffee cups and chocolate cups for Dutch East India and also specialized in coffee pots. The factory produced household ware from 1937 to 1945. From 1941 to 1945, it was owned by Karl Hugo and Willy and Wolfgang Bentz, and was a branch of the firm "Melitta-Werke" Bentz & Son in Minden, Germany. After 1945, it belonged to the 'nar. podnik Thunska' (Thun National Enterprise). In 1946, it burned to the ground , but was rebuilt in 1947. The factory is presently operated as a production plant by **Obchodni Spolecnost Concordia A.S.**

Lubenec (Lubenz) is located 22 miles east of Karlovy Vary. **Franz Lehnert** founded a porcelain factory here in 1846 after he left Kysibl-Stružná. Later, the business was taken over by **Schwab** and its successor was **Porcelain Factory Bros. Kassecker.** Eventually, it was operated as **H. Reinl Porcelain Factory**, which was a branch of the same business in Jeleny. The factory is presently operated as a production plant by **Karlovarský Porcelán A. S. Závod Lubenec**.

Unknown Factory Marks

Many firms used the name Karlsbad or Carlsbad in association with their factory marks, even though the factories were not located in Karlovy Vary. Several of these remain unidentified.

MARKETING AND SALES OF BOHEMIAN PORCELAIN

As potteries developed in Europe, roving tradesmen or peddlers carried the wares in baskets, often on their backs for great distances. These individuals were the first to go "on the road" as traveling men.

Early methods of marketing, a medieval pot-seller. *Crockery and Glass Journal* 72(15): 177 (1910).

The Habsburgs controlled the development of new porcelain factories in Austria-Hungary through the early 1800s. The Viennese wanted to develop the kaolin deposits for the state-owned Imperial and Royal Porcelain Manufactory. Finally, German porcelain makers were able to set up factories in western Bohemia with the help of local nobility. Factories in the Karlovy Vary area were required to register their trademarks at the Chamber of Trade in Cheb (Eger). Occasionally these marks were registered with the United States Office of Patents and Trademarks (see George Borgfeldt & Company advertisement in Appendix 1).

Effect of United States Trade Policies on Porcelain Export

Over an 18-year period, from 1895 to 1913, pottery imports into the United States increased 7.59 percent. Bohemian exports during this time increased 40 percent of which 10 percent went to the United States. Demand for porcelain and hand-decorated ware was cyclical, however. War, politics, and economic depression influenced both supply and demand. In America, manufacturers became increasingly concerned about the volume of cheap foreign goods being imported at the turn of the nineteenth century. The McKinley Tariff Bill of 1890 was vigorously opposed by United States porcelain importers. The merchants organized themselves and went to Washington, D.C., to testify that recent increases in duties had resulted in a decrease in importations during the last nine years. The protest was led by Isidor Straus, son of Lazarus Straus of the New York City china import firm L. Straus & Sons. A strong protest was also made regarding the proposed requirement to identify the country of origin on all imported goods. Both protests failed in changing the provisions of the bill. The cost of imported Bohemian china increased between twenty to fifty percent. In addition, the American Potters Association was successful in getting the United States Customs Office to prohibit the importation of chinaware for four months beginning in February 1907. Industrialists continued to put pressure on Congress to establish tariffs to regulate the shipment of a wide variety of materials including chinaware into the United States. In 1909, President Taft signed a pervasive tariff bill into law. The Payne-Aldrich Act resulted in much higher porcelain prices on foreign imports.

Between July 4, 1789, when the first tariff act levied a duty of 10 percent on imported earthenware, and 1914, there were nineteen tariff laws enacted that related to earthen, stone, and chinaware. From 1867 to 1914, there were seven different tariff acts which resulted in an increase of duty rates for undecorated whiteware from 45 percent of value in 1867, to 55 percent in 1913. The tariff act of October 3, 1913, reduced the import duty on undecorated earthenware from 55 to 35 percent ad valorem (percentage of the customs value as stated on the invoice), decorated earthenware from 60 to 40 percent, undecorated china and porcelain ware from 55 to 50 percent, and decorated china and porcelain wares from 60 to 55 percent. United States potteries had small profits at this time: in 1909, 6.5 percent; 1910, 8 percent; and 1911, 5.5 percent (based on actual capital invested). Given the lower tariffs in 1913, American pottery owners indicated they would have to reduce worker's wages to stay in business.

In 1914, Mr. Frank J. Sheridan, special agent of the Bureau of Foreign & Domestic Commerce, supervised a field study of pottery industries in the United States, England, Germany, and Austria (Bohemia). For purposes of the study pottery products were classified as: 1) white earthenware, 2) chinaware, 3) sanitary ware, 4) porcelain electrical supplies, and 5) stoneware, yellow and Rockingham ware, and red earthenware. The study was limited to table and toilet ware of earthenware and vitreous china (porcelain).

Among the conclusions presented was the finding that a large difference in the cost of chinaware existed between American and European factories. United States costs were in general much higher. In fact, the lowest cost of production in any American pottery exceeded the highest cost of any European factory except for one Austrian factory. Eighty-five percent of the workers in the Austrian potteries earned less than $0.10 per hour in

1914 compared with an average wage of $0.40/hour for American workers.

In 1914, a 100-piece Austrian dinner set had an average factory cost of $5.00. Additional costs to American importers included: crate and packing; inland freight in Europe, consular fees, insurance; ocean freight; import duty on package and ware; and inland freight in the United States. These costs added another 70 percent to the factory cost of the ware. Import duty was 60 percent of the factory cost. With a profit margin added by the retailer, Austrian dinnerware was priced in United States stores at $14–20 per set. With the decrease in tariffs in 1913, prices to American importers decreased by an average of five percent.

Effect of War on Porcelain Export

The Napoleonic wars, harvest failures, and famines in 1816 and 1817 and prohibition of importation of Austrian ware by the Prussian Tariff Union of 1836, all restricted the early expansion of porcelain exports from Bohemia. By 1850, and particularly following the American Civil War in the late 1860s and early 1870s, porcelain exports to the United States steadily increased.

Just at the time the demand for porcelain in America was peaking in 1914, war hit Europe again, and depression followed. Several United States importers, particularly those with Austrian, German, and French connections, closed. Importers, including L. Straus & Sons and Strobel & Wilkin, protested in Washington, urging President Wilson to permit goods to be shipped from warring European countries through neutral ports to the United States. This occurred in response to a British embargo on imports from enemy countries to neutral nations. Few individuals in the porcelain import trade saw the war coming, or at least they didn't discuss it. Many of them had relatives operating factories in Germany and Austria. As a result of the assassination of Austrian Archduke Francis Ferdinand in Sarajevo, Austria declared war on Serbia on July 28, 1914. As Germany came to the aid of Austria, Russia came to the aid of Serbia. By August of 1914, all of Europe was engulfed in war. In the early stages, importers believed the war would be of short duration. No one had more than a year's supply of porcelain in their warehouses. Within a matter of weeks, the German ports were closed, and by the end of the year little or no imports were received from Bohemian factories. In 1918, following the signing of the armistice on November 11th, governments changed hands overnight and so did the names of all the Bohemian towns and villages where much of the export porcelain was produced. Czech names of porcelain producing towns in Bohemia are used throughout this book as the primary name with the German name in parentheses.

Foreign currency exchange rates affected the Bohemian factorys' profits. Factories exporting to the United States invoiced importers in guldens (guilders or florins) and after 1892 krones. For purposes of comparison, in 1892 a gulden was equal to two krones. The exchange rate in 1914 was five Austrian krones to one United States dollar. A gulden was roughly equal to 40 cents. By 1917, the effects of the war in Europe had caused the Austrian krone to drop in value to less than one cent.

By 1918, it became clear that rapid consolidation of the porcelain factories in Bohemia must take place. Unemployment was widespread, and sales had plummeted.

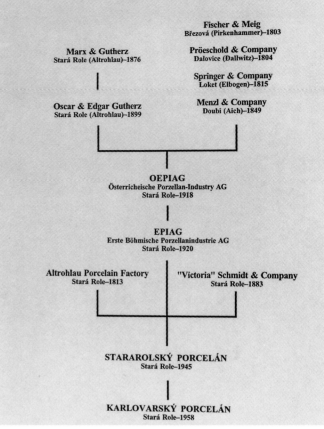

CONSOLIDATION OF KARLOVY VARY AREA PORCELAIN FACTORIES

The economic crisis during and following World War I resulted in the closure and consolidation of many porcelain factories in western Bohemia. The merger of several Karlovy Vary area factories is illustrated in this diagram. The date after each town is the year each factory was established. Later, many other factories outside the Karlovy Vary area also merged into the collective business known as Karlovarský Porcelán.

Exports to the United States and other countries had been cut off by the war and a reduced interest by American consumers in purchasing goods made in Europe created severe economic hardship among these companies. On March 12, 1918, the Vienna government created **OEPIAG** (Österreichische Porzellan-Industrie AG) to centrally manage what was left of the Austrian porcelain industry in Bohemia. On March 3, 1918, the International Bank of Vienna took over and a constitution was approved on April 30, 1918. Later, the Anglo-Czechoslovakian Bank financed the operation.

On June 30, 1920, about a year and a half after the end of World War I, OEPIAG changed its name to **EPIAG** (Erste Böhemische Porzellan Industrie AG or First Bohemian Porcelain Industry Corporation). Several other porcelain factories joined the corporation at this time. These included the Vereinigte (United) porcelain factory (formerly the Benedikt Bros. AG) and the Britannia Porcelain Works-Moser Brothers (formerly Eberhardt & Co.) in Dvory; the 'Alp' GmbH porcelain factory and kaolin processing plant in Hlubany (Lubau) which closed in 1939; Porcelain-Union in Klášterec and Thurn which closed in 1934; and the Metzling Feldspar Works.

By 1925, Bohemian factories began to recover from the effects of World War I. However, the region was soon caught up in the expansion of Hitler's Third Reich (also see chapter on Bohemian Porcelain Production). This part of Czechoslovakia was known as the Sudetenland. It included parts of Bohemia, Moravia, and Austrian Silesia. Approximately 3.5 million Germans lived in the region. In the late 1930s, owners of some of the factories were put into concentration camps and the works confiscated. Prisoners were used as laborers. During this time, the Victoria Porcelain Factory in Stará Role began manufacturing dinnerware for the Waffen SS. In previous centuries, war had passed by the Karlovy Vary area. On September 12, 1944, the Karlovy Vary spa and one-fourth of the train station were bombed, killing 85 men. The suburban areas were largely spared in the attack. On April 17 and 19, 1945, the main train station in Karlovy Vary was bombed and the rail yards in Rybáře and Karlovy Vary were destroyed, effectively immobilizing the transportation of porcelain wares to various destinations.

By the end of the war, porcelain production had largely stopped in most Bohemian factories. In late 1945, local Czechs and Slovaks took over the factories and production resumed. Transportation routes were poor to non-existent, local workers lacked the expertise to run the factories, and not enough raw materials were available. In addition, German workers weren't much interested in working for the new management. Since factory output in the late stages of the war accumulated in warehouses, firms were able to use this inventory to finance the restarting of the factories. Western European countries including Switzerland, Austria, and Belgium were interested in purchasing these wares even if they weren't of first rate quality. Deliveries were quite slow, however. Exports to North America didn't resume until the 1950s.

Exportation Of Bohemian Porcelain

Several porcelain factories in the Karlovy Vary area, as well as other china manufacturers throughout the Austro-Hungarian Empire, exported their wares to other countries. In addition to the United States, much was sold to other European nations. United States importers usually had their trademark placed in red overglaze on the ware. These marks, although treated as proprietary, were rarely registered with the United States Office of Patents and Trademarks. Importer's trademarks, however, were frequently used in advertisements in trade publications.

Exhibitions allowed porcelain factories to demonstrate the quality of their products to the public and especially to potential international buyers. The 1851 Great Exhibition in London was one such event. According to the exhibition catalog, at least five different factories from the Karlovy Vary area displayed porcelain at the Exhibition. The Březová factory, then owned by Christian Fischer, 'displayed dinner, tea and coffee services, vases, toilet services, inkstands, fruit dishes, figures, etc.' The jury gave the factory an 'Honorable Mention.' The Haidinger Brothers in Loket displayed 'dinner, coffee, and tea service, portable service, tea caddy, coffee cups, bread-baskets, writing materials, milk-pots, vases, etc.' They also received an 'Honorable Mention.' The August Nowotny factory in Stará Role displayed vases, flower-pots, dinner and coffee sets, and porcelain figures. Additionally, they exhibited stoneware coffee and tea services. The A. P. Portheim factory in Chodov was another firm that displayed porcelain at the Great Exhibition.

Prospective buyers were entertained by owners of porcelain factories during their visits to the area. Japanese porcelain was first displayed at the International Exhibition of 1862 held in London. Soon after the Exhibition, a period of intense interest in Japanese decoration over took the European Continent. This influence allowed European decorators to move away from the traditional classic designs of border patterns and symmetrical motifs toward asymmetry of design, subtleties of line, and brilliant use of color. One result of this was the construction of the Japanese Porcelain Pavilion (see Carl Knoll Factory, chapter on Karlovy Vary Area Porcelain Factories) in Rybáře.

Late Victorian hospitality in the 1890s and early 1900s centered around the dinner party. For these parties numerous pieces of crockery were required, which included dinner sets for twelve or more and separate sets for serving game, fish, chops, oysters, ice cream, desserts, coffee, tea, and hot chocolate. Bohemian and other factories throughout France, Germany, and England answered the call, manufacturing and exporting thousands of tons of these distinctive pieces.

The demand for china whiteware was greatly stimulated by the popularity of the women's china painting movement which swept America at the end of the nineteenth century. As women become more involved in the arts, many turned to china painting as a way of expression. According to an 1886 article in the *Crockery & Glass Journal* entitled *The Development of China Decoration*, amateur china decorators were unknown in the United States prior to 1876. As the public became more interested in decorated chinaware, both commercial and amateur painting of china increased dramatically. China painting clubs were organized throughout the United States. Large cities in California, Colorado, Illinois, Michigan, New York, and Ohio were locations where china painting was popular. The first ceramic arts club known as the Pottery Club of Cincinnati was found in 1879 by Mary Louise McLaughlin. Another early club was the Manhattan Ceramic Club established in 1892. Susan S. Frackelton, an internationally known award-winning ceramist and china decorator, was elected the honorary president. The club planned on having 1,000 feet of space at the Chicago World's Fair to exhibit pieces of ceramic art. An excellent review of early American china painting may be found in Dorothy Kamm's *American Painted Porcelain: Collector's Indentification & Value Guide.*

China sales room at the Osgood Art School, New York City. Miss A. H. Osgood imported whiteware for her students painting classes. Most, if not all, of the porcelain blanks were purchased through importers. Illustration from 1903 catalog.

Loading porcelain into gas-fired kilns at the Osgood Art School. Illustration from 1903 catalog.

As the market developed for hand-decorated porcelain, the working woman found she could gain employment in large decorating studios, china wholesalers, jewelry stores, and gift shops. China decorator studios sprung up in several cities by the end of the 1800s. The first arts school for china painting was established in 1877 by Adelaide Harriet Osgood (1842–1910). Her studio salesroom provided painting supplies as well as porcelain whiteware from several European factories.

In Milwaukee, Wisconsin, Mrs. Susan S. Frackelton established the Frackelton China Decorating and Color Works in the late 1880s. Her husband, Richard, was a local chinaware dealer. An entrepreneurial woman, she patented a gas-fired kiln in 1886. This made firing china for the amateur painter much easier than using smoky coal-fired kilns.

Another Milwaukee artist, Mrs. Magdalina Kayser established a china decoration business known as the M. Kayser Art Co. It was located in her home at 1227 Twentieth Street. The studio was in business from 1909 to 1916. Lena, as she was then called, purchased Bohemian whiteware from distributors and decorated it in her studio.

Importers and distributors of white china such as the A.H. Abbott Company and Burley & Company in Chicago gave prizes to the decorators that exhibited at the Chicago Ceramic Art Association annual meetings during the early 1900s. In addition, the Burley & Tyrrell Company held competitive exhibitions that further stimulated the sales and decoration of Bohemian produced porcelain. In 1900, Chicago had 10 china decorator studios and by 1910, 44 studios were listed in the city directory. These included well-known names like Bauer, Donath, Pickard, and Stouffer.

As the volume of hand-painted china increased and prices decreased, almost everyone could purchase pieces of hand-decorated porcelain for their homes. As an example, shaving mugs produced by Bohemian factories were sold to distributors who provided them to decorating studios that custom designed mugs for barber shop patrons. Men could select a mug style and decorative pattern from a catalog in the barber shop and have their name placed on it by the decorating studio in gold lettering. When men went to the barber shop for their weekly shave, the barber used the customer's own mug, soap, and brush. The mugs were stored on a mug rack in the shop. An article in the 1899 *Crockery and Glass Journal* details the specialty of decorating shaving mugs.

A WOMAN'S INVENTION.

The Frackelton Portable

GAS·KILN

FOR

FIRING DECORATED CHINA OR GLASS.

◁ NO DUST, SMOKE, OR HOT COALS. ▷

U. S. Patent, Sept. 28, 1886.
U. S. Patent, July 10, 1888.

This kiln can be attached by an India-rubber tube to an ordinary gas-fixture within six inches of a lace curtain.

Needs no chimney.

Simple, and easily managed.

Made now in four sizes.

"The egg form is Nature's choice for the even distribution of heat. All other forms are man's failures."

S. S. FRACKELTON,

Inventor and

Sole Manufacturer.

Small gas-fired kilns made china decorating a possibility for amateur painters. Susan S. Frackelton, *Tried by Fire*. New York: Appleton, 1892.

ART IN THE SHAVING CUP.

OVER on the East side, where all sorts of curious little shops flourish, one of the most curious is a small store on the ground floor of a tenement building, in the window of which is displayed conspicuously a sign bearing the inscription, in English and German, "High Art Decorations on Shaving Cups." Examples of the high art are ranged along under the sign, and it would be difficult to find anywhere a more varied collection. On the curved surface of the mugs are portraits, fancy heads, flags, coats-of-arms, bust of celebrities, mottoes, comic pictures, quotations, and couplets, of what probably is original verse, beside a number of very ornate cups inscribed with the initials of the owners done in text so magnificent that it is quite impossible to make out the letters. These are only a small portion of the stock which the artist keeps on hand, and of which he is very proud. He is an intelligent little old fellow, whose pet maxim is that no man should be without his own shaving mug, and that there is no use in his having one of his own unless it is so decorated that there is no possibility of anybody else getting hold of it by mistake. The tales he tells of the dire results of such mistakes are enough to keep a man from ever entering a barber shop. It is easy, however, to get him switched off from this unpleasant topic to the artistic side of his work, and on that subject he will talk as long as there is any-one to listen.

"In the old times," he said, "it was all initial work. If a man came in and want [sic] a cup decorated, all I had to do was find out his name or initials and put them on in gold or bright colors. But now it is all different, and I have brought about the new fashion, for many years ago I was the first to see that there was room for art in this business. So I made up a few very fine cups and gave them to friends of mine who are big men over here—politicians and brewers and lawyers, an men like that, who start the fashions in this part of the city—and it took right hold, and now I have all the work of a kind that an artist is proud to do. You go into any of the first-class barber shops over here on the East side now, and you'll find the American flag on some of the cups my work. When the war [Spanish-American war] broke out it struck me that there was the place for patriotism, right on a man's shaving cup, so that when he went to get shaved in the morning he'd have something in front of him to make him think of his country, and I turned out a dozen of those. It took like fire, and after that came all sorts of patriotic art.

"The Maine came in for a lot of notice, and I got Dewey down so fine that I can turn out his picture in no time. Mr. McKinley, with "Our President" over his head, makes a very neat piece of work. All the war he-roes have come in for a share, and you could find an art history of the war right on the shaving cups of this part of the city if you went around. There's Roosevelt, Sampson, Schley, and Hobson, Wheeler and Lee, and all the rest of them. I had to get pictures of all of them to reproduce. One of the hardest war jobs I did was the charge of San Juan Hill by the Rough Riders. I put my heart right into that, and I tell you it was too bad to think of staying in a barber shop—it ought to be in a gallery today. The only trouble was that the curve of the cup fixed it so that you couldn't see all the charge at once, but I understand that's the way it was on the hill. So it was all right, and true to life, anyway.

"Now, there's plenty of my customers don't want fancy pictures or anything of that sort, but just pictures of themselves or their families. One fellow had the nerve to come in here the other day with a Coney Island tin-type of himself and his lady friend, and asked me how much I want [sic] to put that on a cup. I told him I didn't reproduce tintypes—not for anybody. But I get plenty of photographs to reproduce, and very nice cups they make. That makes me think of the man that was here lately with a picture of his wife. He wanted it put on with a heavy border of black around it. I asked him how long his wife had been dead, and he said she wasn't dead at all.

'What do you want a morning band put around her for?' I asked.

'Because I wish she was dead,' he says; 'and ev-ery time I look at that it'll make me feel good.'

"First off I thought it was a joke, but it wasn't. If that cup ever gets to his home I bet there'll be trouble. He'll wish it was himself that was dead. Another cus-tomer I had wanted a cup fixed with a picture and in-scription: 'For Governor, P.A. Schmidt,' but didn't bring the picture. I told him I did lots of political work like that, and I'd fix it up for him soon as he brought the photograph, but I said:

'I never heard of any P.A. Schmidt for Governor. Who is he?'

'Oh, that's me,' he said. 'I ain't running yet, but maybe I will some day. I'd like to first-rate.'

"You see, he'll get a lot of harmless satisfaction out of looking at that cup with the inscription on it, even if he never runs, and I haven't heard of anyone nominating him yet. Some queer ones come here, I tell you. Just last week I finished off a mug that was the first of its kind I ever had. It was for a sour old party that didn't like to be bothered with his barber asking him questions, but he couldn't get 'em to remember that in the shop he went to, so he wrote out a list of answers and put 'em all down in a row. His cup read like this when I got it done:

Yes; it is a fine day. Don't talk about it.
What if I am getting bald? Don't talk about that.
Never use any kind of hair tonic.
Water; not very much of it.
It parts on the left side. Look for the place.
N.B.—When I want a shampoo I'll ask for it.

"The old man said he thought that would settle his barber, but a little while after he dropped in and said his barber had got so sore over the inscriptions that he had to go to another barber shop. That isn't the only barber's reminder I had to fix up. One of my oldest customers had me put on, right under his initials, this line: 'Please remember my face is tender.'

"Most of my custom is from the Germans. They're great supporters of the barber shops. That's the reason I have my sign in German, and you'll see that most of the initials are in German letters, though that proves nothing, for nearly all shaving cups are lettered in that way. It seems to be the custom; why I couldn't tell. I must tell you about an old fellow that came in here last winter to get a cup fixed up. He was a typical old Deutscher, and I wasn't all surprised when he asked me if I could affix Emperor William's picture to his shaving cup. That was just after we heard of the Ger-mans making themselves so numerous out at Manila, and the Emperor wasn't exactly popular with me, so I said:

" 'Yes, I can put old Bill's picture on for you, but I'd rather do Admiral Dewey's.'

"As I said it I thought very likely it would lose me a customer, but I didn't much care, for I didn't want the job really. But my old Deutscher looked at me and grinned, and he said: 'Dot's all right, mein freund. You make der Emperor on der ground lying, and Dewey across his back-uff-der-neck gestraddelt, und ofer it all an insgription put.'

"I'll do it,' I said, 'at half price, too. What kind of an inscription will you have?'

"Dis von,' says he: 'Der Emperor himself der Over-Lord calls. Ve put on dis picture, 'Der Under-Lord."

"Well, I made him up a beauty, and I suppose he must have taken it to his barber shop, which was probably largely German, and things must have happened, for a couple of days after it was finished, he sent me the pieces of it and wanted to know if they couldn't be glued together. As soon as he was able to be out he'd come around and see me, he wrote. I made inquiries and found out that he'd got into a row with three men in the barber shop where he was shaved and laid out two of them with the cup before the third one got him. When he came around he was pretty badly bunged up, but still game, and he said as soon as he got his cup back he'd take it around to the shop and spoil some more 'German un-Americans,' as he called them, if they didn't like the design on it. His cup was beyond mending, so I decorated another one for him and charged it up to patriotism, for I didn't want to take money from such a good fighting American. I saw him the other day, and he was in good condition and said the cup was still unbroken and he'd had three fights since and come out all right in all of them. That's what I call a case of the civilizing influence of real art."

Bohemian Porcelain Importers

Numerous chinaware importers established businesses in the United States in the latter half of the nineteenth century especially following the American Civil War. Most of these were located along the east coast and in the Chicago area. The *Crockery & Glass Journal*, which began publishing in 1874, was a favorite place for importers of Bohemian china to advertise. In addition to the *Crockery & Glass Journal*, the trade publication *China, Glass & Lamps* carried importer's advertising. Both journals also published a weekly list of china arriving in New York City, Philadelphia, and Boston from European ports.

These companies imported hundreds of different porcelain items including dinnerware. Many of the pieces were sold as whiteware to china decorators. The purchase of imported porcelain was somewhat seasonal. During the first four months of the year, import houses were busy collecting orders for delivery in

William Frederick Lewis Company advertisement. China trunks for salesmen. *Crockery and Glass Journal* 67(1): 35 (1908).

the fall. European factories would ship samples of their wares to the importers who in turn would feature them in their sales rooms. "Traveling men" or "Drummers" representing these firms toured the country with samples calling on large department stores and

Butler Brothers, New York City, 1905 trade catalog. The firm was a large distributor of Bohemian porcelain. A Royal Austrian cake plate manufactured by the Gutherz factory in Stará Role is illustrated. Many importers attempted to control the purchase of certain shapes or patterns by negotiating exclusive agreements with factories.

65

Plate, 10"d. Cake, relief scalloped gold edge, white ground with central gold medallion, broad red band, transfer decoration. Unsigned. OSCAR & EDGAR GUTHERZ, 1898–1918. $40–50.

regional distributors. Since china samples were subject to frequent packing and unpacking, special sample trunks were used.

Both whiteware and decorated porcelain were sold by Bohemian factories through American china importers or commission merchants to distributors such as Butler Brothers, New York City; Maurer-Campana Art Co., Chicago; L. B. King & Company, Detroit; George B. Peck Dry Goods, Kansas City; and George W. Davis, Rochester, NY; direct to china decorating studios such as W. A. Pickard in Antioch, IL; to large retailers, including Gimbel's; R. H. Macy & Company; Marshall Field's; Wanamaker's; Baily, Banks & Biddle; and mail order firms, such as Sears, Roebuck & Co. and Montgomery Ward. Much of this porcelain was identified in distributor's catalogs (see Appendix 1) as simply "Austrian, Bohemian, Carlsbad or Habsburg China" although Butler Brothers advertised "Royal Austrian" china in their 1905 catalog.

Most American china distributors rarely bought porcelain directly from the factories. A foreign trading company or importer acted as an intermediary. These companies employed buyers who spoke the native language as well as English. They in turn worked with custom brokers who made sure all local and American government regulations were complied with and duties were paid. By 1891, information could be telegraphed to factories in Europe. An article in a December 1891 issue of *China Glass & Lamps* announced that the P. H. Leonard firm had successfully transacted a business matter via trans-Atlantic cable in a few hours on the same day.

Trade fairs were held by European manufacturers to attract American importers. On April 25, 1892, a fair opened in Leipzig, Germany, which according to an article appearing in *China, Glass & Lamps* was attended by owners or employees from Bawo & Dotter, George Borgfeldt & Co., Lazarus & Rosenfeld, A. Klingenberg, C. F. A. Hinrichs, Charles Ahrenfeldt & Son, and L. Straus & Sons. Major crockery businesses in Chicago, St. Louis, Philadelphia, and Boston also attended the fair.

Another method of selling porcelain to china distributors was through wholesale auctioneers. Auction notices were placed in the *Crockery & Glass Journal*. One such firm was Haydock & Bissell located at 83 Chambers Street in New York City.

The Association of Importers and Jobbers of China, Glass, and Earthenware of the City of New York was established in August of 1874. The Executive Committee included Peter H. Leonard from Klingenberg & Leonard, George W. Bassett from George W. Bassett & Co., and Francis H. Bawo from Bawo & Dotter. All of these firms were involved in the importation of Bohemian porcelain. The purpose of the Association was to collect information on the financial standing of customers the members did business with, investigate insolvent estates, provide credit assessment on potential customers, encourage high standards of business principles, protect the city from unjust trade discriminations by freight lines to the South and West, help control freight rates, inform all members of customs regulations, and seek the lowering of tariffs on imports.

Sales of porcelain from Bohemian factories was f.o.b. (free on board, delivery not included) from the factory. Large shipping companies known as "Spediteure" or haulage contractors took the ware from the factories, transported it via rail and water to Hamburg or other ports and delivered it aboard steamers for America. The Augusta Victoria Quay in Hamburg was the most frequently used port for American export in 1914. Factories had the option of shipping their ware by an all rail route or by rail from the Karlovy Vary area to Riesau, Germany, then by water on the Elbe River to Hamburg. The rail-water route was about 35 percent cheaper than the all rail route and took up to 9 days. It is likely that more than half of all the porcelain exported from Karlovy Vary area factories was shipped to New York City. Shipping delays were not uncommon. A short notice in the April 13, 1892 *China, Glass & Lamps* trade journal indicated that Gustave Otto, one of the partners of Bawo & Dotter, had sailed for Bremen, Germany to speed up import orders.

Other factors also affected deliveries of porcelain to American importers. In March of 1900, coal miners in England and Bohemia went on strike at a time when importers were placing large orders with the porcelain factories. Since most factories depended on coal for their kilns, there was grave concern about the factories staying open. Fortunately, the strike in the Bohemian coal fields lasted only a few weeks and did not result in factory closures. When war broke out in Europe in 1914, United States importers had to suspend their pricing from continental factories since only limited quantities of goods were available.

With multiple handling, loading, and transportation of Bohemian porcelain, packing was a critical step to ensure safe passage to the importer. Most of the ware was packed using straw or excelsior and paper in small packages that, in turn, were placed in cases or hogsheads. In 1914, outbreaks of a viral infection in European cattle called "hoof and mouth disease" increased costs of hay and straw used for packing. Inspectors from the United States Department of Agriculture required importers to disinfect all packing material before disposal. Casks or hogsheads, although more expensive, were preferred in some factories to boxes or cases since they could be rolled rather than turned. Skilled packers were employed by the factories for this work. Packers in Bohemian factories earned about $0.09 per hour. Generally 6 to 12 pieces of an article were in each package. Girls and women did the smaller packaging and men and boys packed the cases and casks. This method of shipping resulted in fewer losses due to breakage and was easier for importers to unpack and store. The importer could simply remove the smaller packages from inventory for shipment to the distributor or retailer.

Once the goods arrived in New York City, the importer had to immediately pay the duty. The shipping papers and invoices (generally in the language of the country of origin) were forwarded to the custom broker for "entry." This meant the broker would draw up the proper documents and declarations for the Custom House. The document would list the name of the steamship; date of arrival; marks, numbers, and description of each package; correctly classify the contents of the cases or casks, divided to the cent, under each paragraph; and the rate of duty as the tariff law provided. The factory invoices contained the selling prices of the goods in the currency of the exporting country, any discounts, commissions allowed, packing charges, and other freight costs. The custom broker calculated the exchange rate to convert these costs to United States currency and determined the duty. Often times with poor cash flow importers had to make the rounds on their customers to collect money on their accounts receivable to pay the customs officer. The documents with the declaration were delivered to the Custom House. After two to three hours, if correct, they were returned to the broker with the duty statement attached, following review by the collector's office and naval office. At the time the broker received the shipping papers and invoices from the importer, a bond for the goods was signed by the broker promising redelivery of the cases the importer had received from the wharf to the Custom House, should the appraiser want to examine them. In the case of warehousing, the broker also signed a bond indicating he would pay duty for up to three years if the importer failed to do so. After the payment of duty was received, the dock cases could be delivered to the importer's warehouse. The documents involved in the process of assessing and paying duty on porcelain ware passed through at least twenty-five individuals and were constantly within sight of the custom broker.

The china import business was very competitive. The L. Straus & Sons firm frequently advertised why they could sell their goods so cheaply. Their claim focused on the big discounts the factories would give them for cash purchases; the large orders they placed at the factories, offering direct manufacturer sales from Straus-owned factories; a large number of well-trained buyers; and the small number of traveling salesmen employed by the firm. In spite of this, sooner or later all the firms described in this chapter went out of business due to failure or closure resulting from the deaths of the owners. While excellent

sales and profits occurred in 1899, the United States experienced a financial depression between 1907 and 1908, which hit the catalog houses quite hard. For example, Sears, Roebuck & Company reported a 37 percent decrease in profits from the previous year.

As years passed, the marketing and sale of imported porcelain changed. In 1874, there were 30 jobbing (wholesale) houses in New York City and about 300 country-wide. By 1914, none of the original jobbers were left in New York City and about 100 were still in business in the United States. Many of the larger firms were also importers. As for importers, only the Straus firm remained in business from 1874 through 1914. The Ebeling & Reuss firm continues today as the single recognized name of the early china importers in the United States. Even this firm went through difficult times and was reorganized twice. As the number of importers declined, the number of factory representatives in the United States increased. More and more ware was being sold to wholesalers and retailers directly from the factory through their agents.

Although porcelain was shipped to several ports along the eastern seaboard, most of the Bohemian import business was done in New York City. These businesses were located in the crockery district at the southwest end of Manhattan Island, bounded by Barclay Street on the south, Chambers Street on the north, Broadway on the east, and West Broadway on the west. Other streets in the district included Murray, Warren, and Park Place. Later, many of the crockery and china importers moved their businesses further north to West Thirty-third Street, Sixteenth Street, and East Thirty-seventh Street.

Charles Ahrenfeldt & Son imported Bohemian porcelain from around 1840 to 1910. Charles Ahrenfeldt (1806–1893) was born in Lubeck, Germany. He began his career as a china merchant in his hometown and then established a china import business in New York City in 1831. The business was located on Park Row. Ahrenfeldt was probably the first importer of Bohemian porcelain in the United States. The business then moved to 46 Maiden Lane, then to 56 Maiden Lane. In 1857, a fire destroyed his building and the firm relocated to 50 Murray Street. Herman Trost (1828–1913), also born in Lubeck, Germany, was his partner in the early years until he retired in 1885. Charles spent much of his later years at his home in Dresden, Germany, leaving the American operation to his son, Charles Jules Ahrenfeldt, Jr. (1857–1934).

Crockery District, New York City. Lazarus Straus & Sons is located on the left side of Warren Street. Large numbers of crates are being unloaded off horse-drawn wagons in front of the firm's building. *Crockery and Glass Journal* 66(25): 65 (1907).

Crockery District, New York City. Bawo & Dotter is located on the left side of Barclay Street. The sign over the building advertises the firm's importation of Bohemian china. *Crockery and Glass Journal* 66(25): 79 (1907).

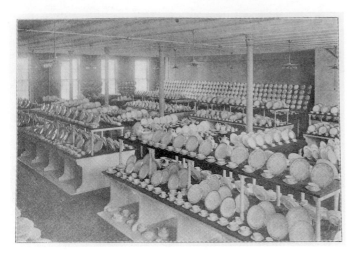

Charles Ahrenfeldt & Son showroom. *Crockery and Glass Journal* 74(25):128 (1911).

The business expanded to include the buildings at 50, 52, & 54 Murray Street. During the 1840s, Ahrenfeldt established a decorating studio in Paris. In the 1860s, he founded a china export business in Limoges, France, and later a decorating studio there around 1884. Prior to his death, he is believed to have started a porcelain factory in Limoges, which was later operated by his son. Ahrenfeldt continued to expand the business, developing a decorating studio in Stará Role in 1886. This was sometimes referred to as the Carlsbad China Factory, although the company never produced porcelain there. Porcelain from this factory was advertised as 'Altrohla Ware.'

Herman C. Kupper, china importer. *Crockery and Glass Journal* 74(18):16 (1911).

Ahrenfeldt advertised Carlsbad dinner, tea and ice cream sets, cups and saucers, plates, and cuspidors, as well as other items. Porcelain manufactured in Limoges was shipped to Stará Role for decorating. In addition, the firm bought porcelain from other Karlovy Vary area factories and from the German company von Schierholz Porcelain Manufactory in Plaue, Thuringia, and decorated it in Stará Role.

The company incorporated in New York State in 1908. In December of 1909, Charles J. Ahrenfeldt, Jr. and M. O. Doering were indicted for fraud under the Customs Administrative Act by a Federal Grand Jury. Both Ahrenfeldt and Doering had left for Europe sometime before the indictment was served and apparently never returned to the United States. Herman C. Kupper (1881– ?) purchased the business in February of 1910.

The decorating studio in Stará Role was sold to Bosshard & Company. Kupper, born in Zurich, Switzerland, was first employed in the Ahrenfeldt factory in Limoges in 1897. He came to New York City in 1904. The business was still an importer of European porcelain in 1981. Additional details concerning the Ahrenfeldt factory are described in the chapter on Karlovy Vary Area Porcelain Factories.

George F. Bassett & Co. imported Austrian porcelain in the late 1800s and early 1900s. The firm began sometime before 1874 as George W. Bassett & Company. By 1879, his son, George F. Bassett (1852–1891), and E. F. Anderson (formerly William Anderson and Son) were successors. The firm known as George F. Bassett & Company and was incorporated in New York State in 1921. The company had a factory in Limoges and purchased porcelain from a variety of Bohemian factories. Company advertising indicated they owned a factory in Austria; however its location could not be confirmed. The firm was located at 52 & 54 Park Place and 49 Barclay Street, later at 920 Broadway and in 1930 at 225 Fifth Avenue. The company also had an office in Chicago at 167 Wabash Avenue. It ceased doing business as a corporation in 1963.

before 1891 — circa 1890–1963

Bawo & Dotter was a large importer, manufacturer, and commission merchant. The firm operated a decorating shop in Rybářě, a suburb of Karlovy Vary, from 1883 to about 1914. The firm was founded in 1864 in New York City by Francis H. Bawo (1834–1899), a native of Haussen, Germany, and Charles T. Dotter from Brooklyn, New York. Both had been employed by C. F. A. Hinrichs (see later in this chapter) as salesmen. They began their new business at 30 Barclay Street.

Initially, they acted as foreign agents for W.T. Copland and W. H. Goss in England and Simon & Halbig, a German factory located in Gräfenhain, Thuringia. In 1872, they purchased the Elite Works, a china decorating shop in Limoges and in 1883 a decorating shop in Rybářě. The factory was identified in advertisements as No. 299 (see chapter on Karlovy Vary Area Porcelain Factories). The factory produced ware marked with the Im-

Francis H. Bawo, china importer. *Crockery and Glass Journal* 47(4): (1898).

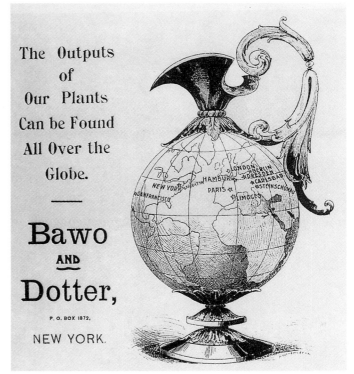

The Outputs of Our Plants Can be Found All Over the Globe.

Bawo AND Dotter,

P. O. BOX 1872,

NEW YORK.

Bawo & Dotter advertisement. *Crockery and Glass Journal* 41(6): 1 (1895).

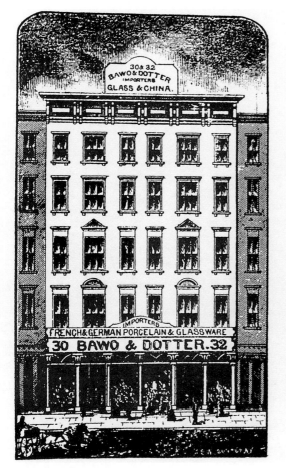

30 & 32
BAWO & DOTTER
IMPORTERS
GLASS & CHINA.

IMPORTERS
FRENCH & GERMAN PORCELAIN & GLASSWARE
30 BAWO & DOTTER 32

Bawo & Dotter building, New York City. *Crockery and Glass Journal* 23(16): 15 (1886).

perial Crown China backstamp. The wares included plates, cakes, salads, comports, teas, coffees, bouillons, after dinner coffees, chop dishes, celery trays, comb and brush trays, mayonnaise boats, and trays.

The firm also purchased locally manufactured porcelain in the Karlovy Vary area for decoration. One of these was the factory located in Klášterec which produced a line of dinnerware called "Vienna China." In Limoges, Bawo & Dotter began producing their own whiteware around 1895. The firm's advertising first appeared in the *Crockery & Glass Journal* in 1874. In 1886, the ware rooms at 30 & 32 Barclay Street occupied 3 floors, including 17,000 sq. ft. of sales space and 40,000 sq. ft. of stock room. The size of the factory in Rybáře was more than doubled in 1891.

By 1895, the firm had expanded into space at 26 & 28 Barclay Street as well. Later, they bought a building at Vesey Street, which extended through to the Barclay Street side. The advertisement below illustrates the global aspect of the company's business.

The company established a glass refinery and decorating workshop in Kamenický Šenov (Steinschönau) in 1888, and an export and import business in Paris in 1894. The company manufactured engraved, decorated table glass and fancy articles in the Kamenický Šenov factory. From the 1870s through the 1890s, the company decorated whiteware made by other Limoges factories. In 1898, the firm purchased the Barjaud de Lafon decorating studio (established 1881) in Limoges. After that, all products from Limoges were exported to the United States until around 1915. When the import firm of P. H. Leonard went into bankruptcy in 1898, Bawo & Dotter obtained the exclusive control of Vienna-brand porcelain produced by the Klášterec factory.

By the mid-1890s, Bawo & Dotter had stores in Paris, London, Berlin, Hamburg, Brussels, and San Francisco, in addition to its New York City import office and store on Barclay Street. The company's European headquarters were located in Kötzchenbroda (a western suburb of Dresden), Germany.

Francis H. Bawo retired in 1888 according to one account, but the article suggested that he seemed to be very active in the business, having just returned from a seven-month trip to Europe. His son, C. F. W. Bawo (?–1934), joined the firm in the same year. In 1898, Dotter retired, and Francis H. Bawo died in Europe in 1899. In 1908, the owners of the Rybáře factory were Henry Witte (New York), Carl Bawo (Brooklyn), Gustave Otto (New Jersey), George S. Lemcke (Brooklyn), and E. L. Max Füssel (Rybáře). Lemcke had married Minnie T. Bawo, Francis Bawo's daughter, in 1882 and was responsible for all outside sales.

The firm was incorporated in New Jersey and was authorized to do business in New York State in 1898. The corporation ceased to do business in 1910 when it was sold to Cassidy & Co., Ltd., a firm located in Montreal, Canada. The business was then known as Bawo & Dotter, Ltd. In 1912, the firm moved to a new building at 18, 20, 22, & 24 West Thirty-third Street which was built by the Astor estate. They occupied seven floors of the twelve-story building. The business went into receivership in 1915 due to the outbreak of war in Europe, the interruption of shipment of porcelain ware from the company's factories in Germany and Austria, and the high cost of rent in the new building. A judge dismissed the firm's bankruptcy claim, indicating the firm failed to prove insolvency, and failed to prove that receivers were put in charge of the assets of the company. Since the corporation was now a Canadian firm (Canada being at war with Germany), its factories in Austria and Germany were seized. The assets of the business were sold to George Borgfeldt & Co. (see later in this chapter). In 1916, after extensive litigation, creditors received 50 cents on the dollar as a settlement.

Benedikt & Friedman operated an import firm at 21 Murray Street. They sold decorated Carlsbad china including dinner sets, tea sets, fruit sets, cups and saucers, plates, mugs, jugs, gift cups, cuspidors, Tom and Jerry sets, and fish and game sets during the 1880s and 1890s. A Tom and Jerry set consisted of a large bowl and several cups or mugs usually lettered with their names. The frothy egg-based alcoholic drink was named after two rather rowdy rogues, Jerry Hawthorne and Corthinian Tom, who were featured in Pierce Egan's *Life in London* in 1821. This warm drink was very popular on cold winter evenings in the United States as early as the 1860s.

Ferdinand Benedikt (1842–1902) was a partner in the business. His son, Harry, later operated the firm which was known as H. Benedikt. It was located at 17 Warren Street in 1894 and 71 & 73 Murray Street in 1915. Benedikt advertised they were the sole agent for the Schwalb Bros. factory in Karlovy Vary. The factory was actually located in Merklín.

Ferdinand Bing & Co., established in 1828, imported porcelain from Karlovy Vary area factories in the 1880s and 1890s. On Bing's retirement in 1873, the firm became known as **Ferdinand Bing & Co.'s Successors.** The business was located at 106 Grand Street.

George Borgfeldt & Co. were large commission merchants located at 425 & 427 Broome Street. George Borgfeldt (1833–1903) was born in Meldorf, Germany, and came to the United States in 1853. He began work as a clerk, and by 1857 had settled in Nashville, Tennessee, where he engaged in the retail business. He moved north to Indianapolis, Indiana, in 1862 during the American Civil War. In 1865, he relocated to New York City where he was employed in the commission business. He established his import business in 1881. The double six-story building featured china and glass on the fourth floor. The firm imported over 300,000 packages a year. All of the items in the showrooms were factory samples from which customers placed orders. In 1892, the company was an agent for the Camill Schwalb factory in Merklín, Bohemia. By 1895, when Borgfeldt

Ferdinand Bing, china importer. *Crockery and Glass Journal* 43(10): 31 (1896).

George Borgfeldt & Company Building, New York City. *Crockery and Glass Journal* 41(4): 18 (1895).

retired, the company was located in a new seven-story building at 18, 20 & 22 Washington Place. In December of 1909, the business moved into a new 50,000 square feet building at Sixteenth Street and Irving Place. The firm acquired about $350,000 of goods at auction for $100,000 from Bawo & Dotter following its failure in 1915. Due to higher tariffs and other trade changes in 1930, Borgfeldt sold off much of its inventory at reduced prices. In January of 1931, the firm moved its business into the William F. Kenny Mercantile Building at 44–60 East Twenty-third Street. The company imported large amounts of Bohemian porcelain from EPIAG factories in Březová, Dalovice, Doubí, Loket, and Stará Role. The business was incorporated in 1893 and dissolved in 1934.

overglaze

└─before 1891─┘ └─circa 1978─┘

H. Burjam was a commission merchant and exporter beginning in 1868 with an office in Haus Moltke and later Haus Bregens in Karlovy Vary. He served as a foreign contact for American importers. In 1901, he moved to Hamburg, Germany, where he continued to engage in German and Bohemian export work through 1905.

A. de Riesthal & Company were importers of Bohemian porcelain from the Karlovy Vary area from 1866 to 1893. The company was incorporated in New York in 1892 with Alphonse de Riesthal (1831–1901) as President, his son, O. J., as Treasurer, F. A. Benedikt as Vice-President and his son, Harry, as Secretary. The business was located at 55 Murray Street. Gustave de Riesthal (1866–1892), also a son of the firm's president, was active in the business until his untimely death from pneumonia. Born in Laurent, France, Alphonse de Riesthal emigrated to the United States in 1864 and was a partner in the S. N. Wolff & Co. In 1881, their partnership was dissolved and the business reorganized as A. de Riesthal & Company. The corporation failed in 1893 following internal disagreements between board members. It was charged that Alphonse de Riesthal had mismanaged the company, taken $1,250 above his salary and refused to refund it, and allowed a $6,143 judgment to be taken against the company in favor of his wife, Helene.

overglaze

└─1891–1893─┘

Charles L. Dwenger imported Bohemian porcelain from the Karlovy Vary area sometime before 1895 to after 1917. Dwenger worked as a clerk for the Klingenberg & Leonard firm in the 1860s.

Pieces with an MZ Classic mark suggest the importer purchased porcelain from the Moritz Zedekauer factory in Stará Role. The business was established in 1895 at 35 & 37 Park Place and then relocated to 41 Barclay Street in 1908. Alexander Klingenberg died in 1894 and Dwenger purchased his import business and factory in 1895. Dwenger advertised whiteware especially for the amateur decorator.

Alphonse de Riesthal, china importer. *Crockery and Glass Journal* 32(24): 181 (1890).

Charles L. Dwenger, china importer. *Crockery and Glass Journal* 49(7): 33 (1899).

overglaze
└── 1912– ───┘ └── circa 1895–1917 ──┘

Haida Lamp and China Co. imported Carlsbad dinner sets, Bohemian glassware, vases, baskets, toilet sets, liquor sets, and biscuit figures in 1890. The business was located at 53 & 55 Warren Street.

Hamburger & Co. were commission merchants for porcelain imported from the Karlovy Vary area from 1885 to 1908. The business was located at 75 & 77 Spring Street in 1895. Simon Hamburger was president when the business filed for bankruptcy in 1908.

Company offices were also located in Nuremberg and Berlin. The firm incorporated and relocated to 20 West Third Street in 1896 and in 1901 to 28 & 30 West Fourth Street. In 1907, the company erected an eight-story department store in San Francisco. Its products included Austrian dinnerware and chinaware for ornamental and table use. In 1910, Simon Hamburger was a china buyer for several firms, including the George H. Bowman Company. His home was in Berlin.

Simon Hamburger, china importer. *Crockery and Glass Journal* 41(26): (1895).

└── 1885–1908 ──┘

Higgins & Seiter imported and distributed French, German, Bohemian, Austrian, and English china from 1887 to 1915. The business incorporated in New York State in March of 1906.

Hamburger & Company Building, New York City. *Crockery and Glass Journal* 52(25): 93 (1900).

Colonel Charles Jacob Seiter, china importer. *Crockery and Glass Journal* 72(15): 33 (1910).

Higgins & Seiter building. *Crockery and Glass Journal* 54:(24): (1901).

Higgins & Seiter advertisement. *Ladies Home Journal*, February 1900.

The firm was founded by Barton B. Higgins (1828–1912), his son, Arthur S., and Colonel Charles Jacob Seiter (1859–1910).

Barton Higgins owned a drugstore and cattle farm in Dixon, Illinois. In 1885, he decided to establish a crockery business for his son in New York City. The business was located at 50, 52, & 54 West 22nd Street.

Although Higgins & Seiter had a retail store at that location, it relied heavily on its mail order catalog business.

The firm's 1899 catalog detailed the profusion of porcelain and cut glass items in their inventory.

Ordering direct from the importer meant a 25 percent price reduction for the purchaser. In 1912, the firm moved to East

Bohemian porcelain in 1899 Higgins & Seiter catalog. The importer purchased porcelain from several Karlovy Vary area factories.

Thirty-seventh Street. Due to the high costs of lease payments in the old location, coupled with their recent relocation and the reduction in business brought on by the outbreak of war in Europe, the business was forced into bankruptcy in 1915. The Camden Corporation formed later that year purchased the stock and assets of Higgins & Seiter. Arthur S. Higgins served as its president. The old name of the firm continued to be used. Creditors received 24 cents on the dollar as a result of the bankruptcy agreement. The corporation was dissolved in 1926.

overglaze

└── circa 1891–1918 ──┘

Charles F. A. Hinrichs (1814–1897) established an import firm at 29, 31, & 33 Park Place in 1844. Hinrichs emigrated from Kleinwiefels, Germany, in 1833.

He first was employed in a fur factory tanning hides and then working as a clerk. Later, he obtained a clerkship in the china, glassware, and toy firm of Michael Werckmeister. This business was New York City's first import firm having been established in 1801. It was located at 115 Broadway and later at 150 Broadway where it remained for many years. On the death of the owner in 1844, Hinrichs took over the business. In 1842, he married Louisa A. Dotter, an aunt of Charles Dotter (see Bawo & Dotter firm). In 1886, his son, Louis, took over the business, along with his brother-in-law, A. C. Meisel. The firm was then known as Hinrichs & Co. At that time, they had offices in Newcastle, England; Paris, Limoges, Nový bor, and Karlovy Vary. The Anton Siegl & Co., established in 1885 in Stará Role, decorated ware for Hinrichs under exclusive contract.

Hinrichs imported both white and decorated Carlsbad china, including dinner, tea, ice cream and fish sets, chamber sets and cuspidors, fruit plates, chocolate pots, cracker jars, and cups and saucers.

Closure of the estate of C. F. A. Hinrichs in 1898 forced the sale of the business. A large auction was held by E. Bissell & Co. and the business closed at the end of May in 1898. Louis Hinrichs then joined the L. Straus & Sons firm and later was employed as their European buyer.

overglaze

└── circa 1886–1891 ──┘ └── 1891–circa 1914 ──┘

Alexander Klingenburg (1830–1894) imported china from the Karlovy Vary area and from Limoges. Klingenberg was born in Iberg, Germany, immigrating to Baltimore and then moving on to New York City. He joined Mr. Kittel in the china import business and the firm became known as Kittel & Klingenberg, located at Maiden Lane. Later, they took on Peter H. Leonard and it was known as Kittel, Klingenberg & Co. On Kittel's retirement the firm was called Klingenberg & Leonard in 1870. It was located at 36 & 38 Barclay Street. The Limoges address was on Rue De La Fonderie. In 1880, the partnership was dissolved, with each member continuing in business for himself. When Klingenberg operated his own import firm, it was located at 35 & 37 Park Place. The business was purchased by Charles L. Dwenger in 1895 following the owner's death. The firm used a mark similar to the Dwenger mark.

Charles F. A. Hinrichs, china importer. *Crockery and Glass Journal* 47(14): 31 (1897).

Alexander Klingenberg, china importer. *Crockery and Glass Journal* 39(5): 32 (1894).

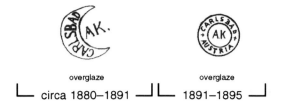

overglaze
circa 1880–1891

overglaze
1891–1895

Koscherak Brothers imported Carlsbad china, glass, and figurines. The firm was founded in 1887 and located at 47 Murray Street. Emanuel Koscherak (?–1907) was one of the owners. In 1895, the firm purchased the entire stock of newly imported goods from the Alexander Klingenberg estate upon the death of that importer. In 1897, they relocated to 29 & 33 Park Place, which was the previous location of C. F. A. Hinrichs. From 1910 to 1915, the firm advertised "Kaiserin Maria Theresia" Carlsbad dinnerware. In 1915, the business moved to 129 & 131 Fifth Avenue in the new crockery district.

Lazarus & Rosenfeld were importers of Bohemian porcelain from their "Victoria" factory in Stará Role (see chapter on Karlovy Vary Area Porcelain Factories). The business was located at 60 & 62 Murray Street. In 1891, they advertised that their factory was the largest in Bohemia employing 2,000 people. Production from this factory was known as Royal Victoria art ware. The firm was still doing business in 1930 at 98 Fifth Avenue.

P. H. Leonard (1848–1904) began his career in the crockery business as a clerk for Herman Trost & Company (see Charles Ahrenfeldt & Son) joining Kittel & Klingenberg around 1855. He became a partner in the firm in 1865 and upon Kittel's retirement in 1866 the business was known as Klingenberg & Leonard. They imported French china and Bohemian glassware.

The firm had offices at 36 & 38 Barclay Street, next door to Bawo & Dotter. They also advertised a Limoges office on Rue De La Fonderie, the same street where Bawo & Dotter's office

Peter H. Leonard building. *China, Glass and Lamps* 3(23): 5 (1892).

was located. By 1880, Leonard and Alexander Klingenberg were operating their own import companies. Leonard's son, Harry P. (1863–1899), joined him at that time. Leonard's business at 18 & 20 Murray Street moved to 76 Reade Street by 1890, and in 1891 he took over the entire building at 76 & 78 Reade Street. The building had eight floors, with 60 front feet on Reade Street, and extended in a L-shape 30 feet down Church Street. Leonard purchased decorated whiteware from Bawo & Dotter's factory in Rybáře and Count Thun's Porcelain Factory in Klášterec, as well as from other factories in the region. His Vienna trademarked china was quite popular, although it was produced in the Klášterec factory. Bohemian factories substituted the Leonard mark for their own whiteware marks.

The business continued until 1898 when a Bremen, Germany, bank forced an assignment. At that time, Leonard had liabilities of $160,000 and assets of $54,000. He owed the Thun factory $24,940. The firm's entire inventory was auctioned off, as well as import shipments received after the assignments were made. Leonard's home in New Jersey was also part of the assignment. Peter Leonard never recovered from his bankruptcy and remained in ill health as a result of it (see Lazarus Straus & Sons). In 1899, a new firm called Leonard, Blakeman & Henderson was formed by the previous employees of P. H. Leonard, including his son, Harry. The business was located at 25 West Broadway in the Crockery Exchange Building. The company featured samples from the Thun factory in Klášterec. The younger Leonard had little to do with this business and died that same year from tuberculosis at the age of 36. The firm then became known as Blakeman & Henderson and only imported Limoges porcelain. According to Röntgen (1981), Anna B. Leonard continued the Leonard part of the business for a few more years.

Anna, who may have been Harry's wife, founded the Denver Pottery Club in 1889 and the Louisville Keramics Club in 1891. Anna was a professional china painter and contributed

Peter H. Leonard, china importer. *Crockery and Glass Journal* 60(13): (1904).

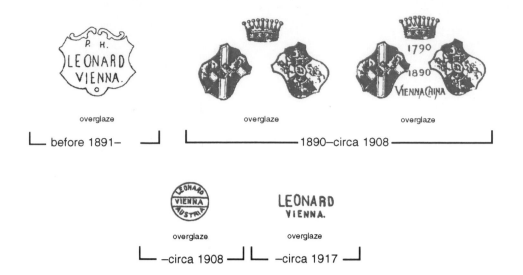

overglaze

└ before 1891– ┘

overglaze

└──── 1890–circa 1908 ────┘

overglaze

overglaze

└ –circa 1908 ┘ └ –circa 1917 ┘

many articles to *Keramic Studio*, a periodical devoted to the china decorator. She served as co-editor along with Adelaide Alsop-Robineau from 1899 to 1903. In 1909 and 1910, Anna had a china decorating studio and tea room on Davis Lane in Edgartown on Martha's Vineyard.

R. Moser imported Bohemian glass and china in 1886 from the Moser Bros. factory in Dvory. The New York City office was located at 932 Broadway.

Julius Palme (1845– ?) was an importer and manufacturer's agent selling Carlsbad dinnerware and other Austrian produced china until the owner's business failed in 1891. Palme was born in Kamenický Šenov, Bohemia, and was in the glass manufacturing business in Europe before emigrating to the United States in 1869. He established his firm in 1871 at College Place, then moved to Murray Street, and by 1890 to 36 & 38 Barclay Street. In 1892, Palme was the General Manager for the recently reorganized J. M. Young Importing Co. After the failure of Young's business in 1897, he again established himself as an importer at 56 & 58 Murray Street. From 1902 to 1907, Palme's firm was located at 35 Barclay Street, extending to 40 Park Place. It was doing business in 1915 at 44 Murray Street.

Paul A. Straub & Co., established in 1915, was located at 85 Fifth Avenue. When one importer lost his contract to control the shape or pattern from a factory another importer would often pick it up. As a result, Straub imported Vienna China from factory 151 and used the crown and double shield mark previously used on porcelain imported by Bawo & Dotter, Charles L. Dwenger, and P. H. Leonard. The business continued until 1970.

Lazarus Straus & Sons established a china and glassware import business in New York City in 1866. Lazarus Straus (1809–1898) and his wife, Sara (1823–1876), who was his brother's (Solmon) daughter, immigrated from Otterberg, Germany, in 1852. He found work as a pushcart peddler and then brought his family to America in 1854. This included their four children

└ circa 1870–circa 1910 ┘

Julius Palme, china importer. *Crockery and Glass Journal* 32(24):177 (1890).

Julius Palme showroom. *Crockery and Glass Journal* 74(7):52 (1911).

Lazarus Straus, china importer. *Crockery and Glass Journal* 47(3): Jan. 20 (1898). Straus was an early importer of Bohemian porcelain from Karlovy Vary area factories.

Isidor (1845–1912), Herman (1846–1923), Nathan (1848–1931), and Oscar (1850–1926). The family settled in Talbotton, Georgia, where Lazarus opened a dry goods store, later moving to Columbus, Georgia.

As a result of anti-Jewish sentiment and the burning of Columbus by Union soldiers during the American Civil War, Lazarus moved his family first to Philadelphia in July of 1865 and then to New York City in 1866, where he purchased the Cauldwell crockery business. As a dry goods merchant in Georgia, Straus had bought crockery from Cauldwell before the war. In 1869, local representatives of Helbing & Straus (Lazarus Straus' brother, Emanuel), a San Francisco crockery and glassware business, asked Lazarus to do their purchasing for them in the eastern market. The firm initially began as L. Straus & Son,

Importers of Crockery, located at 161 Chambers Street. It then moved to 44 Warren Street in 1869. The company expanded to include addresses at 42, 44, 46, & 48 Warren Street in 1886, as well as 116 Chambers Street in 1895.

The business prospered and in 1874 his son, Nathan, who by this time was responsible for outside sales, convinced R. H. Macy to permit the Straus firm to establish a small glass and chinaware department in Macy's department store. This venture later led to a partnership in the firm in 1888 and full ownership in 1896. In 1898, the firm reorganized their method of sales and eliminated their salesmen and traveling representatives. Business was accomplished directly with each customer through the company's several stock departments. Straus was able to offer their customers discounts due to this internal reduction in sales cost. They also dropped products that weren't selling well and moved towards lines of goods in which they had more control. L. Straus & Sons (LS&S) advertised in the 1874 *Crockery and Glass Journal* and took out their first full page ad on the front cover of the April 22, 1875 issue.

The firm had offices or factories in London, Paris, Limoges, Rudolstadt, Kamenický Šenov, and Karlovy Vary. The Karlovy Vary factory was actually located in Stará Role.

In addition to porcelain, LS&S imported clocks, bronzes, and artistic metal goods. Family members in the business during the 1890s included the father and three sons – Isidor, Nathan, and Oscar as well as Lazarus Kohns, his son-in-law. Although Oscar Straus was named on the firm's letterhead, he actually never participated in the business. Instead, he became a lawyer and served as the United States Minister to Turkey and Secretary of Labor and Commerce under the Grover Cleveland administration.

Until 1875, the company purchased their crockery through other importers in New York City (see P. H. Leonard). In the ensuing years, Nathan took charge of buying directly from European porcelain factories. The firm purchased Bohemian porcelain from a number of factories, including the Moritz Zdekauer factory in Stará Role. Straus also imported Bohemian chinaware for several other distributors in cities across America.

During a European buying trip in March of 1875, Nathan met and married Lina Gutherz (1854–1930) on April 28, 1875.

Lazarus Straus & Sons building, New York City. *Crockery and Glass Journal* 32(6):29 (1890).

Lazarus Straus & Sons factory. The factory was owned by Max Marx and Oscar Gutherz, and later by Oscar Gutherz and his brother, Edgar. The factory is shown here with a newly placed L. Straus & Sons sign on the end of the building. *Crockery and Glass Journal* 58(25):202 (1903).

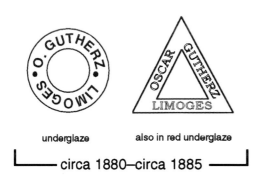

OSCAR GUTHERZ, OF LIMOGES, FRANCE, ASSIGNOR TO L. STRAUS & SONS, OF NEW YORK, N. Y.

DESIGN FOR HOLLOW, FLAT, AND COVERED WARE.

SPECIFICATION forming part of Design No. 14,213, dated August 21, 1883.

Application filed June 29, 1883. Term of patent 7 years.

To all whom it may concern:

Be it known that I, OSCAR GUTHERZ, of Limoges, France, have invented a new and Improved Design for Hollow, Flat, and Covered Ware, of which the following is a full, clear, and exact description.

Reference is to be had to the accompanying photograph, forming a part of this specification, and which represents my new design applied to various articles of ware.

The leading features of my design consist in the diamond-shaped projections upon the surface of the ware and separated by inclined lines, and in the ware having a projection around its base and flared upward and outward from the said base at a gentle curve. The articles of ware are made with a projection around their bases, and with their sides flaring upward and outward from the base at a gentle curve, as shown in the photograph. Upon the surface of the ware are formed diamond-shaped projections separated by inclined lines, as shown in the photograph, giving to the projections the appearance of being arranged in inclined rows.

This design makes the ware very ornamental and attractive.

Having thus fully described my invention, I claim as new and desire to secure by Letters Patent—

The design for hollow, flat, and covered ware herein shown and described, the same consisting of the diamond-shaped projections upon the surface of the ware, said diamond-shaped projections being separated by inclined lines, and of the projection around its base, the sides of the ware being flared upward and outward at a gentle curve.

OSCAR GUTHERZ.

Witnesses:
L. VALLOY,
L. LIMOUSIN.

Description of a United States design patent for porcelain ware produced by Oscar Gutherz in the Lazarus Straus & Sons decorating factory in Limoges awarded August 21, 1883. Gutherz also was awarded a design patent for a porcelain cuspidor the same year.

underglaze   also in red underglaze

└─── circa 1880–circa 1885 ───┘

Jug, 9"h. Diamond quilted design, white ground, gold handle, floral overglaze, hand decoration. Unsigned. *(Oscar Gutherz, Limoges)*. L. STRAUS & SONS, c.1885. $200–250.

Lina's father, Simpson Gutherz, was a successful physician in Ludwigschafen, Germany. Lina was one of nine children. Two of her brothers, Oscar (1856–1938) and Edgar (1859–1928), were assisted in business by their sister's father-in-law. Oscar Gutherz served an apprenticeship in a bank and his brother, Edgar, served one in a business house. Lazarus initially gave Oscar employment in the LS&S decorating studio in Limoges and Edgar in the glassware factory in Kamenický Šenov, Bohemia. In 1893, Edgar served as vice-president of the Straus-owned porcelain factory in Rudolstadt, Germany.

The Straus firm also claimed to have invented the condensed milk or marmalade jar and informed competitors in an advertisement in the June 2, 1892 issue of the *Crockery and Glass Journal* not to infringe on their patent (see Appendix 1).

In 1908, the firm began publishing a monthly periodical entitled *China and Glass Courier*. The purpose was to give their customers a high-quality, illustrated pamphlet that depicted their wares.

Success in business, however, wasn't always without its difficulties. In 1884, Peter H. Leonard and another New York City china importer, John M. Young, accused the Straus firm of failing to pay duty on imported chinaware. This allegation was investigated in detail by the United States Treasury Department and found to be false. Later, Peter Leonard died in an insane asylum. J. M. Young filed bankruptcy, then reorganized in a manner so that his creditors were left empty-handed.

In 1892, the Straus firm was also a partner in Abraham & Straus, a large Brooklyn, New York, retail company. L. Straus & Sons continued as an importer of china, pottery, and glassware until 1924 when it became Nathan Straus & Sons. The business closed in the 1930s.

The firm used a variety of marks. Pieces could also be marked "Designed by L. Straus & Sons," along with their regular circular backstamp. The Rudolstadt mark was R.W. crowned shield.

impressed

└─ before 1891 ─┘ └──── 1891–1917 ────┘

The **Strobel & Wilken Co.** imported dolls and German and Bohemian table and decorative porcelain from around 1864 to about 1925. The firm was established in 1850 by Charles Strobel (1817–1877). Strobel was born in Würzburg, Germany, received a degree in chemistry in Nuremberg, and emigrated to the United States in 1849. Initially, he manufactured leather goods with his brother, Louis, in Cincinnati, Ohio. After the Civil War, they opened a large toy department. The firm was known as Charles Strobel & Brother. George Wilken, a distant relative from Knoxville, Tennessee, joined the firm in 1862. In 1864, he was admitted as a partner and the business changed its name to Strobel & Wilken.

Charles Strobel, china importer. *Crockery and Glass Journal* 51(3): 27 (1900).

George Wilken, china importer. *Crockery and Glass Journal* 51(3): 27 (1900).

Strobel & Wilken Company building, New York City. *Crockery and Glass Journal* 52(25): 47 (1900).

Emil Strobel (1854– ?) served as the second president and was in charge of the foreign department. Later, William R. Strobel, Emil's brother, became involved in European buying. The firm incorporated in 1886 and moved to New York City. The factory at Teplice (Teplitz) supplied a large amount of their porcelain. The firm was located initially at 443 and 445 Broadway, then moved to 501 Broadway in 1889, and in 1896 to 650 Broadway and became only an import and export commission business. In 1908, the firm had a branch office in Chicago at 240 Adams Street. The business moved to 61, 63, & 65 West Twenty-Third Street in 1913. Frank B. Taylor (1858–1901) was associated with Strobel & Wilkin and established his own import firm in Detroit, Michigan, in 1900.

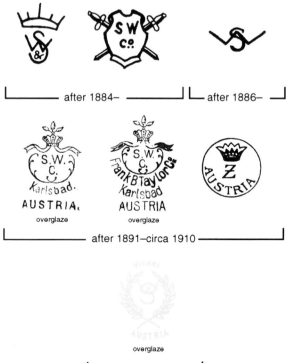

John. M. Young, china importer. *Crockery and Glass Journal* 59(26): 21 (1904).

J. M. Young Importing Co. imported Bohemian china. The firm was owned by John. M. and Thomas P. Young. It was first located at 34 Murray Street and later at 37 & 39 Murray Street.

John M. Young (1837–1904) was born in Ireland and emigrated to the United States in 1854. After a time he was employed by the Herman Trost & Co., the predecessor of the Charles Ahrenfeldt & Son import firm. Young established his own business in 1864. The firm had a European office in Haus Trianon in Karlovy Vary. The firm imported both white and decorated Carlsbad china including dinner, tea, fish, salad, ice cream and berry sets, and cuspidors. Young incorporated his business in 1891 and hired Julius Palme, whose business had recently failed, as his general manager and European buyer. The corporation went into receivership in March of 1897 and reorganized as the New York China, Glass and Toy Co., which was incorporated on April 1, 1897. Creditors took stock in this new corporation with the hopes of recovering their losses from Young. According to Straus family documents, few, if any creditors were paid. Thomas P. Young served as the new president. The business continued until January of 1900 when the firm made an assignment of assets to Walter P. Long. The Snedden-Tallman Co. of New York City was incorporated a week later to continue the operation of the business. Stephen S. Tallman and James W. Snedden were previous employees of the New York City China, Glass and Toy Co. In 1902, the United States Circuit Court awarded John M. Young a $53,700 settlement from his earlier bankruptcy, which was a payment for the personal loans he had made to his business. The Snedden-Tallman Co. closed in 1904.

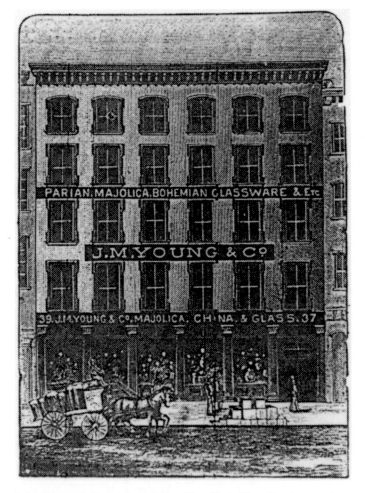

J. M. Young & Company building, New York City. *Crockery and Glass Journal* 33(2): 7 (1891).

Benjamin F. Hunt, Jr., china importer. *Crockery and Glass Journal* 49(23): 29 (1899).

Boston was also a port of delivery for Bohemian porcelain. In 1898, Benjamin Franklin Hunt, Jr. (1844–1931), along with his twin sons, Horace P. and Homer F., founded the import firm **Benjamin F. Hunt & Sons**.

At age 17, Hunt was first employed by the Horace Partridge Company, a large toy importer and later served as treasurer of the business. The firm had an office and showroom at 53 Hanover Street and an office and showrooms at 46 Park Place and 41 Barclay Street in New York City. The importer leased and owned factories in Bohemia (see under Loket and Loučky in the chapter on Karlovy Vary Area Porcelain Factories). In 1898, they closed the factory in Nový bor and shipped its inventory to New York City for disposal. In 1899, the business was located at 122 Pearl Street in Boston, 31 Barclay Street (also Abram French and Co. location) in New York City and at 320 American Express Building in Chicago. The firm closed its New York City office in 1902. Hunt remained at the Loket factory and his sons retired from the business. Following the failure of his own import business and factory in Bohemia, Hunt became the resident European buyer for F. W. Woolworth Co. until he retired in 1925. Later, the twin sons served for a time as eastern representatives for the C. E. Wheelock Co. in Peoria, Illinois, which sold souvenir china produced in Bohemian factories. By 1908, they were associated with George F. Bassett & Co. and in 1913 they were operating as factory representatives under the name H. P. & H. F. Hunt Co. The business continued in Boston until 1971.

The **Abram French Co.** began importing porcelain from Europe as early as 1862 through French, Wells & Co. Later, the firm was known as the Abram French Co. It was initially located 151 and 153 Milk Street in the 1870s and at 89 to 93 Franklin Street and 211 to 215 Devonshire Street by 1898. The firm also had an office at 31 Barclay Street in New York City. Both the Mitchell Woodbury Co. (see p. 82) and Abram French Co. imported large quantities of Carlsbad china including dinner and souvenir ware. By the end of World War I, neither company was in business.

Philadelphia also served as a port for porcelain importation. The **Ebeling & Reuss Co.**, founded in 1886, purchased porcelain from several Bohemian factories. Theodore Reuss (1852–1913), born in Stuttgart, Germany, and Frederick W. Ebeling (1856–1927), born in Hanover, Germany, emigrated to the United States as teenagers.

They both gained employment at the china and glassware firm of Zeh & Schenk in Philadelphia. This business reorganized in 1886 and the two became partners with J. E. F. Zeh. The business was known as Zeh, Ebeling & Reuss and was located at 440 Market Street. Mr. Zeh withdrew from the business in 1900 and the firm continued as Ebeling & Reuss. Mr. Reuss's son, William, took over his share in the business on his death in 1913. William Reuss bought the remainder of the business from the Ebeling estate following the death of Frederick Ebeling in 1927. The business incorporated in 1928, with William Reuss as president and treasurer and Mr. Ebeling's oldest son, Henry,

Frederick W. Ebeling, china importer. *China, Glass and Lamps* August: 32 (1930).

Theodore Reuss, china importer. *China, Glass and Lamps* August: 32 (1930).

Ebeling and Reuss Showrooms, Boston. *China, Glass and Lamps* August: 31 (1930).

as vice president. Ebeling's other son, Robert, served as a board director. By 1930, the business was located at 707 Chestnut Street.

As the depression worsened, Ebeling & Reuss reorganized in 1933. Henry and Robert Ebeling gained controlling interest, although William Reuss remained on the board of directors. As the new president, Henry assumed the role of European buyer. The firm later moved to Devon, Pennsylvania. The business continued through 1987, then went into bankruptcy. Mr. Ronald D. Rapelje joined the company in 1988 to assist in returning the corporation to solvency. In 1992, he purchased the assets of the company and moved it from Royersford to Allentown, Pennsylvania. The Ebeling & Reuss Company continues in business as an importer and distributor of fine gift ware.

overglaze   overglaze
|__ 1918–1939 __| |_____ 1939–1945 _____|

The **Mitchell Woodbury Co.** was an importer of Bohemian porcelain during the 1890s to early 1900s. The business was founded by Jacob Mitchell, C.H. Woodbury, and C.E. Austin. The firm was located 56 Pearl Street and 215 Franklin Street in Boston. It expanded into 25 Hartford Street by 1896. By 1899, the firm had moved to 80–86 Pearl Street. The company merged

overglaze
|__ circa 1891–circa 1917 __|

with the Abram French Co. in 1902 and was located at 76–92 Pearl Street. Things must not have gone well with the merger and by 1906 the firm once again was known as Mitchell Woodbury Co. The company ceased doing business sometime before 1918. Although the company used a mark with the name Royal Austria China, it had no apparent affiliation with the Oscar & Edgar Gutherz factory in Stará Role which also used the Royal Austria name.

As time passed, other cities across the country served as locations for the importation of Bohemian porcelain. Chicago was as a major market in the midwest for Bohemian export porcelain. Porcelain importers and distributors in the Chicago area included the following companies.

A. H. Abbott & Co. an artist supply business, was founded in 1879 by Arthur H. Abbott (?–1915). The firm was located at 147 State Street in 1880. Abbott operated a boarding house along with Albert S. Tyler at this location beginning in 1876. It is not clear if he continued the boarding house operation following the establishment of the art supply business. However, in 1885, he moved his business to 50 Madison Street. In 1910, he relocated to 78 Wabash Avenue, which was across the street from Marshall Field's department store. This address became 119 North Wabash Avenue following a Chicago street numbering change in 1909. In 1925, the business was at 208 South Wabash Avenue and in 1930 at 235 South Wabash Avenue. The business continued until 1931. His wife, Annie E., was a dressmaker with a shop at 70 Madison Street in 1883. Later, she became a china decorator, from 1914 to 1917.

Burley & Co. was established in 1838 as A. G. Burley & Co. Arthur Gilman Burley (1812–1897), a pioneer crockery merchant, was born in Exeter, New Hampshire. He traveled to Chicago in 1837 to make his fortune in a new territory. At that time, the city had no more than 4,000 inhabitants. He was em-

Burley & Tyrrell Co., Chicago. Bohemian porcelain distributor, catalog illustrating Habsburg china, 1904. China sold under the Habsburg name was produced by the Moritz Zdekauer factory in Stará Role.

ployed by Stephen F. Crane, a Chicago book and stationery dealer. Burley saved his money and a year later bought a stock of crockery which had been taken from an Indian trader in part payment of a debt from the State Bank of Illinois. His business was first located at what is now the corner of Lake and State Streets. The building burned in 1842 and he relocated to 105 Lake Street and later to 175 Lake Street. Burley's brother-in-law, John Tyrrell (1820–1903), was a partner in the firm in 1852.

The firm was known as Burley & Tyrrell in 1871 following the Chicago fire and conducted both wholesale and retail business. The company imported Bohemian porcelain beginning around 1880. In 1883, the retail and hotel supply end of the business was sold to a nephew, Frank E. Burley. This business was known as Burley & Co. and was located at 83 & 85 South State Street. The firm engaged in china decorating from 1885 to 1931. The company closed in 1931. Burley & Tyrrell continued in the wholesale china, glass, and lamp business at 42 & 44 East Lake Street.

Both companies continued to exist in different locations in Chicago until 1907 when they re-consolidated the businesses at 118 & 120 Wabash Avenue. The company's last location was at 7 North Wabash Avenue. Burley & Tyrrell continued operating until 1919 when it was purchased by Albert Pick & Co., a competing china and glassware jobber in Chicago. World War I caused Burley & Tyrrell great hardship since the company imported much of their wares from Germany and Austria. Burley & Tyrrell also had a store at 385–389 Jackson Street in St. Paul, Minnesota. In addition to importing tons of European porcelain, the company operated a decorating studio above its salesroom in Chicago. Its institutional customers included numerous hotels, restaurants and railroads, as well as decorating studios such as Pickard. The company used one mark for its Bohemian china.

The **D. M. Campana Art Co.** was founded in 1914 by Domenick Mathews Campana. Born in Venice, Italy, in 1871, he worked as a decorator for the Ceramic Art Company (which later became Lenox China) in Trenton, New Jersey, and then for Pickard China in 1902. He established the D. M. Campana Art Company, an art and china studio in Chicago in 1903. It was located at 431 South Wabash. **W. A. Mauer Co.** was established in 1880 in Council Bluffs, Iowa, and later merged with the D. M. Campana Art Supply Co. in 1929 to become the **Maurer-Campana Art Co.** It was located at 316 & 318 West Grand Avenue. The firm sold large volumes of whiteware to china decorators and provided a teaching studio to aspiring young students. The business continued until 1967.

French & Potter Co., located at the corners of Wabash Avenue and Washington Street imported Bohemian porcelain in addition to French, German, and English ware.

The firm's 1890s catalog featured Carlsbad China during the holiday season. Wares included dinner, tea, ice cream, salad, berry, mush and milk, Tom and Jerry, fish and tête-à-tête sets (including a teapot, sugar, creamer, two cups and saucers, and a porcelain tray), pudding dishes, chocolate pitchers and cracker jars. The business was founded in Boston in 1822 as Abram French & Co. In 1872, the company established its Chicago office at 101 & 103 Wabash Avenue. In 1875, it advertised itself

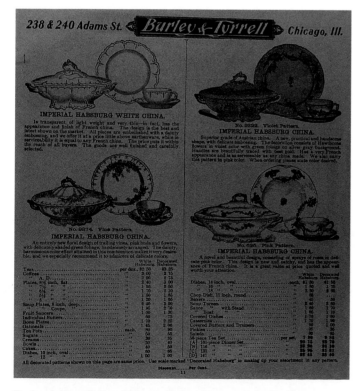

Burley & Tyrrell Co., Chicago. Bohemian porcelain distributor, catalog illustrating Habsburg china, 1904. Four different patterns are shown with blanks that replicated popular Limoges designs.

French & Potter Co., Chicago. Bohemian porcelain distributor, lithograph of building at Wabash Avenue and Washington Street, circa 1890.

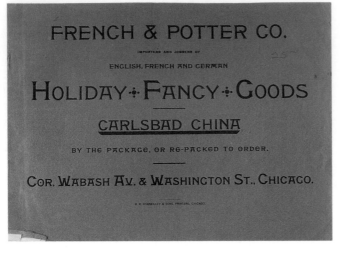

French & Potter Co. Bohemian porcelain distributor, catalog illustrating Carlsbad china, circa 1890.

Jonathan W. Brooks, Jr., china importer. *The Graphic* 4(1): 16 (1891).

as the largest wholesale crockery and glassware house in the United States. Owners at that time were Abram French, L. O. Coburn, John T. Wells, William A. French, L. E. Caswell, and S. Waldo French. From 1879 to 1889, the firm was known as French, Potter & Wilson. Owners were William A. French, Edwin A. Potter, W. Herbert Wilson, and Arthur B. French. The address was 91 & 93 Wabash Avenue. From 1890 to 1898, the firm was known as French & Potter. Edwin Potter, who worked in 1874 as a bookkeeper when the business first started in Chicago, was President, and Henry C. French was Treasurer. In 1899, the firm was known as Thomas French Co., with Henry French as the owner. Edwin Potter became President of the American Trust & Savings Bank. The Abram French & Co. went into receivership in 1902.

Pitkin & Brooks, a wholesaler and retailer of household wares, imported Carlsbad china in the 1880s and 1890s. The firm was located at 56, 58, 60, & 62 Lake Street. The business was established in 1871 following the Chicago fire. Edward Hand Pitkin (1846–1918) was first employed as an office boy by John

Tyrrell at the import house of Burley & Tyrrell Company in 1860. He served in the American Civil War in 1865 and following the war became the manager of the crockery department of Johnson & Abbey in Chicago. His partner, Jonathan W. Brooks, Jr. (1847–?), also had worked at Burley & Tyrrell as a cashier. Brooks was involved in a number of other business activities and served as the president of Hyde Park, Thompson & Houston Electric Co. and as a director of *The Graphic*, a weekly Chicago illustrated newspaper. The firm was first located at 303 Michigan Avenue near the Illinois Central Railroad station, moving several months later to 41 River Street. About 1876, they moved to the State and Lake Street location. By 1891, the business employed 250 workers in addition to 25 traveling salesmen, one local buyer who visited Europe each year, one resident Euro-

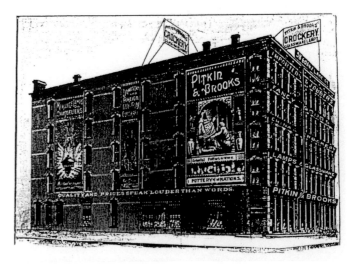

Pitkin & Brooks Building, Chicago. *Crockery and Glass Journal* 34(7): 21 (1891).

Edward H. Pitkin, china importer. *The Graphic 4(1): 16 (1891).*

Pitkin & Brooks ware room, Chicago. *The Graphic* 4(1): 16 (1891).

overglaze

└─ circa 1891–circa 1914 ─┘

pean buyer, and three American buyers. The firm also operated a china decorating studio from 1874 to 1917. The business closed in 1939.

Sears, Roebuck & Co. sold Bohemian china through their mail order catalog, as well as the Chicago store. While companies like Charles Haviland in Limoges catered to the rich and upper-middle classes, producing a 100-piece set of dinnerware for $30 in the 1908 Sears catalog, the Gutherz set of Royal Austria cost $15.50. Sears sold fancy Carlsbad china plates as early as 1897. In 1913 and 1914, the company (see chapter on Porcelain Decoration Methods) featured a Gutherz pattern called Louis XIV similar to Haviland's popular Ranson dinnerware.

Both years of the catalog included numerous pieces of Austrian china. In the 1914 catalog, 13 different patterns of Austrian dinnerware were advertised. Prices for a 100-piece set ranged from $13 to $25. Color pages of chinaware and fancy plates, bowls, and sets also were featured (see Appendix 1).

Thayer & Chandler, founded in 1880, was first located at 46 Madison Street, next door to A. H. Abbott & Co. This wasn't a surprise since Henry J. Thayer (1858–1928) worked as a clerk for Abbott in 1877 and then as a salesman in 1880. Charles H. Chandler was Abbott's bookkeeper. The business initially sold artist supplies and then undecorated whiteware. In 1910, the business was located at 737 & 739 West Jackson Street, in 1916 in the Stevens Building at 17 North State Street, and in 1925 at 913 Van Buren Street. The owner's wives, Miram Chandler and Mary Thayer, were china decorators. The firm did an extensive mail order business in whiteware for china painters. Henry Thayer died March 21, 1928. After his death, C. H. Chandler was President and George E. Ballieff was Secretary-Treasurer. The business begin manufacturing and selling air brushes as well as white china, and expanded into buildings at 913 and 921 Van Buren. Thayer & Chandler continued to sell whiteware through the 1930s. Although the business is no longer family owned, the firm is still a leading manufacturer of air brushes.

Firms in other midwestern cities also distributed Bohemian porcelain. One of these companies was founded by Charles N. Regnier (1850–1930) following the American Civil War. Regnier was born in Bingen, Germany, in the Rhine river valley. He came to the United States in 1867 and settled in Atchison, Kansas. There he established a china and glass business. In 1871, he took in Charles A. Shoup as an employee who later became a partner. The firm was then known as **Regnier & Shoup Mercantile Co.** In 1883, the firm moved to St. Joseph, Missouri. Regnier retired in 1918 and moved to Heidelberg, Germany.

overglaze

└─ circa 1891–circa 1918 ─┘

Porcelain Products Exported to America

Bohemian factories produced hundreds of different porcelain items including decorative objects, figurines, household or utility ware, and tableware for export to the United States. Many of these pieces were produced in different sizes as well, which required maintaining a large inventory of molds. Depending on the decoration applied to the whiteware, many pieces of household or tableware could be identified as art objects. The variety of porcelain ware available through china distributors included:

Decorative Objects

Jardinieres, loving cups, medallions, plates, steins, tankards, rose bowls, and vases.

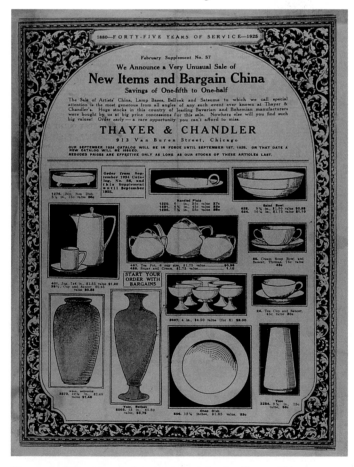

Thayer and Chandler. Bohemian porcelain distributor, Chicago, 1925 catalog.

Household Ware

Ash trays, baskets, bonbon boxes and dishes, bottles, boxes, candlesticks, candy jars, clock holders, comb and brush trays, cookie trays, dresser sets and trays, hair receivers, hatpin holders, ink stands, jewel stands and boxes, jugs, pitchers, perfume bottles, lamps, match stands, pen trays, pin trays, puff boxes, ring trays, smoker's sets, talcum shakers, tobacco jars, toothpick holders, and vanity boxes.

Tableware

Berry bowls and sets, bouillon cups and saucers, breakfast sets, cream soups, butter tubs, cake plates, celery dips, celery trays, chocolate pots and sets, chop dishes, coffee pots and sets, condensed milk and jam jars, condiment sets, covered dishes, cracker jars, cups and saucers, dinnerware, egg cups and sets, fish and games sets, fruit bowls and saucers, grape juice sets, ice cream sets, lemonade jugs and mugs, mayonnaise bowls, muffineers, mustard jars, napkin rings, nut bowls and sets, olive dishes, oyster plates, platters, punch bowls and cups, ramikin and underplates, relish dishes and trays, salad bowls, salt and pepper shakers, salt dips, sandwich trays, sauce dishes, serving trays, sherbet cups, spoon trays, sugar and creamer sets, syrup jugs, teapots and stands, tea sets, tea trays, tumblers, tumbler stands, tureens, and whipped cream bowls.

Victorian living and eating habits required numerous pieces of china designed for a variety of functions. The table below shows the composition of toilet, breakfast, lunch, dinner, tea, chop, roast, fish, game, soup, and salad sets.

127 - PIECE DINNER SET

12 Dinner Plates
12 Soup Plates
12 Breakfast Plates
12 Tea Plates
12 Preserve Saucers
12 Individual Butters
1 10-inch Dish
1 14-inch Dish
1 16-inch Dish
1 Baker
1 Covered Dish
2 Covered Dishes, round
1 Soup Tureen
1 Sauce Tureen and Stand
2 Pickles
1 Salad
12 Tea Cups and Saucers
6 Coffee Cups and Saucers

13 - PIECE CHOP SET

12 Plates, 7 1/2-inch
1 Chop Platter

70 - PIECE LUNCH SET

12 Plates, 7 1/2-inch
12 Individual Butters
1 12-inch Dish
1 14-inch Dish
2 Bakers
2 Bread Plates

12 Saucers
12 Tea Cups and Saucers
2 Casseroles

56 - PIECE TEA SET

12 Plates Tea
12 Preserve Saucers
14 Tea Cups and Saucers
1 Tea Pot
1 Sugar Bowl
1 Creamer
1 Bowl
2 Cake Plates

34 - PIECE ROAST SET

12 Plates (8 1/2 inch)
12 Vegetable Saucers
1 16-inch Dish
2 Bakers
2 Covered Vegetable Dishes (4 pieces)
1 Sauce Tureen (3 pieces)

55 - PIECE BREAKFAST

12 Plates, 7 1/2 inch
12 Breakfast Coffee Cups and Saucers
1 10-inch Dish
1 Baker
12 Individual Butters
1 12-inch Dish
1 Covered Dish
2 Bread Plates

15 - PIECE FISH SET

12 Plates
1 Dish
1 Sauce Tureen (2-pieces)

13 - PIECE GAME SET

12 Plates
1 Platter

14 - PIECE SOUP SET

12 Soup Plates
1 Soup Tureen (2-pieces)

13 - SALAD SET

12 Salad Plates
1 Salad Bowl

12 - PIECE TOILET SET

1 Large Water Pitcher
1 Basin
1 Slop Jar (2 pieces)
1 Chamber (2 pieces)
1 Small Water Pitcher
1 Brush Vase
1 Mug
1 Soap Dish (3 pieces)
(Catalog No. 10. *Fine China Rich Cut Glass*. New York: Higgins & Seiter, 1899)

The Victorians were prodigious eaters with the upper-class, giving frequent dinner parties. *The Requirements of Correct Dinner Service* published in the 1899 *Crockery and Glass Journal* summarized a recent booklet entitled *Hints to the Hostess* issued by the Nathan-Dohrmann Co., San Francisco.

"The service or place plates are purely decorative, and should be in strong colors and rich gold effects. They often bear a gold monogram, crest or other distinctive design.

Since Americans serve bread and butter at every meal, the bread and butter plates should not be omitted. People who think they are out of fashion are misinformed. On these plates one has ample space for both bread and butter. Their convenience commends them to permanent use. In decoration they may match the roast set, or be of a color harmonizing with all the china, preferably in white or gold.

Olives, radishes and celery are most palatable when served cold; consequently the dish for each should be deep enough to hold sufficient cracked ice to bed them in. The mistake of serving celery in high glass stands is sometimes made, but when served in this way soon wilts and loses its flavor. It should be properly served in a tray for that purpose, which, being an odd piece, may be a decorative feature of the table.

Individual celery dips for salt are smaller than an ordinary salt, and especially adapted to individual use.

The oyster course needs no lengthy comment, by reason of its simplicity. Oysters and clams should always be served in their natural shells; otherwise much of the flavor is lost. There are new deep oyster plates in which to imbed shell oysters in crushed ice. They are preferable to the plates heretofore made for the serving of oysters.

Following the oyster course at American dinners, although some famous diners and epicures hold that this order should be reversed, comes the soup course. The kind of soup one should serve depends on the sumptuousness of the courses that follow it. When the dinner courses are light a thick soup should be served in goodly portions, but in heavy course dinners a clear soup is preferable and should be served in smaller portions. The proper way to serve hot or cold bouillon or chicken broth is in a two-handled cup with saucer, the cup being about the size of an ordinary tea cup. Soup plates of the old rim shape are proper for all kinds of soups, but some prefer a coupe shape (without the horizontal rim), and for cream soups two-handled, low-shaped bowls with plates are used. The soup tureen is an important article and may be highly decorated. Tureens are made in various shapes and sizes.

Cracker jars for the oyster cracker or small biscuit are odd pieces of different shapes with wide mouths. Where salted wafers are preferred, very handsome trays may be used for them. Whichever dish is used should harmonize with the articles of the dinner china.

The fish set, which next comes into use, consists of a large fish dish, a sauce boat, and individual plates, all usually elaborately decorated with scenes from fishdom deftly executed.

When scalloped oysters or fish are served, ramekins should be used. They are of fireproof china and the scalloped may be baked in them. They are made with saucers to match and are very practical and satisfactory.

The entree set consists of individual plates and a round dish suitable for serving breaded chops, fricasse of chicken, sweetbread, calves' brains, or whatever else the entree may be. The individual plates should harmonize in color and design with the dish.

Next follows the roast or heavy course, for which there is a special set consisting of a large-size platter, two covered vegetable dishes, a gravy tureen and plates to match. The roast course is the main feature of the dinner, and the china for it should be more elaborately decorated than that used for the other courses. A very effective dinner service is that in which the decorations of the china increase in color and design with the progress of the dinner from the oysters to roast, the roast set being a fitting climax to the preceding sets in richness of design.

When game or fowl follows the roast the colors of the service may be as strong as those of the roast set, but naturally of a different character. The game dish and plates comprising this set are capable of the finest decorations on china. They usually bear paintings of birds or hunting scenes by high-class artists, no two pieces having the same picture.

The set for asparagus consists of a platter with a drainer, a boat for dressing, and individual compartment plates, all beautifully decorated in rich colors.

The salad should be served after the roast or game courses, but may be served with roast or fowl when the asparagus is not made a separate course. It should be dressed at the table and never until guests are ready to be served, as the lettuce loses its brittleness and becomes less palatable if allowed to remain in the vinegar and oil. The salad may be served from a cut-glass bowl or fine porcelain bowl modeled for the purpose. Besides the bowl the set consists of individual salad plates, mayonnaise bowl, and vinegar and oil cruets of cut glass, and servers of ivory, silver or wood.

For the pudding course a special dish, sauce boat and individual plates are necessary. The pudding dish has been very much improved in recent years and is now made with a separate fireproof lining in which the baking may be done, in consequence of which the dish itself may be beautifully decorated, and run no risk of being cracked or stained by the heat of the oven. Ramekins, which are now to be had in the finest decorations, with little plates to match, are often used for individual puddings as well as for scalloped oysters, sweetbreads, etc.

The ice cream set, consisting of a tray, individual plates and cake plates, may show pleasing contrasts in gold and color. Cake plates are very necessary adjuncts to the proper serving of ice cream. They should blend fittingly with the ice cream set.

The cheese course is served with a set consisting of a cheese dish, individual plates and cabarets, the latter having three or four compartments for radishes, celery, watercress or young onions. Some kinds of cheese need to be kept moist and should be dispensed from a wedge-shaped or round glass stand with a cover, made for the purpose. Brie, Camembert and other like cheeses are served from a small plate. The custom of serving, with the cheese, lettuce, radishes, and other vegetables of the same family in cabarets, which is popular in England, might well be adopted in America, for the combination of the flavors is quite palatable.

The cafe noir course is served with a special set consisting of a coffee-maker or coffee pot, cups saucers, sugar bowl and spoon tray. Cups of moderate size, admitting of fantastic decorations in high colors, are most satisfactory.

The last course is usually of light indulgence in either liqueurs, cordials or crème de menthe. At weddings, banquets or state dinners punch is dispensed.

After this the ladies withdraw, leaving the gentlemen to enjoy their cigars. Candlesticks and ash trays, the latter of various shapes, should be placed before each smoker."

With needs for dinnerware and accessory pieces to compliment all these courses, it was no wonder that Bohemian porcelain factories found a ready market for their wares.

PHOTOGRAPHS/VALUE GUIDE

Numerous types of porcelain objects were produced by Bohemian factories for American export. This chapter shows many of these pieces, some of which were factory decorated or sold as whiteware, and many of which were studio or individually decorated by American china painters. The pieces are grouped as Decorative Objects, Household Ware, and Tableware. Since much of the porcelain shipped was whiteware for the American china painting market, each group is subdivided into Bohemian and American decorated ware. Values are derived from asking prices at antique shops, actual prices paid, and published antique price guides. Unless otherwise stated, values shown for multiple items are for entire sets. Although sizes of porcelain objects were originally produced using metric units, these have been converted to inches for American readers. Size is indicated as diameter (d), length (l), and height (h).

Decorated Objects

Bohemian Decorated Porcelain

Plate, 10.75"d. Cake, gold and silver gilded feather relief, center medallion, hand decoration. Unsigned. CARL KNOLL CARLSBAD, 1848–1868. $75–85.

Plate, 9"d. Coupe, orange poppies, white ground, festooned gold band, hand-decorated transfer. Signed: *Martin.* OSCAR & EDGAR GUTHERZ, 1898–1918. $50–60.

Cake plate, 10.75"d. Coupe, multicolored leaves, ivory ground, gold band, scalloped edge, hand-decorated transfer. Signed: *Raymond.* OSCAR & EDGAR GUTHERZ, 1898–1918. $35–45. Plate, 9.75"d. Coupe, multicolored leaves, ivory ground, gold band, scalloped edge, hand-decorated transfer. Signed: *Raymond.* OSCAR & EDGAR GUTHERZ, 1898–1918. $30–40. Plate, 6.2"d. Coupe, multicolored leaves, ivory ground, gold band, scalloped edge, hand-decorated transfer. Signed: *Raymond.* OSCAR & EDGAR GUTHERZ, 1898–1918. $10–12.

Plate, 8.9"d. Coupe, green grapes, yellow roses, green leaves, multicolored ground, gold band, hand-decorated transfer. Signed: *Laporte*. OSCAR & EDGAR GUTHERZ, 1898–1918. $50–60. Plate, 6.2"d. Coupe, green grapes, yellow roses, green leaves, multicolored ground, gold band, hand-decorated transfer. Signed: *Fann*. OSCAR & EDGAR GUTHERZ, 1898–1918. $20–25.

Plate, 8.75"d. Coupe, orange gooseberries, white ground, gold edge, transfer decoration. Unsigned. PFEIFFER & LOWENSTEIN, c.1914–1918. $25–30.

Plate, 8.9"d. Coupe, pink roses, tan red leaves, brown ground, gold band, hand-decorated transfer. Signed: *Georges*. OSCAR & EDGAR GUTHERZ, 1898–1918. $50–60.

Plate, 13"d. Coupe, orange gooseberries, ivory ground, gold edge, hand-decorated transfer. Unsigned. PFEIFFER & LOWENSTEIN, c.1914–1918. $50–60.

89

Plate, 8.75"d. Coupe, beaded relief border, scalloped edge, yellow and red roses, hand-decorated transfer, gold band. Unsigned. OSCAR & EDGAR GUTHERZ, 1898–1918. $25–30. Plate, 6"d. Coupe, beaded relief border, scalloped edge, yellow and red roses, hand-decorated transfer, gold band. Unsigned. OSCAR & EDGAR GUTHERZ, 1898–1918. $15–20.

Plate, 8.75"d. Coupe, red and pink roses, green leaves, multicolored ground, gold band, hand-decorated transfer. Signed: *Martin*. OSCAR & EDGAR GUTHERZ, 1898–1918. $40–50. Plate, 6"d. Coupe, red and pink roses, green leaves, multicolored ground, gold band, hand-decorated transfer. Signed: *Georges* OSCAR & EDGAR GUTHERZ, 1898–1918. $40–50. Ramekin with underplate, 4.25"d. Rim, red and pink roses, green leaves, multicolored ground, festooned edge, gold band, hand-decorated transfer. Signed: *Georges* OSCAR & EDGAR GUTHERZ, 1898–1918. $30–40.

Plate, 7.5"d. Coupe, scalloped edge, pink roses, green leaves, pale gray ground, gold band, hand-decorated transfer. Signed: *Martin*. OSCAR & EDGAR GUTHERZ, 1898–1918. $30–40. Plate, 6.2"d. Coupe, scalloped edge, pink roses, green leaves, pale gray ground, gold band, hand-decorated transfer. Signed: *Martin*. OSCAR & EDGAR GUTHERZ, 1898–1918. $20–25.

Plate, 9.6"d. Coupe, red and pink roses, green leaves, ivory ground, gold band, transfer decoration. Unsigned. OSCAR & EDGAR GUTHERZ, 1898–1918. $30–40. Plate, 6.2"d. Coupe, red and pink roses, green leaves, ivory ground, gold band, transfer decoration. Unsigned. OSCAR & EDGAR GUTHERZ, 1898–1918. $10–15.

Plate, 9.6"d. Coupe, red roses, green leaves, white ground, gold band, scalloped edge, transfer decoration. Unsigned. OSCAR & EDGAR GUTHERZ, 1898–1918. $40–50.

Plate, 8.9"d. Coupe, white and yellow roses, green leaves, ivory ground, gold band, hand-decorated transfer. Signed: *Fann*. OSCAR & EDGAR GUTHERZ, 1898–1918. $40–50.

Plate, 8.9"d. Coupe, yellow roses, hand-decorated transfer, pale green ground, gold band. Signed: *Fann*. OSCAR & EDGAR GUTHERZ, 1899–1918. $40–50.

Plate, 8.75"d. Coupe, white and yellow roses, hand-decorated transfer, ivory ground, gold band. Signed: *Laporte*. OSCAR & EDGAR GUTHERZ, 1899–1918. $40–50. Plate, 6.1"d. Coupe, white and yellow roses, hand-decorated transfer, ivory ground, gold band. Signed: *Raymond*. OSCAR & EDGAR GUTHERZ, 1899–1918. $15–20.

Plate, 8.75"d. Coupe, scalloped edge, yellow and white roses, green leaves, white ground, gold band, hand-decorated transfer. Signed: *Martin*. OSCAR & EDGAR GUTHERZ, 1898–1918. $40–50. Plate, 8.9"d. Coupe, yellow and white roses, green leaves, white ground, gold band, hand-decorated transfer. Signed: *Martin*. OSCAR & EDGAR GUTHERZ, 1898–1918. $40–50.

Plate, 8.9"d. Coupe, yellow roses, green leaves, ivory ground, gold band, hand-decorated transfer. Signed: *Raymond*. OSCAR & EDGAR GUTHERZ, 1898–1918. $40–50.

Plate, 9"d. Coupe, yellow, white and pink roses, green leaves, multicolored ground, gold filigree band, hand-decorated transfer. Signed: *Laporte*. OSCAR & EDGAR GUTHERZ, 1898–1918. $40–50.

Plate, 9.75"d. Coupe, gold roses, green leaves, ivory frosted ground, gold band, hand-decorated transfer. Signed: *Georges*. OSCAR & EDGAR GUTHERZ, 1898–1918. $50–60.

Plate, 7.6"d. Coupe, beaded relief border, scalloped edge, pink and white phlox, ivory ground, gold band, transfer decoration. Unsigned. OSCAR & EDGAR GUTHERZ, 1898–1918. $10–15.

Plate, 8.9"d. Coupe, pink roses, white ground, festooned gold edge, transfer decoration. Unsigned. OSCAR & EDGAR GUTHERZ, 1898–1918. $40–50.

Plate, 9.6"d. Coupe, red pink roses, blue violets, hand-decorated transfer, white ground, gold band. Signed: *Martin*. OSCAR & EDGAR GUTHERZ, 1899–1918. $50–60

Plate, 8.5"d. Coupe, beaded relief border, scalloped edge, pink roses, hand-decorated transfer, gold fleur-de-lis band. Signed: *Fann*. OSCAR & EDGAR GUTHERZ, 1898–1918. $40–50. Plate, 7.5"d. Rim, beaded relief border, scalloped edge, pink roses, hand-decorated transfer, gold band. Signed: *Martin*. OSCAR & EDGAR GUTHERZ, 1898–1918. $30–40.

Plate, 8.9"d. Coupe, pink roses, green leaves, ivory ground, gold band, hand-decorated transfer. Signed: *Raymond*. OSCAR & EDGAR GUTHERZ, 1898–1918. $40–50.

Plate, 6"d. Coupe, beaded relief border, scalloped edge, pink roses, green leaves, ivory ground, gold band, hand-decorated transfer. Signed: *Laporte*. OSCAR & EDGAR GUTHERZ, 1898–1918. $25–30.

Plate, 8.9"d. Coupe, white and pink roses, green leaves, white ground, gold checkered band, hand-decorated transfer. Signed: *Laporte*. OSCAR & EDGAR GUTHERZ, 1898–1918. $50–60.

Plate, 8.2"d. Coupe, pink roses, green leaves, white ground, gold band, "Ranson" relief edge, transfer decoration. Unsigned. OSCAR & EDGAR GUTHERZ, 1898–1918. $30–40.

Plate, 6.2"d. Coupe, white pink roses, green leaves, white ground, gold band, transfer decoration. Unsigned. OSCAR & EDGAR GUTHERZ, 1898–1918. $10–15.

Plate, 9"d. Coupe, pink roses, green leaves, ivory ground, gold band, hand-decorated transfer. Signed: *Martin*. OSCAR & EDGAR GUTHERZ, 1898–1918. $50–60.

Plate, 9.5"d. Coupe, pink and white roses, white ground, double filigree gold band, beaded relief border, scalloped edge, transfer decoration. Unsigned. OSCAR & EDGAR GUTHERZ, 1898–1918. $30–40.

Decorative plates. *Left*, 9.5"d. $50–60. *Right*, 7.5"d. $20–30. Coupe, floral chains of pink roses and blue and white flowers, white ground, beaded relief border, gold filigree rim, scalloped edge. Unsigned. OSCAR & EDGAR GUTHERZ, 1899–1918.

Plate, 6"d. Coupe, pink roses, red and green bands, white ground, fleur-de-lis relief scalloped edge, transfer decoration. Unsigned. OSCAR & EDGAR GUTHERZ, 1898–1918. $8–10.

Decorative plate, 8.5"d. Pink roses, gold filigree ornamentation, central gold medallion, green band on festooned edge, transfer decoration. Unsigned. OSCAR & EDGAR GUTHERZ, 1898–1918. $45–55.

Plate, 6.2"d. Rim, pink roses, gold laurel wreath band, white ground, gold festooned edge, transfer decoration. Unsigned. OSCAR & EDGAR GUTHERZ, 1898–1918. $8–10.

Plate, 9.75"d. Coupe, white grapes, colored leaves, ivory ground, gold filigree rim, gold band, hand-decorated transfer. Signed: *Raymond*. OSCAR & EDGAR GUTHERZ, 1898–1918. $50–60. Plate, 8.9"d. Coupe, white grapes, colored leaves, ivory ground, gold filigree rim, gold band, hand-decorated transfer. Signed: *Martin*. OSCAR & EDGAR GUTHERZ, 1898–1918. $50–60. Tray, 12.1"l. Celery, white grapes, colored leaves, ivory ground, gold filigree rim, gold band, hand-decorated transfer. Signed: *Raymond*. OSCAR & EDGAR GUTHERZ, 1898–1918. $45–55.

Left, plate, 8.75"d. Coupe, white grapes, green leaves, hand-decorated transfer, ivory ground, wide gold band with hand painted apple blossoms. Signed: *Raymond. (A. Gunck).* OSCAR & EDGAR GUTHERZ, 1899–1918. $85–100. *Right,* plate, 8.75"d. Coupe, white grapes, green leaves, hand-decorated transfer, ivory ground, gold band. Signed: *Raymond.* OSCAR & EDGAR GUTHERZ, 1899–1918. $40–50.

Plate, 7.6"d. Coupe, lily of the valley, green ground, gold edge, beaded relief border and scrollwork, scalloped edge, hand decoration. Signed: *Fann.* OSCAR & EDGAR GUTHERZ, 1898–1918. $30–40.

Plate, 9"d. Coupe, multicolored floral, white ground, gold edge, hand-decorated transfer. Signed: *Martin.* OSCAR & EDGAR GUTHERZ, 1898–1918. $40–50.

Plate, 8.9"d. Coupe, multicolored clematis, green leaves, white ground, gold filigree band, hand-decorated transfer. Signed: *Raymond.* OSCAR & EDGAR GUTHERZ, 1898–1918. $40–50.

Plate, 8.9"d. Coupe, white daisies, green leaves, ivory ground, gold band, transfer decoration. Unsigned. OSCAR & EDGAR GUTHERZ, 1898–1918. $40–50.

Plate, 9"d. Coupe, pale pink roses, green leaves, ivory ground, wide gold filigree band, hand-decorated transfer. Signed: *Laporte*. OSCAR & EDGAR GUTHERZ, 1898–1918. $50–60.

Plate, 8.9"d. Coupe, multicolored poppies, hand-decorated transfer, ivory ground, gold band. Signed: *Fann*. OSCAR & EDGAR GUTHERZ, 1899–1918. $40–50. Plate, 6.1"d. Coupe, multicolored poppies, hand-decorated transfer, ivory ground, gold band. Signed: *Fann*. OSCAR & EDGAR GUTHERZ, 1899–1918. $15–20.

Plate, 8.75"d. Coupe, pale pink poppies, green leaves, white ground, gold filigree band, hand-decorated transfer. Signed: *Raymond*. OSCAR & EDGAR GUTHERZ, 1898–1918. $50–60.

Decorative plates. Coupe, purple and white violets, pale green ground, gold band, hand-decorated transfer. *Left*, 8.75"d. Signed: *Raymond*. $40–50. *Center*, 12.25"d. Signed: *Martin*. $50–60. *Right*, 7.75"d. Signed: *Georges*. $35–40. OSCAR & EDGAR GUTHERZ, 1899–1918.

Plate, 9.75"d. Coupe, magenta and white, hand-decorated transfer, ivory ground, double gold band. Signed: *Raymond*. OSCAR & EDGAR GUTHERZ, 1899–1918. $40–50.

Plate, 8.9"d. Coupe, pink and white phlox, green leaves, ivory ground, gold band, transfer decoration. Unsigned. OSCAR & EDGAR GUTHERZ, 1898–1918. $30–40. Plate, 7.6"d. Coupe, beaded relief border, scalloped edge, pink and white phlox, ivory ground, gold band, transfer decoration. Unsigned. OSCAR & EDGAR GUTHERZ, 1898–1918. $10–15.

Plate, 8.9"d. Coupe, lavender chrysanthemum, green leaves, ivory ground, gold band, hand-decorated transfer. Signed: *Georges*. OSCAR & EDGAR GUTHERZ, 1898–1918. $40–50.

Plate, 8.6"d. Coupe, pink poppies, green leaves, ivory and brown ground, gold band with black diamonds, hand-decorated transfer. Signed: *Martin*. OSCAR & EDGAR GUTHERZ, 1898–1918. $40–50.

Decorative plate, 12.25"d. Coupe, white apple blossoms, pale green ground, gold band, hand-decorated transfer. OSCAR & EDGAR GUTHERZ, 1899–1918. $50–60.

Portrait plate, 9.5"d. Coupe, unknown woman, red banding, gold filigree ornamentation, transfer decoration. Unsigned. OSCAR & EDGAR GUTHERZ, 1898–1918. $100–150.

Plate, 8.9"d. Coupe, ripening blackberries, multicolored leaves, ivory ground, gold band, hand-decorated transfer. Signed: *Laporte*. OSCAR & EDGAR GUTHERZ, 1898–1918. $40–50.

Plate, 8.9"d. Coupe, purple iris, green leaves, ivory ground, gold band, hand-decorated transfer. Signed: *Martin*. OSCAR & EDGAR GUTHERZ, 1898–1918. $40–50.

Plate, 9.9"d. Rim, festooned edge, multicolored variegated tulips, white ground, gold band, hand-decorated transfer. Unsigned. OSCAR & EDGAR GUTHERZ, 1899–1918. $20–25.

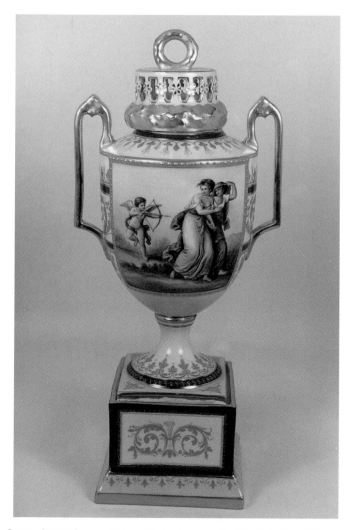

Large decorative amphora style vase, curved gilded handles with pedestal stand and swivel square base, 12.5"h. Central panel is hand painted mythological scene of cupid and two maidens. Signed: *A. Heer*. Beehive mark attributed to CARL KNOLL CARLSBAD, Rybáře, c.1895. *Courtesy of Richard Rendall*. $400–500.

Lidded vase, gilded cover, 8.5"h. Woman with ostrich plume bonnet. Signed: *F. Tenner*. Beehive mark attributed to CARL KNOLL CARLSBAD, Rybáře, c.1895. *Courtesy of Richard Rendall*. $550–650.

Vase, 16.5"h. Detail, "Portia's plea for mercy" in *Merchant of Venice*, transfer decoration.

Vase, 16.5"h. Amphora, Shakespearean scenes, red ground, gold handles and ornamentation, transfer decoration. Unsigned. "VICTORIA" SCHMIDT & COMPANY, 1891–1918. $250–300.

Vase, 16.5"h. Detail, "Death of King Lear," in *King Lear*, from an illustration by Walter Paget (1863–1935), transfer decoration.

Decorative steins, Vienna style, cobalt ground, raised paste gilding. *Left*, 6.5"h. Braumeister portrait. Unsigned. *Right*, 4"h. Beer drinker with stein. Unsigned. CARL KNOLL CARLSBAD, c.1885. *Courtesy of Milwaukee Art Museum.* $2,500–3,000.

Decorative stein, 6.5"h. Vienna style, detail frontal view. CARL KNOLL CARLSBAD, c.1885. *Courtesy of Milwaukee Art Museum.*

American Decorated Porcelain

Plate, 8.75"d. Coupe, yellow roses, green leaves, beaded relief border, gold scalloped edge, hand decoration. Unsigned. OSCAR & EDGAR GUTHERZ, 1898–1918. $30–40.

Plate, 9.75"d. Coupe, yellow roses, beaded relief border, scalloped edge, hand decoration, gold rim. Signed: *A. Stuewe.* OSCAR & EDGAR GUTHERZ, 1898–1918. $20–25.

Plate, 6"d. Coupe, pink apple blossoms, beaded relief border, scalloped edge, hand decoration. Signed: *B. R. E.* OSCAR & EDGAR GUTHERZ, 1898–1918. $15–20. Plate, 6"d. Coupe, forget-me-nots, beaded relief border, scalloped edge, hand decoration. Unsigned. OSCAR & EDGAR GUTHERZ, 1898–1918. $20–25.

Plate, 7.5"d. Coupe, forget-me-nots, beaded relief border, scalloped edge, hand decoration, gold edge. Signed: *B. N.* OSCAR & EDGAR GUTHERZ, 1898–1918. $20–25.

Plate, 7.9"d. Rim, forget-me-nots, beaded relief border, scalloped edge, hand decoration, gold edge. Signed: *L.E.* OSCAR & EDGAR GUTHERZ, 1898–1918. $25–30.

Plate, 6.9"d. Coupe, forget-me-nots, white ground, gold edge, hand decoration. Signed: *T.* OSCAR & EDGAR GUTHERZ, 1898–1918. $10–15.

Plate, 7.9"d. Soup, rim, red, yellow, pink roses, beaded relief border, scalloped edge, wide gold band, hand-decorated dinnerware. Signed: *L. S.* OSCAR & EDGAR GUTHERZ, 1898–1918. $25–30.

Plates, 8.75"d. Rim, pink roses and pink peonies, white ground, gold band, hand decoration. Signed: *P.H.* OSCAR & EDGAR GUTHERZ, 1899–1918. $40–50.

Plate, 9.75"d. Coupe, purple violets, white ground, gold edge, hand decoration. Signed: *M.M.* OSCAR & EDGAR GUTHERZ, 1898–1918. $20–30.

Plate, 8.5"d. Rim, festooned edge, pink and violet sedum, green leaves, gold edge, hand decoration. Signed: *F. Neary.* OSCAR & EDGAR GUTHERZ, 1898–1918. $25–35.

Plate, 8.9"d. Coupe, yellow and blue floral, Art Deco style, pale blue ground, gold edge, hand decoration. Signed: *E. C. O.* OSCAR & EDGAR GUTHERZ, 1899–1918. $20–25.

Plate, 7.6"d. Coupe, goldfinch and pink apple blossoms, hand decoration. Signed: *Morselaan*. OSCAR & EDGAR GUTHERZ, 1898–1918. *Courtesy of Dorothy Kamm*. $20–30.

Plate, 7.75"d. Coupe, flying song birds, hand decoration. Signed: *P. K.* BASSETT LIMOGES AUSTRIA, c.1915. *Courtesy of Dorothy Kamm*. $20–30.

Plate, 9.75"d. Rim, yellow quince, beaded relief border, scalloped edge, gold band, hand decoration. Unsigned. OSCAR & EDGAR GUTHERZ, 1898–1918. $25–30.

Vase, 4"h. Scalloped floral relief with clamshell-footed base, green leaves, gold ornamentation, hand decoration. Signed: *Mabel Urban–1908*. OSCAR & EDGAR GUTHERZ, 1898–1918. $50–55.

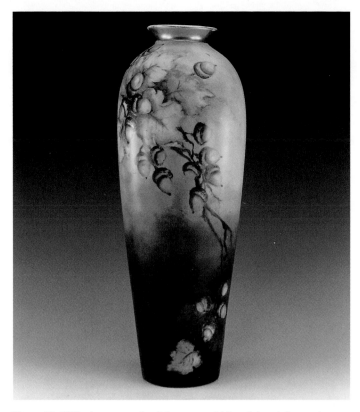

Vase, 12.25"h. Acorns and oak leaves, gold band, hand decoration. Unsigned. OSCAR & EDGAR GUTHERZ, 1899–1918. $100–120.

Vase, 10.5"h. Pastoral scene, gold band, hand decoration. Unsigned. OSCAR & EDGAR GUTHERZ, 1898–1918. $70–90.

Vase, 9.6"h. Forget-me-nots, pale blue ground with double gold band, hand decoration. Unsigned. OSCAR & EDGAR GUTHERZ, 1898–1918. $50–60.

Vase, 7.25"h. Fluted shape, pink roses, ivory and pale blue ground, gold edge, hand decoration. Unsigned. OSCAR & EDGAR GUTHERZ, 1898–1918. $20–25.

Bud vase, 5.5"h. Woman's portrait, gold edge, hand decoration. Unsigned. OSCAR & EDGAR GUTHERZ, 1898–1918. $20–30.

Vase, 6.3"h. Cylindrical, sparrows, gold edge, hand decoration. Unsigned. OSCAR & EDGAR GUTHERZ, 1898–1918. $30–35.

Vase, 7"h. Yellow daffodils, pale blue ground, gold band on fluted edge, hand decoration. Signed: *E. H.* OSCAR & EDGAR GUTHERZ, 1898–1918. $55–60.

Vase, 9.9"h. Rust floral with green leaves, white ground, hand decoration. Signed: *E. Reed.* OSCAR & EDGAR GUTHERZ, 1898–1918. $40–50.

Household Ware

Bohemian Decorated Porcelain

Dish, 6.25"l. Bonbon, oval, ribbed, red and white roses (*Gloire de Dijon*), multicolored ground, scalloped gold edge, hand-decorated transfer. Signed: *Fann*. OSCAR & EDGAR GUTHERZ, 1898–1918. $15–25.

Dish, 5"l. Bonbon, oval, footed, beaded relief border, gold handle and scalloped edge. Unsigned. OSCAR & EDGAR GUTHERZ, 1898–1918. $10–15.

Dish, 6.25"l. Bonbon, oval, ribbed, red roses (*Rose du Barry*), green ground, scalloped gold edge, hand-decorated transfer. Signed: *Fann*. OSCAR & EDGAR GUTHERZ, 1898–1918. $15–25.

Dish, 8.25"l. Bonbon, oval, handled, pink roses, white ground, scalloped edge, transfer decoration. Unsigned. OSCAR & EDGAR GUTHERZ, 1898–1918. $20–25.

Soap dish, 5.25"l. $30–35. Shaving brush vase with drain, 4.25"h. Pink dogwood, transfer decoration, hand painted rural scenes. Unsigned. BAWO & DOTTER, c.1883–1891. $60–70.

Dish, 8.25"l. Pickle, oval, acorns and oak leaves, tan ground, gold edge, hand-decorated transfer. Signed: *Laporte*. OSCAR & EDGAR GUTHERZ, 1898–1918. $30–40.

Button box, 3"d. Gold edge, white ground, hand decoration. Unsigned. OSCAR & EDGAR GUTHERZ, 1898–1918. $15–20. Pomade, 2.5"d. Derby shape, white ground, relief ornamentation. Unsigned. OSCAR & EDGAR GUTHERZ, 1898–1918. $15–20.

Card tray, 5.25"l. Gold filigree and edge, dark green band, white ground, transfer decoration. Unsigned. OSCAR & EDGAR GUTHERZ, 1898–1918. $15–20. Bonbon, 4"d. Handled, footed, lobulated, gold filigree and edge, dark green band, white ground, transfer decoration. Unsigned. OSCAR & EDGAR GUTHERZ, 1898–1918. $20–30.

Dresser set. Talcum shaker, 4.25"h., pin tray, 4.5"l., puff box, 3.25"d., hair receiver, 3.25"d., dresser tray, 12.5"l., yellow roses, ivory ground, transfer decoration. Unsigned. OSCAR & EDGAR GUTHERZ, 1898–1918. $130–150.

Chamberstick, 2.5"h. Gold handle and filigree ornamentation, red ground, transfer decoration. Unsigned. OSCAR & EDGAR GUTHERZ, 1898–1918. $15–25.

Calling card tray, 5.5"d. Napkin fold, pink, yellow and blue floral, gold filigree ornamentation, hand decoration. Unsigned. COUNT THUN'S PORCELAIN FACTORY, 1880–1898. *Courtesy of Dorothy Kamm.* $20–30.

American Decorated Porcelain

Dish, 6.9"d. Bonbon, coupe, handled, yellow daisies, gold edge, pale blue ground, hand decoration. Signed: *J. Hanke.* ROYAL EPIAG, 1920–1945. $35–40.

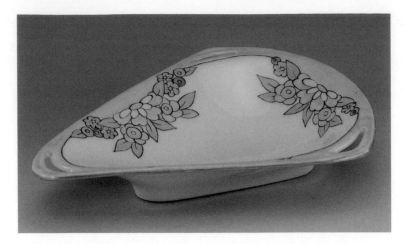

Dish, 5"l. Bonbon, triangular, open handles, yellow and blue floral, gold edge, white ground, hand decoration. Unsigned. OSCAR & EDGAR GUTHERZ, 1898–1918. $20–25.

Dish, 9.9"l. Bonbon, leaf-shape, red strawberries, white ground, scalloped gold edge, hand decoration. Signed: *L. Soutter*. OSCAR & EDGAR GUTHERZ, 1898–1918. $20–25.

Dish, 6.75"l. Bonbon, footed, oval, purple floral, multicolored ground, beaded relief border, scalloped edge, hand decoration. Signed: *J. Arthur*. OSCAR & EDGAR GUTHERZ, 1898–1918. $15–20.

Dish, 8.25"l. Bonbon, oval, handled, forget-me-nots, ivory ground, scalloped gold edge, hand decoration. Unsigned. OSCAR & EDGAR GUTHERZ, 1898–1918. $20–25.

Shaving mug, 3.5"h. Pink carnations, "A. Behrendt" inscribed in gold, gold trim, hand-decorated transfer. Unsigned. OSCAR & EDGAR GUTHERZ, 1898–1918. $45–50.

Shaving mug, 3.5"h. Front view.

Hair receiver, 4.25"d. Forget-me-nots, ivory ground, wide gold band, hand decoration. Unsigned. OSCAR & EDGAR GUTHERZ, 1898–1918. $25–30.

Hair receiver, 4.75"d. Iowa shape, raised gold filigree ornamentation, pale blue and white ground, footed, hand decoration. Signed: *Eller.* OSCAR & EDGAR GUTHERZ, 1898–1918. $55–65.

Puff box, 4.75"d. Iowa shape, multicolored floral, pale blue ground, luster glaze interior, footed, hand decoration. Signed: *E.A.M. '9.* ROYAL EPIAG, 1920–1945. $35–45.

Hair receiver, 4"d. $25–35. Puff box, 4"d. $25–30. Pink apple blossoms, ivory ground, ball-footed, gold ornamentation, hand decoration. Unsigned. OSCAR & EDGAR GUTHERZ, 1898–1918.

Hair receiver, 4"d. $25–30. Puff box, 4"d. $25–30. Blue violets, hand decoration. Unsigned. Dated: *10/13* OSCAR & EDGAR GUTHERZ, 1898–1918.

Puff box, 5"d. Pink roses, wide blue and pink banding, crenelated base, gold ornamentation, hand decoration. Unsigned. OSCAR & EDGAR GUTHERZ, 1898–1918. $25–35.

Puff box, 5"d. Orange and violet pansies, ivory ground, crenelated base, hand decoration. Unsigned. OSCAR & EDGAR GUTHERZ, 1898–1918. $30–35.

Puff box, 3.5"d. $35–45. Button box, 3"d. $25–35. Pink and red roses, ivory ground, hand decoration. Signed: *J. Koch.* OSCAR & EDGAR GUTHERZ, 1898–1918.

Lidded pin box, 3.75"d. Pink apple blossoms, gold border, white ground, hand decoration. Unsigned. OSCAR & EDGAR GUTHERZ, 1898–1918. $15–20.

Ring tree, 4.5"l. Oval base, forget-me-nots, gold ornamentation, hand decoration. Unsigned. OSCAR & EDGAR GUTHERZ, 1898–1918. *Courtesy of Dorothy Kamm.* $35–45.

Collar button box, 2.5"d. Floral design, silver ornamentation, hand decoration. Unsigned. OSCAR & EDGAR GUTHERZ, 1898–1918. $60–70.

Dresser set, child's: hatpin holder, tray, hair receiver, puff box. Pale yellow and lavender floral, gold banding, hand decoration. Signed: *PPP, Atlan, LCD(unknown).* OSCAR & EDGAR GUTHERZ, 1898–1918 *Courtesy of Alan Reed.* $225–265.

Perfume bottle, stoppered, 5.5"h. OSCAR & EDGAR GUTHERZ, 1898–1918. Puff box, 4.75"d. Iowa shape, footed. COUNT THUN'S PORCELAIN FACTORY, c.1891–c.1908. Button box, 2.75"d. OSCAR & EDGAR GUTHERZ, 1898–1918. Pin tray, 5.25"l. OSCAR & EDGAR GUTHERZ, 1898–1918. Unsigned. Gold Art Deco ornamentation, pink floral, ivory and pale blue ground, gold edge, hand decoration $175–180.

Perfume bottle, 5.5"h. Pink apple blossoms, hand decoration. Signed: *Frederick Walters*. OSCAR & EDGAR GUTHERZ, 1898–1918. $60–65.

Perfume bottle, 4.75"h. Forget-me-nots, ivory and pale blue ground, gold edge, hand decoration. Unsigned. OSCAR & EDGAR GUTHERZ, 1898–1918. $30–35.

Talcum shaker, 3"h. Pink and purple floral design, gold top, hand decoration. Unsigned. OSCAR & EDGAR GUTHERZ, 1898–1918. $15–20.

Talcum shaker, 4.75"h. Forget-me-nots, gold top, hand decoration. Unsigned. *(Stouffer Studio, Chicago)*. OSCAR & EDGAR GUTHERZ, 1898–1918. $80–100.

Hatpin holder, 4.25"h. Pink roses with green leaves, gold top with round flared base, hand decoration. Unsigned. OSCAR & EDGAR GUTHERZ, 1898–1918. $50–60.

Talcum shaker, 4.4"h. Oval gold top with round flared base, pink apple blossoms with green leaves, hand decoration. Signed: *Cora Dickie*. OSCAR & EDGAR GUTHERZ, 1898–1918. $50–60.

Cruet, 6.5"d. Pink and white floral, gold stopper and handle, ivory ground, hand decoration. Signed: *R. A. S.* OEPIAG, 1919–1920. *Courtesy of Dorothy Kamm*. $50–60.

Card tray, 6.1"l. Open handles, forget-me-nots, pale blue ground, gold edge, hand decoration. Signed: *Mary E. Hargraves*. OSCAR & EDGAR GUTHERZ, 1898–1918. $25–30.

Nut cup, 3.5"d. Club shape, blue violets, gold edge, ivory ground, hand decoration. Signed: *M. Burnet*. OSCAR & EDGAR GUTHERZ, 1898–1918. $20–25.

Dresser clock, 4.9"h. Pink roses with blue ribbon, transfer decoration. Unsigned. OSCAR & EDGAR GUTHERZ, 1898–1918. $50–60.

Boudoir clock, 5.6"h. Pink and blue floral, gold ornamentation, hand decoration. Signed: *B. J. S. 1924*. OSCAR & EDGAR GUTHERZ, 1898–1918. *Courtesy of Dorothy Kamm*. $100–150.

Candlesticks, 4.4"h. Round base, pink apple blossoms, ivory ground, gold edge and top, hand decoration. Unsigned. OSCAR & EDGAR GUTHERZ, 1898–1918. $30–35.

Candlesticks, 8.9"h. Square base, forget-me-nots, white ground, gold top, hand decoration. Unsigned. OSCAR & EDGAR GUTHERZ, 1898–1918. $50–60.

Candlesticks, 6.4"h. Square base, pale blue ground, gold trim and "FA" monogram, hand decoration. Unsigned. OSCAR & EDGAR GUTHERZ, 1898–1918. $40–50.

Lidded inkwell, 2.75"h. Forget-me-nots, gold top, pale blue ground, hand decoration. Signed: *Eckstrom*. OSCAR & EDGAR GUTHERZ, 1898–1918. *Courtesy of Maureen Farmer*. $50–60.

Vase, 5.5"h. Urn-shape, gold band, white ground, hand decoration. Unsigned. OSCAR & EDGAR GUTHERZ, 1898–1918. $20–30.

Tableware

Undecorated Bohemian Porcelain

Covered butter dish, 7.5"d. Beaded relief border, scalloped edge. OSCAR & EDGAR GUTHERZ, 1898–1918. $30–40.

Dinner rim plate, 9.9"d. $10–15. Tea cup and saucer, 3.75"d. $10–15. Beaded relief border, scalloped edge. OSCAR & EDGAR GUTHERZ, 1898–1918.

Demi-tasse cup and saucer, 2.3"d. Beaded relief border, scalloped edge. Unsigned. OSCAR & EDGAR GUTHERZ, 1898–1918. $15–20.

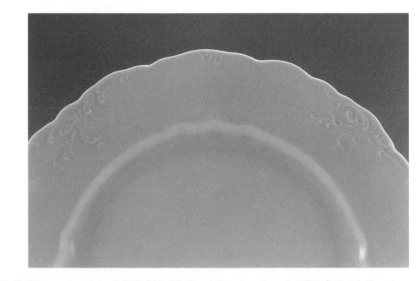

(*Left*) Dinner rim plate, 9.9"d. $15–20. Breakfast rim plate, 8.75"d. $10–15. Tea rim plate, 7"d. $10–15. Bread and butter rim plate, 6.25"d. $5–10. Butter dish, 3.5"d. $5–10. Scrolled relief, scalloped edge. OSCAR & EDGAR GUTHERZ, 1898–1918. (*Above*) Dinnerware pattern. Detail. Scrolled relief border, scalloped edge.

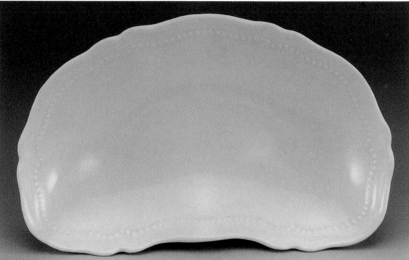

Sauce boat with underplate, 7.75"l. Scalloped edge. OSCAR & EDGAR GUTHERZ, 1898–1918. $25–30.

Bone dish, 6"l. Scalloped edge, beaded relief border. OSCAR & EDGAR GUTHERZ, 1898–1918. $15–20.

Bohemian Decorated Porcelain

Bowl, 8.25"d. Footed. Dish, 5.25"d. Berry, *boule de neige* (hydrangia), pale tan ground, gold rim. Signed: *Fann*. OSCAR & EDGAR GUTHERZ, 1898–1918. $125–175.

Plate, 8.9"d. Coupe, white roses, gold edge and filigree ornamentation, white and cobalt ground, hand-decorated transfer. Signed: *Raymond*. OSCAR & EDGAR GUTHERZ, 1898–1918. $40–50. Sauce bowls, 5"d. Conical, gold edge and filigree ornamentation, white roses, white and cobalt ground, hand-decorated transfer. Signed: *Raymond, Fann, Laporte*. OSCAR & EDGAR GUTHERZ, 1898–1918. $100–150.

Bouillon cup and saucer, 3.6"d. Pink roses, white ground, gold banding with red daisies, transfer decoration. Unsigned. OSCAR & EDGAR GUTHERZ, 1898–1918. $12–15.

Bouillon cup and saucer, 3.6"d. Gold leaf band, white ground, hand decoration. Unsigned. OSCAR & EDGAR GUTHERZ, 1898–1918. $15–20.

Cake plate, 10"d. Coupe, pink roses, central gold medallion, figure-eight festooned beaded relief border, transfer decoration. Unsigned. OSCAR & EDGAR GUTHERZ, 1898–1918. $90–100.

Cake plate, 10.75"d. Coupe, pink roses, scalloped relief rim, white ground, gold trim, transfer decoration. Unsigned. MORITZ ZDEKAUER, 1884–1909. $20–25.

Cake plate, 11.5"d. Coupe, Ranson shape, twig relief, white ground, scalloped gold edge. Unsigned. OSCAR & EDGAR GUTHERZ, 1898–1918. $40–50.

Cake plate, 10.25"d. Coupe, pink floral, white ground, gilded floral relief, scalloped edge, transfer decoration. Unsigned. OSCAR & EDGAR GUTHERZ, 1898–1918. $40–50.

Cake plate, 10.75"d. Coupe, Ranson shape, pink roses, white ground, gold trim, transfer decoration. Unsigned. OSCAR & EDGAR GUTHERZ, 1898–1918. $40–50.

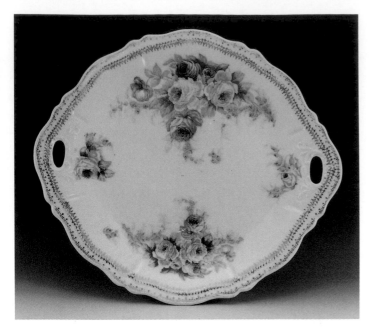

Cake plate, 11"d. Coupe, pink and white roses, double gold filigree band, beaded relief border, scalloped edge, transfer decoration. Unsigned. OSCAR & EDGAR GUTHERZ, 1898–1918. $40–50.

Cake plate, 11"d. Coupe, central gold medallion, double gold filigree band, beaded relief border, scalloped edge, transfer decoration. Unsigned. OSCAR & EDGAR GUTHERZ, 1898–1918. $40–50.

Cake plate, 11.5"d. Coupe. $40–50. Lidded syrup, 3.5"h. Donatello shape. $25–30. Yellow roses, gold handle, hand-decorated transfer. Signed: *Fann*. OSCAR & EDGAR GUTHERZ, 1898–1918.

Pancake dish, 9.75"d. $70–100. Cake plate, 11"d. Coupe. $50–60. Burgundy thistle, gold edge and handle, beaded relief border, scalloped edge, hand-decorated transfer. Signed: *Fann*. OSCAR & EDGAR GUTHERZ, 1898–1918.

Celery tray, 12.1"l. Salt dips, 3.5"l. Oval rim with gold band, hand decoration. Unsigned. OSCAR & EDGAR GUTHERZ, 1898–1918. $80–90.

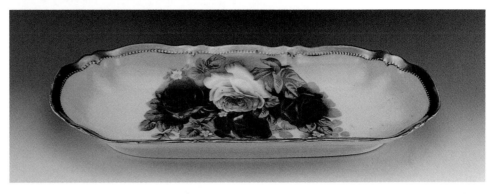

Celery tray, 12.25"l. Red and pink roses, scalloped gold edge and beaded relief border, hand-decorated transfer decoration. Signed: *Martin.* OSCAR & EDGAR GUTHERZ, 1898–1918. $35–50.

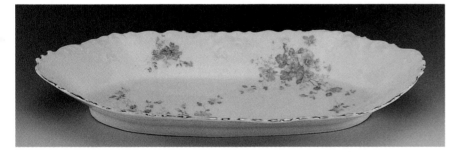

Celery tray, 11.75"l. Yellow petunias, scrolled relief, scalloped gold edge, transfer decoration. Unsigned. OSCAR & EDGAR GUTHERZ, 1898–1918. $35–50.

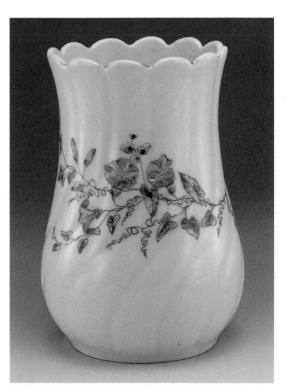

Celery vase, 6.25"h. Yellow morning glory, festooned gold rim, hand-decorated transfer. Unsigned. MARX & GUTHERZ, 1884–1898. $35–40.

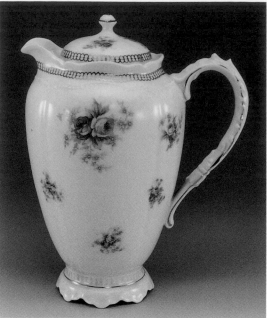

Plate, 9.4"d. Square cake, pink and red American Beauty roses, scalloped gold rim, hand-decorated transfer. Signed: *Fann*. OSCAR & EDGAR GUTHERZ, 1898–1918. $20–30. Celery tray, 12.1"d. Pink and red American Beauty roses, beaded relief border, scalloped gold rim, hand-decorated transfer. Signed: *Fann*. OSCAR & EDGAR GUTHERZ, 1898–1918. $50–60. Bonbon, 7"d. Pink and red American Beauty roses, festooned gold edge, hand-decorated transfer. Signed: *Fann*. OSCAR & EDGAR GUTHERZ, 1898–1918. $35–40.

Chocolate pot, 8.5"h. Pink and white roses, beaded relief border, scalloped-footed base, gold ornamentation, transfer decoration. Unsigned. OSCAR & EDGAR GUTHERZ, 1898–1918. $120–150.

Celery tray, 12.25"l. Lily of the valley, ivory ground, gold scalloped edge, hand-decorated transfer. Signed: *Martin*. OSCAR & EDGAR GUTHERZ, 1898–1918. $50–60. Sauce bowl, 5.3"d. Lily of the valley, ivory ground, gold scalloped edge, hand-decorated transfer. Signed: *Martin*. OSCAR & EDGAR GUTHERZ, 1898–1918. $10–15. Plate, 8.75"l. Coupe, Lily of the valley, ivory ground, gold edge, hand-decorated transfer. Signed: *Martin*. OSCAR & EDGAR GUTHERZ, 1898–1918. $40–50.

Coffee pot, 9"h. Pink roses, white ground, gold trim, burgundy band on top, transfer decoration. Unsigned. OSCAR & EDGAR GUTHERZ, 1898–1918. $85–150. Demi-tasse cup and saucer, 3"h. Gold handle and filigree ornamentation, red and white ground, transfer decoration. Unsigned. OSCAR & EDGAR GUTHERZ, 1898–1918. $40–50.

Coffee pot, 9"h. Multi-color floral, white ground, gold ornamentation, blue banding, transfer decoration. Unsigned. OSCAR & EDGAR GUTHERZ, 1898–1918. $85–150. Plate, 9.75"h. Rim, multi-color floral, scalloped gold edge and filigree ornamentation, blue banding, transfer decoration. Unsigned. OSCAR & EDGAR GUTHERZ, 1898–1918. $40–50.

Coffee pot, 9"h. Gold handle, trim and filigree ornamentation, green ground, transfer decoration. Unsigned. OSCAR & EDGAR GUTHERZ, 1898–1918. $85–150.

Chocolate pot, 9"h. Acorns and oak leaves, tan ground, gold trim and handle, hand-decorated transfer. Signed: *Martin*. OSCAR & EDGAR GUTHERZ, 1898–1918. $100–150. Chocolate cups and saucers, 3"h. Acorns and oak leaves, tan ground, gold handle, band and filigree ornamentation, hand-decorated transfer. Signed: *Fann*. OSCAR & EDGAR GUTHERZ, 1898–1918. $90–120.

Cake plate, 11.25"d. $35–40. Lidded sugar, 7"h. $35–40. Creamer, 6"h. $35–40. Coffee pot, 8.75"h. $60–80. Tan willow leaves, pink Allegheny-vine, hand-decorated transfer, white ground. Unsigned. BRUDER SCHWALB, 1884–1898.

Coffee pot, 8"h. Red roses, green ground, gold ornamentation, beaded relief border, hand-decorated transfer. Signed: *Fann.* OSCAR & EDGAR GUTHERZ, 1898–1918. $100–150.

Lidded condensed milk jar with underplate, 6"h. Red and pink roses, gold ornamentation, beaded relief border, scalloped edge, hand decoration. Unsigned. OSCAR & EDGAR GUTHERZ, 1898–1918. $100–150.

Muffin dish, 7.5"d. Pink and violet floral, gold ornamentation, white ground, scalloped edge, hand decoration. Unsigned. OSCAR & EDGAR GUTHERZ, 1898–1918. $50–60.

Lidded cracker jar, 9"d. Ranson shape, acorns and oak leaves, tan ground, gold handles, hand-decorated transfer. Signed: *Georges* OSCAR & EDGAR GUTHERZ, 1898–1918. $100–150.

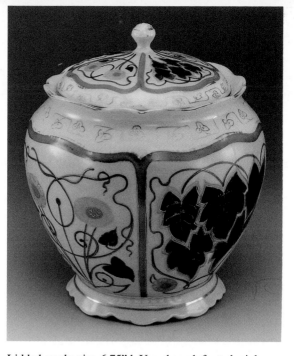

Lidded cracker jar, 6.75"d. Urn-shaped, footed, pink floral design with green ivy leaves in four panels, pink and pale blue ground, hand decoration. Unsigned. *(Carl Friedrich Boseck & Co., Nový bor).* OSCAR & EDGAR GUTHERZ, 1898–1918. $100–125.

Lidded cracker jar, 7"d. Six panels, green geometric design, white ground, gold handles, transfer decoration. Unsigned. OSCAR & EDGAR GUTHERZ, 1898–1918. $100–175. Cup and saucer, 3.5"d. Six panels, green bands and gold filigree ornamentation, transfer decoration. Unsigned. OSCAR & EDGAR GUTHERZ, 1898–1918. $15–20.

Cracker jar, 7"d. Donatello shape, orange poppies, gold edge and handles, hand-decorated transfer. Signed: *Fann.* OSCAR & EDGAR GUTHERZ, 1898–1918. $125–175. Plate, 7"h. Coupe, orange poppies, gold edge, hand-decorated transfer. Signed: *Georges.* OSCAR & EDGAR GUTHERZ, 1898–1918. $40–50.

Tea cup and saucer 3.75"d. Derby shape, pink roses, floral relief, transfer decoration. Unsigned. OSCAR & EDGAR GUTHERZ, 1898–1918. $10–20.

Tea cup and saucer 3.75"d. *Rose pompadour*, red and pink roses, forget-me-nots, beaded relief border, scalloped gold edge, hand-decorated transfer. Signed: *Fann.* OSCAR & EDGAR GUTHERZ, 1898–1918. $50–60.

Plate, 9.75"d. Rim, wide red band, gold central medallion, beaded scalloped edge and filigree ornamentation, transfer decoration. Unsigned. OSCAR & EDGAR GUTHERZ, 1899–1918. $30–40.

Plate, 9.5"d. Rim, wide red band, gold central medallion, beaded relief border and filigree ornamentation, scalloped edge, transfer decoration. Unsigned. OSCAR & EDGAR GUTHERZ, 1899–1918. $30–40.

Plate, 9.5"d. Rim, wide red band, gold central medallion, beaded relief border and filigree ornamentation, scalloped edge, transfer decoration. Unsigned. OSCAR & EDGAR GUTHERZ, 1899–1918. $30–40.

Dinnerware pattern. Detail. Purple violets, scrolled relief border, scalloped edge.

Dinner rim plate, 9.75"d. Purple violets, white ground, scrolled relief, scalloped edge, transfer decoration. OSCAR & EDGAR GUTHERZ, 1898–1918. $15–20.

Dinnerware pattern. Detail. Lavender foral pattern, daisy relief border, scalloped edge.

Dinner rim plate, 9.75"d. Lavender floral pattern, white ground, floral daisy relief, scalloped edge, transfer decoration. OSCAR & EDGAR GUTHERZ, 1898–1918. $15–20.

Plate, 9"d. Rim, pink and purple violets, transfer decoration, white ground. Unsigned. OSCAR & EDGAR GUTHERZ, 1898–1918. $15–20.

131

Dinner rim plate, 9.75"d. $15–20. Tea rim plate, 7.9"d. $10–15. Violet pansies, scrolled relief, transfer decoration. Unsigned. OSCAR & EDGAR GUTHERZ, 1898–1918.

Dinnerware pattern. Detail. Pink moss rose, beaded relief border, scalloped edge.

Plate, 9.6"d. Rim, $15–20. Sauce boat, 7.3"l. $25–30. Tea cup and saucer, 3.6"d. $15–25. Pink moss rose, beaded relief border, white ground, transfer decoration. Unsigned. OSCAR & EDGAR GUTHERZ, 1898–1918.

(*Above*) Dinnerware pattern. Detail. Yellow floral, scalloped edge. (*Left*) Dinner rim plate, 9.9"d. $10–20. Covered butter dish, 7."d. $25–35. Tea cup and saucer, 3.75"d. $20–30. Yellow floral pattern, white ground, scalloped gold edge, transfer decoration. OSCAR & EDGAR GUTHERZ, 1898–1918.

Dinner rim plate, 9.75"d. $15–20. Covered vegetable bowl, 11.6"l. $50–60. Tea cup and saucer, 3.75"d. $20–30. Derby shape, clover leaf border pattern, white ground, transfer decoration, similar to Schleiger no. 98. OSCAR & EDGAR GUTHERZ, 1898–1918.

Dinnerware pattern. Detail. Clover leaf border, similar to Schleiger no. 98.

Covered vegetable, 10.1"d. Donatello shape. $30–40. Plate, 8.75"d. Rim. Tea cup and saucer, 3.5"d. $10–15. Bouillon cup and saucer, 3.6"d. $10–15. Gold Greek key edge, white ground, hand decoration. Unsigned. OSCAR & EDGAR GUTHERZ, 1898–1918.

Dinnerware pattern. Detail. Gold Greek key border.

Plate, 9.6"d. Rim, pink roses, scrolled relief, gold edge, white ground, transfer decoration. $15–20. *Left*, tea cup and saucer, 2.9"d. Kermes shape with ring handle, pink roses, gold edge, white ground, transfer decoration. $10–15. *Right*, tea cup and saucer, 3.6"d. Ovide shape, pink roses, white ground, transfer decoration. $10–15. Unsigned. OSCAR & EDGAR GUTHERZ, 1898–1918.

Dinnerware pattern. Detail. Pink roses, scrolled relief, scalloped edge.

Dinnerware pattern. Detail. Pink roses, Ranson shape, similar to Schleiger no. 1.

Plate, 9.75"d. Rim, dinner. $15–20. Covered round vegetable, 9.6"d. $50–60. Tea cup and saucer, 3.6"d. $15–25. Ranson shape, pink roses, white ground, transfer decoration. Unsigned. OSCAR & EDGAR GUTHERZ, 1898–1918.

Plate, 9.6"d. Rim. $15–20. Plate, 7.75"d. Rim. $15–18. Plate, 6.25"d. Rim. $5–10. Tea cup and saucer, 3.4"d. $10–15. Bouillon cup and saucer, 3.5"d. $10–15. Demi-tasse cup and saucer, 2.3"d. Ranson shape (Louis XIV), gold edge, white ground, hand decoration. Unsigned. OSCAR & EDGAR GUTHERZ, 1898–1918.

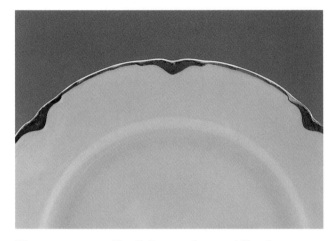

Dinnerware pattern. Detail. Ranson shape, gold band.

Dinnerware pattern. Detail. Pink rose, lattice chain border, similar to Schleiger no. 152.

Covered vegetable bowl, 11.75"l. Pink roses, figure-eight chain border, gold edge. $50–60. Dinner rim plate, 9.6"d. $15–20. Tea cup and saucer, 3.5"d. $20–30. Pink roses, lattice border, white ground, gold edge, transfer decoration, similar to Schleiger no. 150. OSCAR & EDGAR GUTHERZ, 1898–1918.

Tea set. Teapot, 4-tasse. Latice border, pink roses, white ground, transfer decoration. Unsigned. ROYAL EPIAG, 1920–1939. $50–60. Lidded sugar and creamer, 2-tasse. Figure-eight chain link border, pink roses, white ground, transfer decoration, 2-tasse. Unsigned. OSCAR & EDGAR GUTHERZ, 1898–1918. $20–30.

Milk jug, 7"h. $20–30. Unsigned. L. STRAUS & SONS, 1884–1898. Lidded sugar, 7"h. $30–40. Coffee pot, 8.5"h. $40–60. Gray-brown hand-decorated floral transfer, white ground. Unsigned. MARX & GUTHERZ, 1884–1898.

Covered vegetable bowl. $40–60. Platter. $30–40. Gray-brown hand-decorated floral transfer, white ground. Unsigned. MARX & GUTHERZ, 1884–1898.

Bowl, 10"d. Salad. $30–40. Baker, with underplate, 8"l. $10–15. Gray-brown hand-decorated floral transfer, white ground. Unsigned. MARX & GUTHERZ, 1884–1898.

136

Sauce boat, 9"l. Handled with drainer, gray-brown hand-decorated floral transfer, white ground. Unsigned. MARX & GUTHERZ, 1884–1898. $50–60.

Covered butter dish, 8.25"d. $25–35. Covered vegetable bowl, 11.5"l. $60–80. Floral relief, pink floral transfer decoration OSCAR & EDGAR GUTHERZ, 1898–1918.

Covered vegetable, 12.1"l. Lavender floral, scalloped relief border, white ground, transfer decoration. $60–80. Salad bowl, 9.5"d. Lavender floral, beaded relief border, scalloped edge, white ground, transfer decoration. $30–40. Unsigned. OSCAR & EDGAR GUTHERZ, 1898–1918.

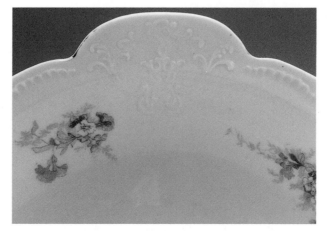

Dinnerware pattern. Detail. Lavender floral, beaded and scroll relief border, scalloped edge.

Covered vegetable bowl. $40–60. Platter. $30–40. Gray-brown hand-decorated floral transfer, white ground. Unsigned. RUDOLF & EUGEN HAIDINGER, 1833–1860.

Covered round vegetable, 10"d. Pink roses, white ground, transfer decoration. Unsigned. OSCAR & EDGAR GUTHERZ, 1898–1918. $60–80.

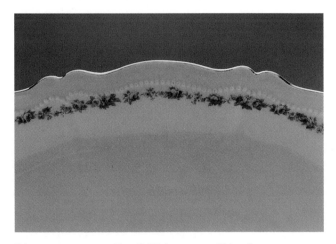

Dinnerware pattern. Detail. Pink roses and blue forget-me-nots, beaded relief border, scalloped edge.

(*Left*) Covered vegetable bowl, 11.5"l. $50–60. Platter, 15.5"l. $60–80. Pink roses and forget-me-nots, beaded relief border, scalloped gold edge, transfer decoration. Unsigned. OSCAR & EDGAR GUTHERZ, 1898–1918.

Covered vegetable bowl, 11"l. Pink roses and yellow floral, scalloped gold edge, transfer decoration. Unsigned. OSCAR & EDGAR GUTHERZ, 1898–1918. $50–60.

Left, butter dish, 3.5"d. Pink and white roses, white ground, relief border, scalloped edge, transfer decoration. $5–10. *Right*, butter dish, 3.25"d. Pink roses, white ground, scalloped edge, transfer decoration. $5–10. OSCAR & EDGAR GUTHERZ, 1898–1918.

Left, butter dish, 3.5"d. Pink moss rose, white ground, beaded relief border, scalloped edge, transfer decoration. $5–10. *Right*, butter dish, 3.5"d. Pink rose, white ground, beaded relief border, scalloped edge, transfer decoration. $5–10. OSCAR & EDGAR GUTHERZ, 1898–1918.

Left, butter dish, 3.5"d. Double gold band and central medallion, beaded relief border, scalloped edge, transfer decoration. $5–10. *Right*, butter dish, 3.6"d. Clover leaf border, white ground, gold edge, transfer decoration. $10–15. OSCAR & EDGAR GUTHERZ, 1898–1918.

Left, butter dish, 3.6"d. Ranson shape, yellow floral, gold edge, transfer decoration. $10–15. *Right*, butter dish, 3.6"d. Ranson shape, white ground, gold edge, transfer decoration. $10–15. OSCAR & EDGAR GUTHERZ, 1898–1918.

Left, butter dish, 3"d. Ranson shape, pink roses, transfer decoration. $5–10. *Right*, butter dish, 3.6"d. Green and gold filigree border, gold edge, transfer decoration. $10–15. OSCAR & EDGAR GUTHERZ, 1898–1918.

Left, butter dish, 3.3"d. Pink and white floral with green leaves, white ground, relief border, scalloped edge, transfer decoration. L. STRAUS & SONS, c.1885–1917. $10–15. *Right*, butter dish, 3"d. Forget-me-nots, white ground, transfer decoration. $10–15. (Strobel & Wilken, Importer) c.1891–1910.

Bone dish, 6.25"l. Clover leaf border, gold band on scalloped edge, transfer decoration. Unsigned. OSCAR & EDGAR GUTHERZ, 1898–1918. $10–15.

Sauce boat with underplate, 7.75"l.
Scalloped gold edge, white ground.
OSCAR & EDGAR GUTHERZ,
1898–1918. $30–40.

Sauce boat with underplate, 7.6"l.
Yellow floral, scalloped gold edge,
white ground. OSCAR & EDGAR
GUTHERZ, 1898–1918. $40–50.

Plate, 8.5"d. Rim, chains of yellow and pink roses and forget-me-nots, white ground, gold festooned edge, transfer decoration. Unsigned. OSCAR & EDGAR GUTHERZ, 1898–1918. $15–20.

Plate, 7.9"d. Rim, central gold medallion, gold filigree band, beaded relief border, scalloped gold edge, transfer decoration. Unsigned. OSCAR & EDGAR GUTHERZ, 1898–1918. $25–30.

Plate, 8.5"d. Oyster, pink roses, transfer decoration, white ground, gold edge. Unsigned. OSCAR & EDGAR GUTHERZ, 1899–1918. 1884–1898. $125–175.

Plate, 8.25"d. Oyster, scarlet pimpernel, hand-decorated transfer, white ground, gold trim. Unsigned. MARX & GUTHERZ, 1884–1898. $150–200.

Plate, 8.5"d. Oyster, floral decoration, ivory ground, gilded relief and edge, hand decoration. Unsigned. *(Oscar Gutherz, Limoges).* L. STRAUS & SONS, c.1880. $200–300.

Plate, 8.5"d. Oyster, gold band, white ground with central gold medallion, festooned edge, transfer decoration. L. STRAUS & SONS, c.1890. $200–250.

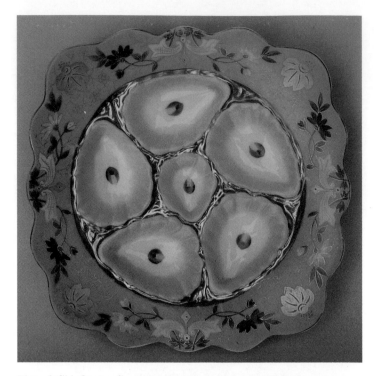

Plate, 8.75"d. Coupe. Signed: *Martin*. $40–50. Plate, 6"d. Coupe. Signed: *Georges*. $15–20. Ramekin with underplate, 4.25"d. Signed: *Georges*. $30–40. Red and pink roses, festooned edge, ivory ground, gold band, hand-decorated transfer. OSCAR & EDGAR GUTHERZ, 1899–1918.

Plate, 8.6"d. Oyster, floral motif, gilding, pink ground, festooned edge, hand decoration. MARX & GUTHERZ, 1884–1898. $250–300.

Ramekin with underplate, 4.25"d. Pink roses, white ground, festooned edge, transfer decoration. Unsigned. OSCAR & EDGAR GUTHERZ, 1899–1918. $30–40. Ramekin with underplate, 3.75"d. Pink floral, light blue and white ground, gold filigree ornamentation, scalloped edge, transfer decoration. Unsigned. OSCAR & EDGAR GUTHERZ, 1899–1918. $30–35. Ramekin with underplate, 4.25"d. Red and pink roses, light green ground, gold band, festooned edge, hand-decorated transfer. Signed: *Georges*. OSCAR & EDGAR GUTHERZ, 1899–1918. $30–40.

Lunch tray, 11.5"d. Handled, three compartment, gold scalloped edge, pink roses, ivory ground, transfer decoration. Unsigned. "VICTORIA" SCHMIDT & COMPANY, 1883–1918. $50–60.

149

Bowl, 10.5"d. Ribbed, salad, pink roses, tan ground, pointed scalloped gold edge, transfer decoration. Unsigned. MORITZ ZDEKAUER, 1884–1909. $50–60.

Bowl, 9.25"d. Rim, salad, lily of the valley, gold edge, hand-decorated transfer. Unsigned. OSCAR & EDGAR GUTHERZ, 1898–1918. $80–85.

Bowl, 10.25"l. Rim, salad daffodils with multicolored leaves, white ground, gold edge hand-decorated transfer. Signed: *Fann*. OSCAR & EDGAR GUTHERZ, 1898–1918. $60–80. Lidded sugar and creamer, 2-tasse. Donatello shape, gold handles and daffodils with multi-colored leaves, white ground, hand-decorated transfer. Signed: *Raymond/Martin*. OSCAR & EDGAR GUTHERZ, 1898–1918. $30–40.

Bowl, 10.5"d. Rim, salad, red roses, green leaves, multicolored ground, gold edge, hand-decorated transfer. Signed: *Laporte*. OSCAR & EDGAR GUTHERZ, 1898–1918. $50–60.

Bowl, 9.5"d. Ribbed, salad, pink roses, scalloped, gold edge, hand-decorated transfer. Signed: *Martin*. OSCAR & EDGAR GUTHERZ, 1898–1918. $60–80.

Bowl, 10.5"d. Rim, salad, multicolored oak leaves, tan ground, gold edge, hand-decorated transfer. Signed: *Martin*. OSCAR & EDGAR GUTHERZ, 1898–1918. $50–60.

Plate, 8.9"d. Coupe, pink roses, green leaves, brown ground, gold band, hand-decorated transfer. Signed: *Raymond*. OSCAR & EDGAR GUTHERZ, 1898–1918. $50–60.

Plate, 8.9"d. Coupe, acorns and multicolored leaves, gold band, hand-decorated transfer. Signed: *Martin*. OSCAR & EDGAR GUTHERZ, 1899–1918. $40–50.

Bowl, 10.5"d. Rim, salad, purple violets and lily of the valley, green leaves, white ground, gold edge, transfer decoration. Unsigned. OSCAR & EDGAR GUTHERZ, 1898–1918. $50–60.

Plate, 8.9"d. Coupe, purple violets and lily of the valley, white ground, gold edge, hand-decorated transfer. Signed: *Laporte*. OSCAR & EDGAR GUTHERZ, 1898–1918. $50–60.

Bowl, 9.1"d. Rim, salad, pink roses, green leaves, ivory ground, wide gold edge, hand-decorated transfer. Signed: *Martin*. OSCAR & EDGAR GUTHERZ, 1898–1918. $45–50.

Bowl, 10.5"d. Rim, salad, pink roses, green leaves, white ground, gold edge, hand-decorated transfer. Signed: *Fann*. OSCAR & EDGAR GUTHERZ, 1898–1918. $50–60.

Salt dip, 1.75"d. Footed, gold band, hand decoration. Pepper shaker, 1.75"h. Gold band and top. Unsigned. OSCAR & EDGAR GUTHERZ, 1898–1918. $25–30.

Plate, 8.9"d. Coupe, white pink roses, green leaves, ivory ground, gold band, hand-decorated transfer. Signed: *Laporte*. OSCAR & EDGAR GUTHERZ, 1898–1918. $40–50.

Orange bowl, 10.5"l. Clamshell shape, scalloped edge, scrolled relief design, footed base, floral transfer decoration. Unsigned. (*Bawo & Dotter*) SPRINGER & COMPANY, 1889–1918. $30–40.

Salt dip, 2"d. Footed, gold hexagonal edge, hand decoration. Unsigned. OSCAR & EDGAR GUTHERZ, 1898–1918. $15–20.

Salt dip, 2"d. Pink roses, gold octagonal fluted edge, transfer decoration. Unsigned. OSCAR & EDGAR GUTHERZ, 1898–1918. $20–25.

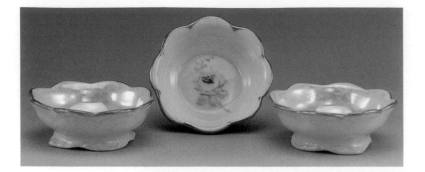

Salt dip, 2"d. Footed, gold scalloped edge, interior luster glaze, hand decoration. Unsigned. OSCAR & EDGAR GUTHERZ, 1898–1918. $15–20. Salt dip, 2"d. Footed, pink rose, gold scalloped edge, hand decoration. Unsigned. OSCAR & EDGAR GUTHERZ, 1898–1918. $15–20.

Salt dip, 1.9"d. Gold band and ball feet, hand decoration. Unsigned. OSCAR & EDGAR GUTHERZ, 1898–1918. $15–20. Salt dip, 2.25"d. Gold band and ball feet, hand decoration. OSCAR & EDGAR GUTHERZ, 1898–1918. $15–20.

Salt and pepper shaker, 2.6"h. Fluted, pink roses, ivory ground, gold band, hand-decorated transfer. Unsigned. OSCAR & EDGAR GUTHERZ, 1898–1918. $15–20.

Lidded sugar and creamer, 2-tasse. Ranson shape, pink roses, white ground, gold trim on handles, transfer decoration. Unsigned. OSCAR & EDGAR GUTHERZ, 1898–1918. $10–15.

Lidded sugar and creamer, 2-tasse. Thomas shape, acorns and oak leaves, tan ground, gold trim and handles, hand-decorated transfer. Signed: *Raymond*. OSCAR & EDGAR GUTHERZ, 1898–1918. $25–30.

Tea set, Hexagonal shape, red and white ground, gold filigree ornamentation, transfer decoration. Teapot, 4.5"h. Creamer, 2-tasse. Lidded sugar, 2-tasse. Unsigned. OSCAR & EDGAR GUTHERZ, 1898–1918. $100–125.

Creamer, 4-tasse. Pink and yellow floral, gold trim, white ground, transfer decoration. Unsigned. "VICTORIA" SCHMIDT & CO., 1918–1939. $25–30.

Covered soup tureen, 12.75"l. White roses and green leaves, white ground, floral relief, scalloped gold edge, transfer decoration. OSCAR & EDGAR GUTHERZ, 1898–1918. $75–85.

Tea tile, 5.75"d. Yellow-brown floral, gold edge, transfer decoration. Unsigned. MARX & GUTHERZ, 1884–1898. $10–15.

Dinnerware pattern. Detail. White roses, floral relief border, scalloped edge.

Tumbler stands, 2.9"d. Gold edge, white ground, hand decoration. OSCAR & EDGAR GUTHERZ, 1898–1918. $10–15.

American Decorated Porcelain

Oatmeal set. Plate, coupe, 6.9"l. Bowl, rim, 6.25"d. Creamer, 2-tasse. Pink roses, gold ornamentation, hand decoration. Signed: *George Gast*. OSCAR & EDGAR GUTHERZ, 1898–1918. $50–60.

Butter tub with drainer, 5.25"d. Pail-shape, yellow roses, pale green ground, hand decoration. Signed: *N. Peck*. OSCAR & EDGAR GUTHERZ, 1898–1918. $40–50.

Cream soup and saucer, 4"d. Beaded relief border, pale green and white ground, gold edge, hand decoration. Signed: *A. F. B.* OSCAR & EDGAR GUTHERZ, 1898–1918. $10–15.

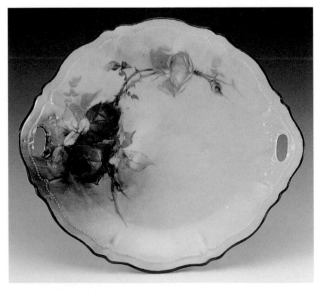

Plate, 12.5"d. Cake, red and white roses, beaded relief border, scalloped edge, hand decoration. Signed: *Brosius*. OSCAR & EDGAR GUTHERZ, 1898–1918. $40–50.

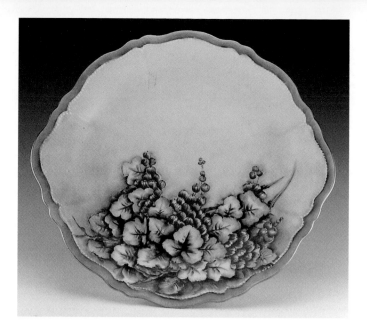

Charger, 10.9"d. Red currents and green leaves, beaded relief border, scalloped edge, hand decoration. Signed: *Mrs. E. Roeder*. OSCAR & EDGAR GUTHERZ, 1898–1918. $40–50.

Celery tray, 12"l. Red cherries, scalloped gold edge and beaded relief border, hand decoration. Signed: *E. Schmidt*. OSCAR & EDGAR GUTHERZ, 1898–1918. $30–40.

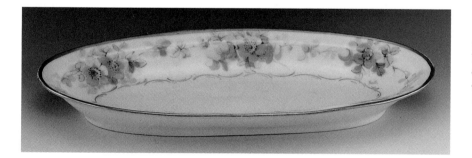

Celery tray, 12.1"l. Yellow floral, white and pale blue ground, oval rim with gold band, hand decoration. Signed: *Keates (Keates Art Studio, Chicago)*. OSCAR & EDGAR GUTHERZ, 1898–1918. $35–50.

Celery tray, 12.2"l. Pink roses and forget-me-nots, gold edge, hand decoration. Signed: *McKee*. OSCAR & EDGAR GUTHERZ, 1898–1918. *Courtesy of Dorothy Kamm.* $35–45.

Lidded condensed milk jar with underplate, 5.5"h. Red currents, green leaves, gold ornamentation, hand decoration. Signed: *Lydia Treviranus.* PFEIFFER & LOWENSTEIN, c.1914–1918. *Courtesy of Maureen Farmer.* $100–150.

Lidded cracker jar, 9"d. Ranson shape, white wild roses, pale green ground, gold handles, hand decoration. Signed: *A. S. S.* OSCAR & EDGAR GUTHERZ, 1898–1918. $100–175.

Lidded cracker jar, 6.5"d. Pink roses, yellow ground, gold handles, hand decoration. Unsigned. OSCAR & EDGAR GUTHERZ, 1898–1918. $100–175.

Tea cup and saucer, 4"d. Pink blossoms, beaded relief border, scalloped edge, hand decoration. Signed: *R.* OSCAR & EDGAR GUTHERZ, 1898–1918. $15–25.

Tea cup and saucer, 3.5"d. Red currents and green leaves, hand decoration. Unsigned. OSCAR & EDGAR GUTHERZ, 1898–1918. $15–25.

Pedestal cup and saucer, 2.5"h. White apple blossoms and green leaves, hand decoration. Signed: *G. A.* OSCAR & EDGAR GUTHERZ, 1898–1918. $20–25.

Pedestal cup and saucer, 3.6"h. Lavender grape bunches and light green leaves outlined in black, gold ornamentation with "Frank" inscribed on bottom of double-waisted pedestal, hand decoration. Signed: *N. Ellis.* OSCAR & EDGAR GUTHERZ, 1898–1918. $60–65.

Pedestal cup and saucer, 3.6"h. Detail illustrating fitted pedestal base.

Tea cup and saucer, 3.5"d. Art deco pink floral design, hand decoration. Unsigned. *(Diana Mutual China Co.).* OSCAR & EDGAR GUTHERZ, 1898–1918. $20–25.

Tea cup and saucer, 3.75"d. Ball-footed, pink roses, gold edge and handle, ivory ground, hand decoration. Unsigned. OSCAR & EDGAR GUTHERZ, 1898–1918. $25–30.

Tea cup and saucer, 3.75"d. Ball-footed, pink and red roses, gold edge, white ground, hand decoration. Unsigned. OSCAR & EDGAR GUTHERZ, 1898–1918. $25–30.

Plate, 9"d. Coupe, raised gold floral, hand decoration. Unsigned. FISCHER & MIEG, circa 1914–1918. $25–30. Cup, 3.6"d. Ball-footed, raised gold floral, hand decoration. Unsigned. OSCAR & EDGAR GUTHERZ, 1899–1918. $10–15.

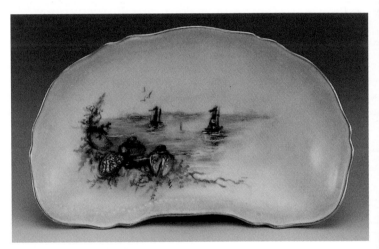

Bowl, 9.5"l. Baker, pink apple blossoms, ivory ground, oval, beaded relief border, scalloped gold edge, hand decoration. Unsigned. OSCAR & EDGAR GUTHERZ, 1898–1918. $60–75.

Bone dish, 6"l. Sea shells and sailing boats, beaded relief border, scalloped edge, hand decoration. Unsigned. OSCAR & EDGAR GUTHERZ, 1898–1918. $15–20.

Bowl, 8.9"d. Footed, pine needles and cones, scalloped edge, gold rim, hand decoration. Signed: *A. C. Storm*. OSCAR & EDGAR GUTHERZ, 1898–1918. $140–150.

Gravy boat with underplate, 7"l. Footed base, forget-me-nots, blue and yellow ground, bow scroll relief, hand decoration. Unsigned. OSCAR & EDGAR GUTHERZ, 1898–1918. $35–45.

Pitcher, 7"h. Donatello shape, white daisies, pale blue ground, gold ornamentation, hand decoration. Signed: *H. E. D.* OSCAR & EDGAR GUTHERZ, 1898–1918. $50–100.

Plate, 6.25"d. Pink and yellow roses, white ground, beaded relief border, scalloped edge, "EBD" monogram, hand decoration. Signed: *MBLR*. OSCAR & EDGAR GUTHERZ, 1898–1918. $15–20.

Napkin rings, 2"d. Footed, forget-me-nots and daisies, white ground, gold trim, hand decoration. Unsigned. OSCAR & EDGAR GUTHERZ, 1898–1918. $30–40.

Nut bowl, 6.2"d. Hexagonal, pink floral art deco, green leaves, tan and brown ground, gold edge, hand decoration. Unsigned. OSCAR & EDGAR GUTHERZ, 1898–1918. $60–80.

Nut bowl, 5.5"d. Pink apple blossoms, green leaves, pale green ground, gold relief and edge, hand decoration. Unsigned. OSCAR & EDGAR GUTHERZ, 1898–1918. $25–35.

Nut bowl, 8"d. Footed, acorns, green leaves, tan ground, hand decoration. Signed: *A. A.* OSCAR & EDGAR GUTHERZ, 1898–1918. $60–80.

Nut bowl, 7"d. Victoria shape, footed, chestnuts, green leaves, interior luster glaze, gold edge, hand decoration. Unsigned. OSCAR & EDGAR GUTHERZ, 1898–1918. $50–60. Nut dishes, 5"l. Oval, footed, chestnuts, beaded relief border, gold scalloped edge. Signed: *L. V.* OSCAR & EDGAR GUTHERZ, 1898–1918. $50–75.

Plate, 7.75"d. Rim, yellow roses, green leaves, tan band, gold edge, hand decoration. Unsigned. OSCAR & EDGAR GUTHERZ, 1898–1918. $30–40. Nut bowl, 5.75"d. Victoria shape, yellow roses, green leaves, scalloped edge, gold band, hand decoration. Unsigned. OSCAR & EDGAR GUTHERZ, 1898–1918. $40–50.

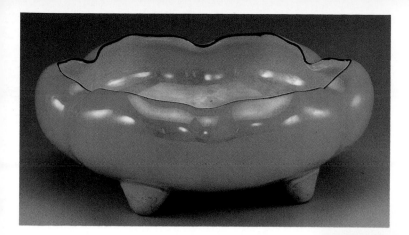

Nut bowl, 5.75"d. Victoria shape, footed, tan ground, interior luster glaze, black edge, hand decoration. Signed: *M. A. M.* OSCAR & EDGAR GUTHERZ, 1898–1918. $30–40.

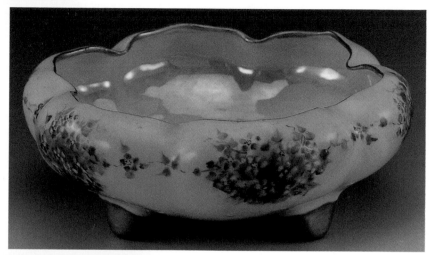

Nut bowl, 7"d. Victoria shape, footed, forget-me-nots, green leaves, interior luster glaze, gold edge, hand decoration. Unsigned. OSCAR & EDGAR GUTHERZ, 1898–1918. $50–60.

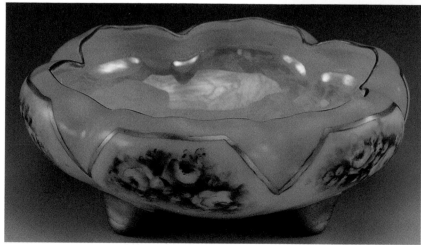

Nut bowl, 7"d. Victoria shape, footed, yellow roses, interior luster glaze, gold edge, hand decoration. Unsigned. OSCAR & EDGAR GUTHERZ, 1898–1918. $50–60.

Nut bowl, 7"d. Victoria shape, footed, pine needles and cones, interior luster glaze, gold edge, hand decoration. Unsigned. OSCAR & EDGAR GUTHERZ, 1898–1918. $50–60.

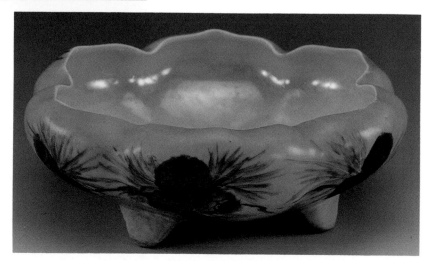

Nut bowl, 4.75"d. Huyler shape, ball-footed, pink apple blossoms, green leaves, gold edge, hand decoration. Unsigned. OSCAR & EDGAR GUTHERZ, 1898–1918. $35–45.

Nut bowl, 4.75"d. Huyler, detail. Bottom view with nautical scene.

Bulb bowl, 8.25"d. Geometric design, Art Deco style, tan ground, hand decoration. Unsigned. OSCAR & EDGAR GUTHERZ, 1898–1918. $40–50.

Oval bowl, open handles, 8.5"d. Donatello shape, Russian design, hand decoration. Signed: *E. Tolpin*. OSCAR & EDGAR GUTHERZ, 1898–1918. *Courtesy of Alan Reed.* $235–285.

Dish, 5.9"l. Olive, handled, forget-me-nots, triangular shape, rolled edge, hand decoration. Signed: *A. V. D.* OSCAR & EDGAR GUTHERZ, 1898–1918. $30–35.

164

Plate, 8.6"d. Oyster, gold relief band, festooned edge, hand decoration. Signed: *C. T. Chase, 1908*. OSCAR & EDGAR GUTHERZ, 1898–1918. $200–250.

Bowl, 9"d. Rim, salad, floral Art Deco style, green band, gold edge, hand decoration. Unsigned. OSCAR & EDGAR GUTHERZ, 1898–1918. $25–50.

Bowl, 9"d. Rim, salad, pink apple blossoms, gold edge, hand decoration. Unsigned. OSCAR & EDGAR GUTHERZ, 1898–1918. $25–50.

Bowl, 9.25"d. Fluted, red cherries, gold scalloped edge, hand decoration. Unsigned. MORITZ ZDEKAUER, 1884–1909. *Courtesy of Dorothy Kamm.* $60–80.

Salt dip, 2.25"d. Footed, pink and red roses with green leaves, interior luster glaze, hand decoration. Signed: *A. E. B.* OSCAR & EDGAR GUTHERZ, 1898–1918. $20–25.

Salt dip, 1.25"d. Pail-shaped, gold band and handles, hand decoration. Unsigned. OSCAR & EDGAR GUTHERZ, 1898–1918. $15–20.

Salt dip, 2.25"d. Pink roses, oval with gold eared handles and edge, hand decoration. Unsigned. OSCAR & EDGAR GUTHERZ, 1898–1918. $15–20. Salt dip, 2.25"d. Footed, gilded, clam-shaped, interior luster glaze, hand decoration. OSCAR & EDGAR GUTHERZ, 1898–1918. $20–25.

Salt dip and spoon, 1.5"d. Gilded, octagonal fluted edge, hand decoration. Signed: *A. L. W.* OSCAR & EDGAR GUTHERZ, 1898–1918. $15–20.

Nut cups, 2.75"d. Club and spade shaped, pink roses and forget-me-nots, gold edge, hand decoration. Unsigned. OSCAR & EDGAR GUTHERZ, 1898–1918. $40–50.

Muffineer, 4.4"h. Square pedestal base, forget-me-nots, white ground, gold top, hand decoration. Signed: *E. V. C.* (*Stouffer Studio*) OSCAR & EDGAR GUTHERZ. 1898–1918. $35–50. Salt and pepper shakers, 3.1"h. Square pedestal base, forget-me-nots, white ground, gold top, hand decoration. Unsigned. OSCAR & EDGAR GUTHERZ, 1898–1918. $15–20.

Muffineer, 4.75"h. Pink roses, ivory and pale blue ground, gold top, hand decoration. Unsigned. OSCAR & EDGAR GUTHERZ, 1898–1918. $95–100.

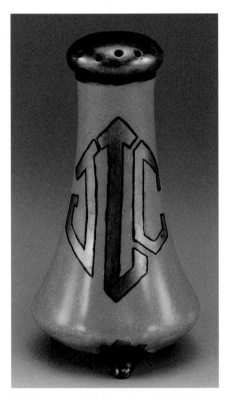

Salt and pepper shaker, 3"h. Forget-me-nots, white and pale blue ground, gold top, hand decoration. Signed: *May Jioske.* OSCAR & EDGAR GUTHERZ, 1898–1918. $15–20.

Muffineer, 4.5"h. Footed, gold "JLC" monogram, dark pink ground, hand decoration. Unsigned. OSCAR & EDGAR GUTHERZ, 1898–1918. $20–30.

Salt and pepper shaker, 3.1"h. Pear shape, forget-me-nots, white ground, gold top, hand decoration. Signed: *Minnie A. Luken.* OSCAR & EDGAR GUTHERZ, 1898–1918. $15–20.

Salt and pepper shaker, 3"h. Flared base, pink floral, ivory and pale blue ground, gold top, hand decoration. Unsigned. OSCAR & EDGAR GUTHERZ, 1898–1918. $15–20.

Salt and pepper shaker, 3.1"h. Square, floral art deco, white ground, gold top and ornamentation, hand decoration. Unsigned. *(Pickard Studio, Antioch, Illinois)*. OSCAR & EDGAR GUTHERZ, 1898–1918. $15–20.

Salt and pepper shaker, 3"h. Hexagonal, forget-me-nots, white interior luster glaze, gold top, hand decoration. Signed: *Esther D. Lierman*. OSCAR & EDGAR GUTHERZ, 1898–1918. $10–15.

Salt and pepper shaker, 3"h. Cylindrical, forget-me-nots, pale blue and ivory ground, gold band, hand decoration. Unsigned. OSCAR & EDGAR GUTHERZ, 1898–1918. $10–15.

Salt and pepper shaker, 3"h. Cylindrical, blue birds and daisies, white ground, gold top, hand decoration. Unsigned. OSCAR & EDGAR GUTHERZ, 1898–1918. $10–15.

Salt and pepper shaker, 3.75"h. Flared base, violets, multicolored ground, gold top, hand decoration. Signed: *M. Burnes*. OSCAR & EDGAR GUTHERZ, 1898–1918. $30–40.

Salt and pepper shaker, 3.1"h. Depressed sides, pink floral, white ground, gold top, hand decoration. Signed: *Luella Cooke*. OSCAR & EDGAR GUTHERZ, 1898–1918. $15–20.

Salt and pepper shaker, 2.4"h. Mushroom shape, tan ground, gold top, hand decoration. Unsigned. OSCAR & EDGAR GUTHERZ, 1898–1918. $10–15.

Salt and pepper shaker, 2.9"h. Barrel shape, orange floral, ivory ground, gold top, hand decoration. Unsigned. OSCAR & EDGAR GUTHERZ, 1898–1918. $10–15.

Salt and pepper shaker, 2.5"h. Footed, forget-me-nots, white ground, gold top, hand decoration. Signed: *Sumares McDyer*. OSCAR & EDGAR GUTHERZ, 1898–1918. $45–50.

Salt and pepper shaker, 3"d. Barrel shape, white ground, gold top and "H" monogram, hand decoration. Signed: *K. M. H. '13*. OSCAR & EDGAR GUTHERZ, 1898–1918. $10–15.

Tray, 14.5"l. Sandwich, purple daisies, ivory pale blue ground, gold handles and edge, hand decoration. Unsigned. OSCAR & EDGAR GUTHERZ, 1898–1918. $40–65.

Plate, 7.75"d. Soup, seashells, gold beaded relief band and scalloped edge, hand decoration. Unsigned. OSCAR & EDGAR GUTHERZ, 1898–1918. Courtesy *of Dorothy Kamm*. $35–45.

Plate, 8"d. Soup, purple plums, beaded relief band and gold scalloped edge, hand decoration. Signed: *E. Mil.* OSCAR & EDGAR GUTHERZ, 1898–1918. *Courtesy of Dorothy Kamm*. $10–20.

Plate, 7.9"d. Soup, red cherries, beaded relief border, scalloped edge, hand decoration. Signed: *Emily Chase*. OSCAR & EDGAR GUTHERZ, 1898–1918. $20–25.

Punch cups, 4"h. Gold footed, forget-me-nots, interior luster glaze, hand decoration. Unsigned. OSCAR & EDGAR GUTHERZ, 1898–1918. $110–120.

Punch cups, 3.25"h. Footed, pink floral, wide gold band, hand decoration. Signed: *F. L. C.* OSCAR & EDGAR GUTHERZ, 1898–1918. $90–105.

Left, punch cups, 3.25"h. Footed, forget-me-nots, gold rim, hand decoration. Unsigned. *Center,* yellow and white roses, wide gold band, hand-decorated transfer, Signed: *Martin. Right*, yellow floral, hand decoration. Unsigned. OSCAR & EDGAR GUTHERZ, 1898–1918. $75–90.

Lidded sugar and creamer, 4-tasse. Nasturtiums with gold ornamentation, ivory ground, hand decoration. Unsigned. OSCAR & EDGAR GUTHERZ, 1898–1918. $70–80.

Lidded sugar and creamer, 8-tasse. White daisies with gilded ornamentation, white ground, beaded relief border, hand decoration. Signed: *Ugalde*. OSCAR & EDGAR GUTHERZ, 1898–1918. $85–100.

Lidded sugar and creamer, 6-tasse. White ground, gold handles and trim, beaded relief border, hand decoration. Unsigned. OSCAR & EDGAR GUTHERZ, 1898–1918. $25–30.

Lidded sugar and creamer, 4-tasse. Ranson shape, gold trim. Unsigned. OSCAR & EDGAR GUTHERZ, 1898–1918. $30–35.

Lidded sugar and creamer, 2-tasse. Currents and green leaves, gold handles, hand decoration. Unsigned. OSCAR & EDGAR GUTHERZ, 1898–1918. $40–50.

Lidded sugar and creamer, 2-tasse. Donatello shape, pink apple blossoms, ivory ground, gold handles and trim, hand decoration. Signed: *Skitt*. OSCAR & EDGAR GUTHERZ, 1898–1918. $30–40.

Lidded sugar and creamer, 2-tasse. Donatello shape, blue violets, ivory ground, gold handles and trim, hand decoration. Unsigned. (*Kayser Studio*). OSCAR & EDGAR GUTHERZ, 1898–1918. $30–40.

Lidded sugar and creamer, 2-tasse. Pink and red roses, pale green ground, gold trim, hand decoration. Unsigned. OSCAR & EDGAR GUTHERZ, 1898–1918. $30–35.

Lidded sugar and creamer, 2-tasse. Derby shape, forget-me-nots, pale blue ground, gold handles and trim, hand decoration. Signed: *L. Kuecker*. OSCAR & EDGAR GUTHERZ, 1898–1918. $25–30.

Lidded sugar and creamer, 2-tasse. Derby shape, white ground, gold handles and edge, hand decoration. Signed: *L. E. M.* OSCAR & EDGAR GUTHERZ, 1898–1918. $15–20.

Sugar and creamer, 4-tasse. Yellow roses, ball-footed, gold handles, hand decoration. Signed: *M. P.* OSCAR & EDGAR GUTHERZ, 1898–1918. $25–30.

Lidded sugar and creamer, 4-tasse. Donatello shape, floral Art Deco design, gold trim, hand-decorated transfer. Unsigned. OSCAR & EDGAR GUTHERZ, 1898–1918. $25–30.

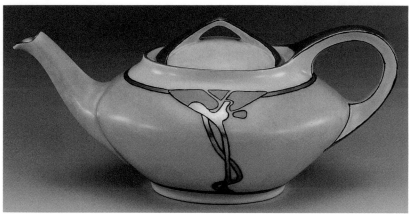

Teapot, 2-tasse. Donatello shape, Art Deco design, gold ornamentation, hand decoration. Unsigned. OSCAR & EDGAR GUTHERZ, 1898–1918. $90–100.

Tea set, Thomas shape, red and pink roses, gold handles, hand decoration. Teapot, 2-tasse. Creamer, 2-tasse. Lidded sugar, 2-tasse. Signed: *Louis.* OSCAR & EDGAR GUTHERZ, 1898–1918. $100–125.

Tumbler, 3.25"h. Orange poppies, gold edge, hand decoration. Signed: *C. S.* OSCAR & EDGAR GUTHERZ, 1898–1918. $10–15.

Tea set, Donatello shape, blue chicory, hand decoration. Teapot, 4.5"h. ROSENTHAL, 1908–1953. Creamer, 2-tasse. Lidded sugar, 2-tasse. Cup, 3.1"d. Saucer, 6.6"d. Unsigned. OSCAR & EDGAR GUTHERZ, 1898–1918. $100–125.

Tea set, Donatello shape, pink roses, pale blue and ivory ground, Art Deco gold ornamentation, hand decoration. Teapot, 4.75"h. COUNT THUN'S PORCELAIN FACTORY, c.1891–c.1908. Signed: *C. E. Tolchard, 1914*. Creamer, 2-tasse. Lidded sugar, 2-tasse. Signed: *C. E. Tolchard, 1914*. MORITZ ZDEKAUER, 1884–1909. Courtesy *of Dorothy Kamm.* $400–500.

Handled mug, 4.75"h. Donatello shape, red currents and green leaves, ivory ground, hand decoration. Unsigned. COUNT THUN'S PORCELAIN FACTORY, circa 1891–circa 1908. *Courtesy of Dorothy Kamm.* $45–65.

175

APPENDIX 1:
TRADE CATALOG ADVERTISEMENTS

Charles Ahrenfeldt & Son advertisement. *Crockery and Glass Journal* 41(4):1 (1895).

George F. Bassett & Co. advertisement. *Crockery and Glass Journal* 57(10):12 (1902).

Bawo & Dotter advertisement. *Crockery and Glass Journal* 62(12):31 (1905).

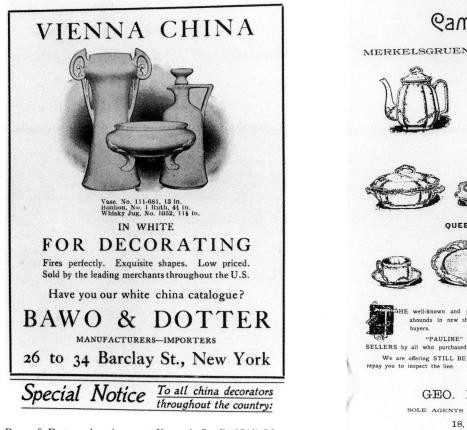

Bawo & Dotter advertisement. *Keramic Studio* 10(4):96 (1908).

George Borgfeldt & Co. advertisement for Camill Schwalb factory produced porcelain. *Crockery and Glass Journal* 40(5):10 (1894).

Benedikt & Friedman advertisement. *Crockery and Glass Journal* 24(5):6 (1886).

H. Benedikt advertisement. *Crockery and Glass Journal* 40(5):10 (1894).

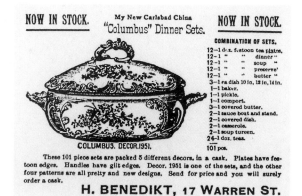

Austria.
REGISTERED
Trade Mark
No. 31435

Carlsbad Clover Leaf China.

"The highest in quality.   The lowest in price."

The Majestic,
The Bijou,
The St. Elmo,

are the leading 1896 shapes in

Carlsbad China Tea and Dinner Ware,

and this season's decorations in the way of dainty and delicate flower designs by far surpass anything ever made heretofore and are bound to please every buyer, since they are particularly suited for *Open Stock Patterns.* Do not fail to see them before placing your orders elsewhere. *"We control this line."*

GEO. BORGFELDT & CO.
18 TO 24 WASHINGTON PLACE   NEW YORK
PARIS   BERLIN   VIENNA
SONNEBERG   FURTH   SOLINGEN   BODENBACH   LIMOGES   STOKE-UPON-TRENT

George Borgfeldt & Co. advertisement for porcelain produced in Merklín, Bohemia by the Camill Schwalb factory. *Crockery and Glass Journal* 43(4):20 (1896).

The A. DE RIESTHAL COMPANY
55 Murray Street, New York.
READY FOR IMPORT.

We invite your attention to a few of our specialties :

CARLSBAD CHINA.—In three beautiful shapes, "CROWN," "ISABELLA" and our new set "COLUMBUS," in white and decorated. TEA SETS, CUSPADORES, CUPS and SAUCERS, FISH SETS, etc.

COLUMBUS. DECOR.1951.

Here is a cut of our new "COLUMBUS" dinner set, which we promised to show you. Now judge for yourself if it isn't the prettiest Carlsbad se you ever saw.

ST. LOUIS GLASSWARE—The finest line yet shown for the money. Must be seen to be appreciated.

BISQUE FIGURES, GERMAN CHINA, VASES, and an endless variety of novelties in china and glass from all of the leading factories of Europe.

All we ask is that you call. We can safely depend upon your orders.

Our Mr. A. C. Stutts is still at the Tremont House, Chicago, with a complete assortment of china, glass and fancy goods for stock and import.

A. de RIESTHAL, *President.*   O. J. de RIESTHAL, *Treasurer.*   H. BENEDIKT, *Secretary.*   F. A. BENEDIKT, *Vice-President.*

A. de Riesthal Co. advertisement. *Crockery and Glass Journal* 37(6):22 (1893).

WORTH NOTING.

IMPORT SAMPLES READY.

Charles L. Dwenger,
IMPORTER,

35 and 37 Park Place,   New York,

Successor to A. KLINGENBERG, Limoges.

FRENCH CHINA.
White and Decorated,

In endless variety, comprising all the latest novelties from my Limoges house.

CARLSBAD CHINA.
"OLIVET."

The above shape is pronounced unequalled for quality of china, beauty of form and tasty decorations. If you doubt it, come and see for yourself.

Specialties in Pottery. Tall Bohemian Glass Lily Vases in gold relief decors.
Early spring stock in great shape. Full line of White China for Amateur decorating.
Price list and illustrations on application.

A. de Riesthal Co. advertisement. *Crockery and Glass Journal* 37(6):22 (1893).

NEW HABSBURG
AK
CD
AUSTRIA

LIMOGES
AK
CD
FRANCE

THE New World's capacity for designing and originating and the Old World's capacity for executing are most happily combined in the famous "A. K." French China and the New Habsburg China. The French line is confined to fancy things, while the New Habsburg is confined to Dinner Ware, as is well known. Each has its distinctive features—so distinctive that they conflict with no other makes. That's why you will find the "A. K." and New Habsburg on sale in the best retail stores, even though other brands are also displayed.

The 1903 Import Samples will be ready in January, and we can safely promise just as striking an individuality among the new things as has heretofore characterized the lines. A greater variety of decorations will also be in evidence.

We wish you the Compliments of the Season most heartily.

C. L. DWENGER.
35 Park Place,   New York.

Charles L. Dwenger advertisement. *Crockery and Glass Journal* 57(24):103 (1902).

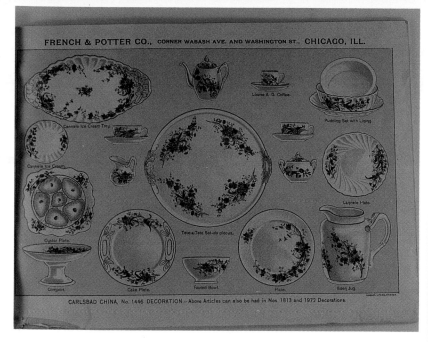

French & Potter Co. Bohemian porcelain distributor catalog circa1890.

Hamburger & Co. advertisement. *Crockery and Glass Journal* 57(6):3 (1903).

Oscar & Edgar Gutherz advertisement. *Crockery and Glass Journal* 49(1):3 (1899).

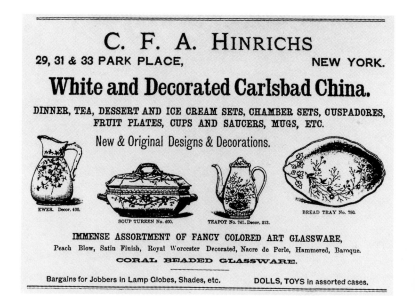

C. F. A. Hinrichs advertisement. *Crockery and Glass Journal* 24(5):10 (1886).

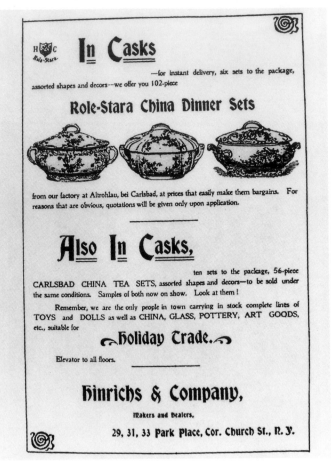

Benjamin F. Hunt & Sons advertisement. *Crockery and Glass Journal* 43(10):16 (1896).

Hinrichs & Co. advertisement. *Crockery and Glass Journal* 41(6):7 (1895).

Lazarus & Rosenfeld advertisement. An importer with offices in London and New York City, they also were owners of the "Victoria" Schmidt porcelain factory in Stará Role (Altrohlau). *China, Glass and Lamps* 2(22):2 (1891).

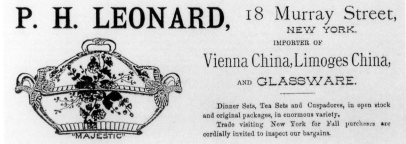

Koscherak Brothers advertisement. *Crockery and Glass Journal* 57(24):101 (1902).

Peter H. Leonard advertisement. *Crockery and Glass Journal* 32(22):15 (1890).

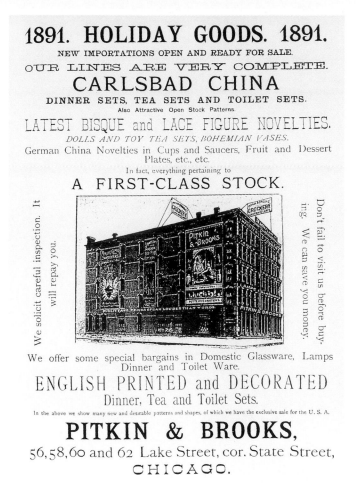

Phillips cocoa advertisement, circa 1885. The common practice of drinking hot chocolate during Victorian times stimulated the production of porcelain chocolate pots and cups by many Bohemian factories. *Courtesy of the Strong Museum.*

Pitkin & Brooks advertisement. *Crockery and Glass Journal* 34(7):21 (1891).

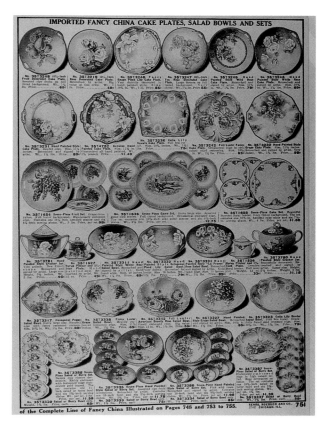

Fancy china novelties, ornaments, toilet articles. Sears, Roebuck & Co. catalog 1914.

Imported fancy china cake plates, salad bowls and sets. Sears, Roebuck & Co. catalog 1914.

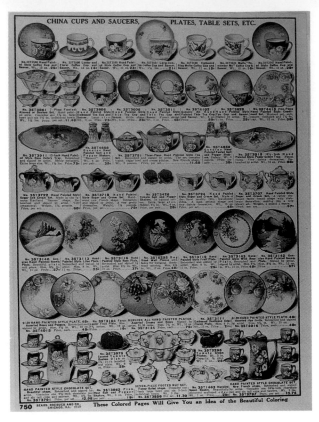

China cups and saucers, plates, table sets, etc. Sears, Roebuck & Co. catalog 1914.

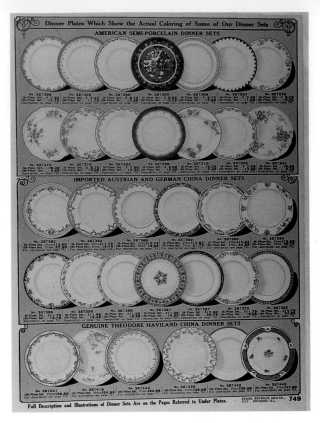

Imported Austrian and German china dinner sets. Sears, Roebuck & Co. catalog 1914.

NOTICE.

The above cut shows the Condensed Milk and Marmalade Receptacle, of which we are the inventors and the sole owners.

We hereby give notice to all infringers that we have instructed our solicitors to take action and to bring suit for accounting and damages.

No one has authority to sell or buy this article unless they obtain that right from us.

There is no other patent in existence covering this article, though several efforts have been made to evade it without warrant of law.

We are receiving weekly shipments of the latest NOVELTIES in Glassware, Art Pottery and Staple Goods.

During the past week we have received an immense new line of Elite Ware from the well-known Rudolstadt Art Pottery, and also many new decorations in Fancy Goods from the Royal Dresden.

L. Straus & Sons.

Importers and Manufacturers,

42, 44, 46 and 48 Warren Street,

NEW YORK.

L. Straus & Sons advertisement claiming to be the inventors of the condensed milk and marmalade jar. *Crockery and Glass Journal* 35(22):27 (1892).

DECOR 3277, CARLSBAD CHINA — OPEN STOCK.

In QUALITY equal to French China; In PRICE lower than Domestic

Full Lines in EMPIRE GREEN, PINK, CANARY YELLOW, MAROON and ROYAL BLUE

These goods, hitherto made in Limoges, are now for the first time produced in Austrian China of the highest grade.

The prices are within the reach of all, and price-list and full particulars can be obtained on application.

The goods must be seen to be appreciated, as the richness of colorings has never been surpassed in china making.

They will be in stock during the Spring, and orders can now be placed either for Import or for delivery from stock upon arrival.

L. STRAUS & SONS,

IMPORTERS AND MANUFACTURERS,

42, 44, 46 and 48 Warren Street, and 116 Chambers Street,   NEW YORK.

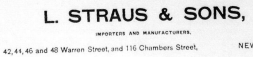

Limoges, France.   Carlsbad, Bohemia.   Rudolstadt, Thuringia.   Paris, 3 Avenue de l'Opera.   Steinschenau, Bohemia.
Cut Glass Works, Hoboken, N. J.

Lazarus Straus & Sons advertising Carlsbad china. The woman is pouring from a chocolate pot. *Crockery and Glass Journal* 45(9):1 (1897).

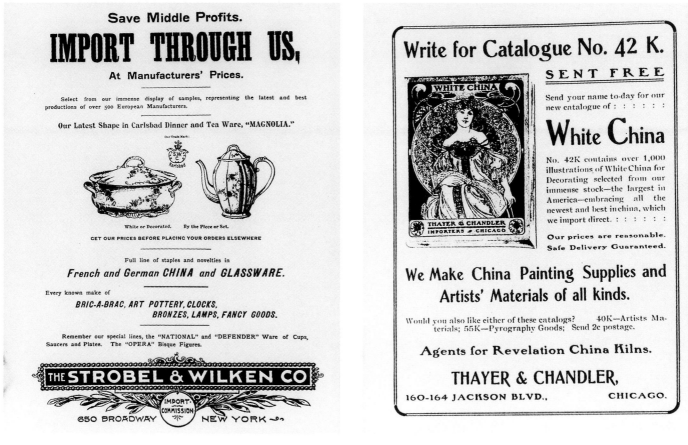

The Strobel & Wilken Co. advertisement. *Crockery and Glass Journal* 43(7):13 (1896).

Thayer and Chandler advertisement. *Keramic Studio* 6(12):VI (1905).

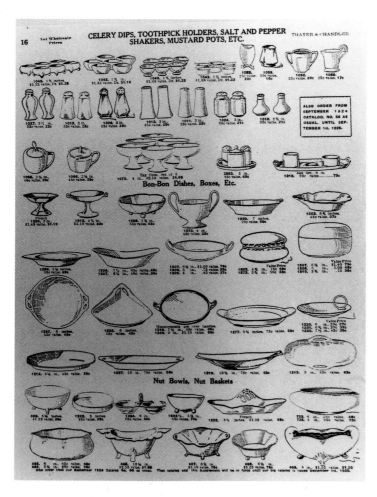

Thayer and Chandler 1925 catalog, page 16.

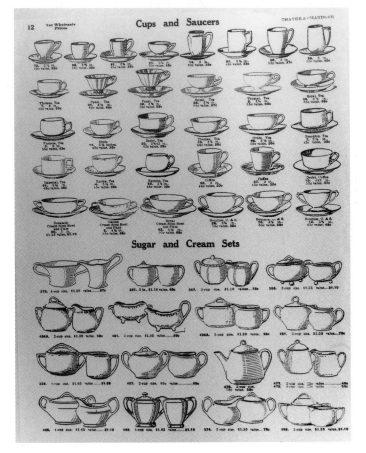

Thayer and Chandler 1925 catalog, page 17.

Thayer and Chandler 1925 catalog, page 18.

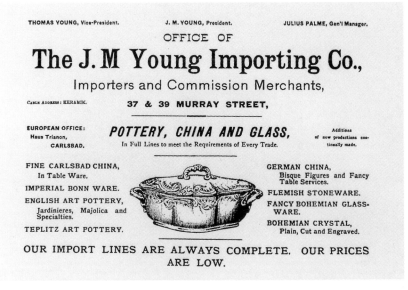

The J. M. Young Importing Co. advertisement. *Crockery and Glass Journal* 39(15): 12 (1894).

APPENDIX 2:
HAAS & CŽJŽEK EXPORT DECORATIONS

Floral pattern for American export porcelain, plate design 11290. HAAS & CŽJŽEK, c. 1890. *Courtesy of Dagmar Braunová.*

Floral patterns for American export porcelain, plate designs 119 and 120. HAAS & CŽJŽEK, c.1890. *Courtesy of Dagmar Braunová.*

Floral patterns for American export porcelain, plate design 129. HAAS & CŽJŽEK, c.1890. *Courtesy of Dagmar Braunová.*

Floral rim pattern for American export porcelain. HAAS & CŽJŽEK, c.1890. *Courtesy of Dagmar Braunová.*

Floral pattern for American export porcelain. HAAS & CŽJŽEK, c.1890. *Courtesy of Dagmar Braunová.*

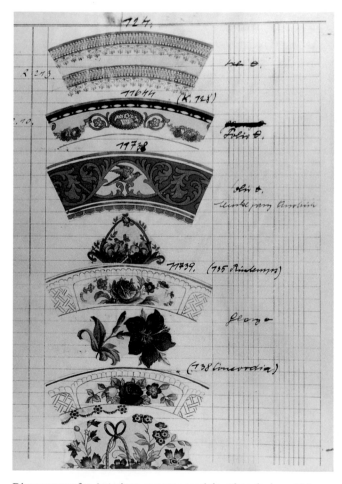

Rim patterns for American export porcelain, plate designs 124, 11644, 19738, 11739 and 138. HAAS & CŽJŽEK, c.1890. *Courtesy of Dagmar Braunová.*

Rim patterns for American export porcelain, plate designs 167, 170, 175, 166 and 185. HAAS & CŽJŽEK, c.1890. *Courtesy of Dagmar Braunová.*

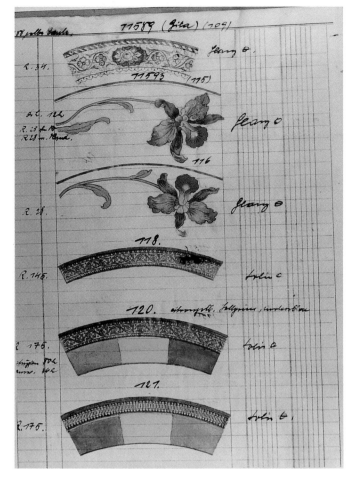

Rim patterns for American export porcelain, plate designs 164, 165, 175, 166 and 185. HAAS & CŽJŽEK, c. 1890. *Courtesy of Dagmar Braunová.*

Rim patterns for American export porcelain, plate designs 11589, 11593, 116, 118, 120 and 121. HAAS & CŽJŽEK, c.1890. *Courtesy of Dagmar Braunová.*

Rim patterns for American export porcelain, plate designs 11288 and 11289. HAAS & CŽJŽEK, c.1890. *Courtesy of Dagmar Braunová.*

187

Rim patterns for American export porcelain, plate designs 117 and 118. HAAS & CŽJŽEK, c.1890. *Courtesy of Dagmar Braunová.*

Rim patterns for American export porcelain, plate designs 123 and 124. HAAS & CŽJŽEK, c.1890. *Courtesy of Dagmar Braunová.*

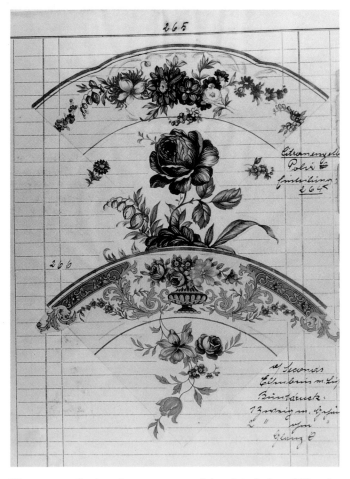

Rim patterns for American export porcelain, plate designs 265 and 266. HAAS & CŽJŽEK, c.1890. *Courtesy of Dagmar Braunová.*

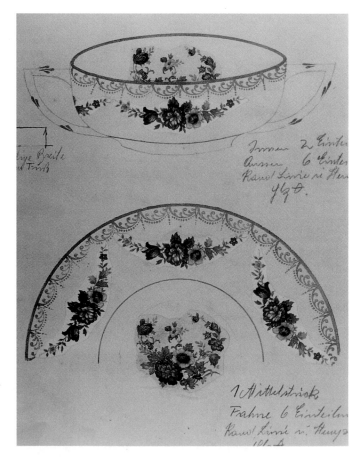

Patterns for American export porcelain, cream soup and plate. HAAS & CŽJŽEK, c.1890. *Courtesy of Dagmar Braunová.*

Patterns for American export porcelain, form 1910. HAAS & CŽJŽEK, c.1890. *Courtesy of Dagmar Braunová.*

Patterns for American export porcelain, form 1910. HAAS & CŽJŽEK, c.1890. *Courtesy of Dagmar Braunová.*

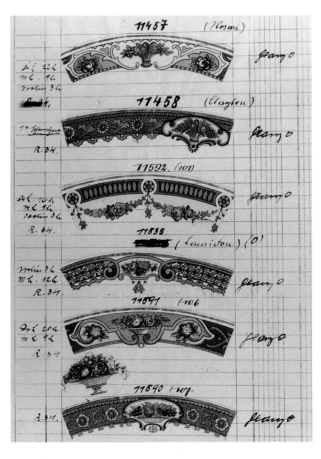

Rim patterns for American export porcelain, plate designs 11457, 11458, 11592, 11533, 11591 and 11590. HAAS & CŽJŽEK, c.1890. *Courtesy of Dagmar Braunová.*

APPENDIX 3.
DURATION OF BOHEMIAN PORCELAIN FACTORY OPERATION
IN KARLOVY VARY AREA

Town Name (German)	Date Founded	Factory Name	Date Closed	Factory Name
Horní Slavkov (Schlaggenwald)	1792	Johann GeorgPaulus	Open	Haas & Cžjžek
	1901	Anton Waldmann	1945	Sommer & Matschak
	1919	Bernhart & Co.	1928	Bernhart & Co.
Klášterec (Klösterle)	1794	Johann Nikolaus Weber	Open	Karlovarský Porcelán
Miřetice (Meretitz)	1910	Venier & Company	1921	Porcelain Union
	1910	August Wolf & Co.	1921	Porcelain Union
	1921	Porcelain Union	1939	EPIAG
	?	Julius Neuman Factory	ca. 1915	Julius Neuman Factory
Březová (Pirkenhammer)	1802	Höcke & List	Open	Artporcel, s.r.o. Manufaktura Pirkenhammer
Stružná (Gießhübel)	1803	Nonne & Rösch	1945	Porcelain Factory Gießhübel Johann Schuldes
Dalovice (Dallwitz)	1804	Ritter von Schönau Brothers	Open	EPIAG D.F. Porcelán Dalovice
Chodov (Chodau)	1811	Franz Mießl	Open	Karlovarský Porcelán
	1883	Richter, Fenkl & Hahn	1945	Fenkl & Langner
Stará Role (Altrohlau)	1811	Benedikt Haßlacher	Open	Starorolský Porcelán Moritz Zdekauer A. S.
	1870	William Pistor & Co.	1946	Franz Manka
	1876	Carl Weidermann	1946	Herbert Manka
	1883	"Victoria" Schmidt & Co.	Open	Karlovarský Porcelán
	1884	Marx & Gutherz	Open	Karlovarský Porcelán
	1886	Charles Ahrenfeldt & Son	1949	"Gloria" Porcelain Manufacturing Factory
	1904	J. Schneider & Co.	1949	Josef Lenhart
Loket (Elbogen)	1815	Haidinger Brothers	Open	Karlovarský Porcelán
	1886	Winter & Co.	1942	Johann Hoffman
	1890	Winter, Lochschmidt & Co.	1945	Porag, Porcelain Radiator GmbH
Rybáře (Fischern)	1848	Carl Knoll	1945	Carl Knoll
	1883	Bawo & Dotter	1913	Bawo & Dotter
Doubí (Aich)	1849	Johann Möhling	1933	EPIAG
Duchov(Dux)	1853	Edward Eichler	Open	Porcelánova Manufaktura Royal Dux Bohemia A. S.
	1883	C. Riese	Closed	C. Riese Porcelain, Terra Cotta and Majolica Factory
Merklín(Merkelsgrün)	1868	Becher & Stark	1945	Zettliz Kaolin Works
Ostrov (Schlackenwerth)	1873	Pfeiffer & Löwenstein	1949	Porcelain Factory Schlackenwerth Josef Pfeiffer
Dvory (Meierhöfen)	1883	Benedikt Brothers	Open	Hotelovy Porcelán A. S.
	1898	Moser Brothers	1918	Benedikt Brothers
Božičany (Poshetzau)	1890	I.S. Maier & Co.	1945	Poschetzau Porcelain Factory
Hory (Horn)	1897	Louise Klier	1930	H. Wehinger & Co. AG.
Karlovy Vary (Karlsbad)	1918	OEPIAG	1945	EPIAG
	1900	Josef Kuba	1945	Josef Kuba
Bochov (Buchau)	1902	Alfred Pollak	1945	Buchau Porcelain Factory Plaß & Roesner
Loučky (Grünlas)	1907	Benjamin Hunt	Open	Leander 1946 s.r.o.
Nová Role (Neurohlau)	1921	"Bohemian" Ceramic Works	Open	Karlovarský Porcelán

BIBLIOGRAPHY

A Biographical History of Prominent Men of the Great West. Chicago: Manhattan Publishing Company, 1894.

Karl Baedeker (Firm). *Austria-Hungary, including Dalmatia and Bosnia; Handbook for Travellers*, 10th ed. New York: Charles Scribner's Sons, 1905.

Karl Baedeker (Firm). *Baedeker's Czech/Slovak Republics.* New York: Prentice Hall, 1994.

Bagdade, Susan, and Al Bagdade. *Warman's English & Continental Pottery & Porcelain*, 2d ed. Radnor, Pennsylvania: Wallace-Homestead Book Company, 1991.

Baker, Lillian. *The Collector's Encyclopedia of Hatpins and Hatpin Holders.* Paducah, Kentucky: Collector Books, 1993.

Baker, Lillian. *Hatpins and Hatpin Holders. An Illustrated Value Guide.* Paducah, Kentucky: Collector Books, 1994.

Boger, Louise Ade. *The Dictionary of World Pottery and Porcelain.* New York: Charles Scribner's Sons, 1971.

Braunová, Alena. "The Origin and Development of Bohemian China Production Before the End of the Eighteenth Century." *Glass Review* 32(4) (1977): 11–17.

Braunová, Alena. "The Origin and Development of Bohemian China Production Before the End of the Eighteenth Century. The China Works at Klášterec nad Ohři." *Glass Review* 32(11) (1977): 13–18.

Braunová, Alena. *Kouzlo keramiky a porcelánu.* Praha: Delfin, 1978.

Braunová, Alena. *Kouzlo keramiky a porcelánu.* 2d ed. Praha: Delfin, 1985.

Braunová, Dagmar. *Porcelánová tradice.* Karlovy Vary: Haas & Czjzek, 1992.

Burley & Tyrrell (Firm). *English, Habsburg China and French Dinnerware.* Chicago: Burley & Tyrrell. Catalog No. 6, September, 1904.

Burley & Company (Firm). *White China for Decorating.* Chicago: Burley & Tyrrell. Catalog No. 19, circa 1910.

Butler Brothers (Firm). New York: Butler Brothers. Catalog, 1905.

Cameron, Elisabeth. *Encyclopedia of Pottery and Porcelain 1800–1960.* New York: Facts on File Publications, 1986.

Carek, Jiří. *MĚSTÉ ZNAKY v českých zemích.* Praha: Academia, 1985.

Celebrating 150 Years of Haviland China 1842–1992. Milwaukee, Wisconsin: Villa Terrace Decorative Arts Museum, 1992.

České menšiny, Oblast Národni Jednoty Severočeské. Národnostní menšiny, 1910.

China, Glass and Lamps (August 1930): 31–34.

China, Glass and Lamps (1933): 32.

Chládek, Jiří, and Ilona Nová. *Monografie Manufaktury v Březové (Pirkenhammer).* Karlovy Vary: Karlovarský porcelán, 1990.

Chládek, Jiří, and Ilona Nová. *Porcelán kolemnás.* Praha: Karlovarský porcelán, 1991.

Danckert, Ludwig. *Directory of European Porcelain.* 4th ed. London: N.A.G. Press, Ltd., 1981.

Downes, Richard. *History of Transfer Printing.* Society of Glass and Ceramic Decorators Meeting. Personal Communication, 1995.

Fą-Hallé, Antoinette, and Barbara Mundt. *Porcelain of the Nineteenth Century.* New York: Rizzoli, 1983.

Frackelton, Susan S. *Tried By Fire.* New York: D. Appleton and Company, 1892.

French & Potter Company (Firm). *Holiday Fancy Goods, Carlsbad China.* Chicago: French & Potter Co., Catalog, circa 1890.

Gaston, Mary Frank. *The Collector's Encyclopedia of Limoges Porcelain.* Paducah, Kentucky: Collector Books, 1992.

Godey's Ladies Book, (March 1859): 267.

Godden, Geoffrey A. *Godden's Guide to European Porcelain.* New York, London, Paris: Cross River Press, 1993.

Grandville, J. J. *Les fleurs animees.* Translated by Peter A. Wick as *The Court of Flora: the engraved illustrations of J. J. Grandville.* New York: G. Braziller, 1981.

Hamer, Frank. *The Potter's Dictionary of Materials and Techniques.* New York:Watson-Guptill Publications, 1975.

Hardmeyer, J. *Illustrated Europe. Carlsbad.* Zürich:Art. Institut Orell Füssli, 1888.

Higgins & Seiter (Firm). *China and Cut Glass–1899, Illustrated Catalog and Historical Introduction.* Princeton: The Pyne Press, 1971.

Hofmeisterová, Jana. "180 Years of Bohemian China." *Glass Review* 27(12) (1972): 371–380.

Kamm, Dorothy. *American Painted Porcelain: Collector's Indentification and Value Guide.* Paducah, Kentucky: Collector Books, 1997.

Karell, Viktor. "Die Unfänge der Zettlizer Kaolingewinnung," in *Karlsbader historiches Jahrbuch fur das Jahr 1939.* (Drud: Eger Verlag und Druderei, Gmb, 1939): 148–156.

Karell, Viktor. "Die Entwicklung der Zettlizer Kaolingewinnung," in *Karlsbader historiches Jahrbuch fur das Jahr 1941.* (Drud: Eger Verlag und Druderei, Gmb, 1941), Folge 4, 160–176.

Karell, Viktor. *Karlsbad von A bis Z, Ein Stadtlexikon.* München: Aufstieg-Verlag, 1971.

Karsnitz, Jim, and Vivian Karsnitz. *Oyster Plates.* Atglen, Pennsylvania: Schiffer Publishing, Ltd., 1993.

Kovel, Ralph, and Terry Kovel. *Kovel's New Dictionary of Marks.* New York: Crown Publishers, Inc., 1986.

Kraus, R. Mario. "The Březová China Factory." *Glass Review* 27(11) (1972): 333–339.

Ladies Home Journal (February 1900): 19–20.

Ladies Home Journal (November 1910): 24.

Mauer-Campana Art Company (Firm). Chicago: Mauer-Campana Art Co., Catalog No. 100, August, 1929.

W. A. Mauer Company. Chicago: W. A. Mauer Company, Catalog No. 210, January 1951.

Machatá, Olga. "125 Years Existence of the Duchcov China Works." *Glass Review* 33(7) (1978): 2–5.

Machatá, Olga. "The Thun Mark – Known Throughout the World." *Glass Review* 34(9) (1979): 21–24.

Machatá, Olga. "In the Beginning is Kaolin ... ." *Glass Review* 38(4) (1983): 5–7.

Machatá, Olga. "Two Crossed Hammers – A Trademark Known for 180 Years." *Glass Review* 38(5) (1983): 6–11.

Machleidtová, Vlasta. "The 170th Anniversary of the Dalovice Works." *Glass Review* 27(5) (1972): 141–143.

Machleidtová, Vlasta. "The 180th Anniversary of the China Works at at Klášterec nad Ohři (Klösterle)." *Glass Review* 29(12) (1974): 5–6.

Maršiková, J. "Loket and China." *Glass Review* 27(8) (1972): 241–245.

Meyer, Hans. *Böhmisches Porzellan und Steingut*. Leipzig: Verlag Karl W. Hiersemann, 1927.

Moore, Ralph. *Porcelain and Pottery Tea Tiles*. Marietta, Ohio: Antique Publications, 1994.

Neuwirth, Waltraud. *Porzellanmaler-Lexikon 1840–1914*, 2 vols. Braunschweig: Klinkhardt & Biermann, 1977.

Osgood, A. H. *Catalog and Price List of Supplies Required for China Decoration*. New York: Osgood Art School, 1903.

Poche, Emanuel. *Bohemian Porcelain*. Praha: Artia, 1954.

Ray, Marcia. *Collectible Ceramics*. New York: Crown Publishers, Inc., 1974.

Reed, Alan. *Collector's Encyclopedia of Pickard China*. Paducah, Kentucky: Collector Books, 1995.

Řehořík, E. "175 Years of Existence of the China Works at Březová." *Glass Review* 33(5) (1978): 2–5.

Röntgen, Robert E. *Marks on German, Bohemian and Austrian Porcelain–1710 to the Present*. Atglen, Pennsylvania: Schiffer Publishing, Ltd., 1981.

Rudolph, H. *Vollständstes geographisch-topgraphisch-statistisches ORTS-LEXIKON von DEUTSCHLAND sowie der unter Oesterreichs und Preussens Botmässsigkeit stehenden nichtdeutschen Länder*, 2 vols. Leipiz: Louis Zander, 1870.

Strejc, Josef. "Kaolin–Czechoslovakia's White Gold." *Glass Review* 29(9) (1974): 8–10.

Savage, George, and Newman, Harold. *Illustrated Dictionary of Ceramics*. New York: Van Nostrand Reinhold Co., 1974.

Schleiger, Donna. *Two Hundred Patterns of Haviland China*. Book VI. Redlands, California: Donna Schleiger Publisher, 1991.

Schleiger, Donna. *Handbook for Identifying Haviland China*. Redlands, California: Donna Schleiger Publisher, 1991.

Sears, Roebuck & Company (Firm). Chicago: Sears, Roebuck & Co. Catalog No. 104, 1897, 685.

Sears, Roebuck & Company (Firm). Chicago: Sears, Roebuck & Co. Catalog No. 117, 1908, 355.

Sears, Roebuck & Company (Firm). Chicago: Sears, Roebuck & Co. Catalog No. 127, 1913, 655.

Sears, Roebuck & Company (Firm). Chicago: Sears, Roebuck & Co. Catalog No. 129, 1914, 734–755.

Straus Family Papers 1810–1962. New York Public Library Archives, 1992.

Thayer & Chandler (Firm). *Artist's China, Parchment Shades*. Chicago: Thayer & Chandler, Catalog No. 54, 1923.

Thayer & Chandler (Firm). Chicago: Thayer & Chandler, February Supplement Catalog No. 57, 1925.

Thayer & Chandler (Firm). *Artist's China, China, Parchment Shades, Lustrcraft, Oriental Lacquers*. Chicago: Thayer & Chandler, Catalog No. 58, 1925.

U.S. Department of Commerce, Bureau of Foreign and Domestic Commerce, *The Pottery Industry, Report on the Cost of Production in the Earthenware and China Industries of the United States, England, Germany, and Austria*. 1915 Miscellaneous Series, no. 21.

Wakefield, David. *Fragonard*. London: Oresko Books Ltd., 1976.

Ware, George W. *German & Austrian Porcelain*. New York: Crown Publishers, Inc., 1963.

Weiss, Gustav. *The Book of Porcelain*. New York: Praeger Publishers, 1971.

Wendler, Ljuboš. "The Research Institute of Fine Ceramics at Karlovy Vary-Březová." *Glass Review* 28(2) (1973): 12–15.

Williams, Laurence W. *Collector's Guide to Souvenir China*. Paducah, Kentucky: Collector Books, 1998.

Williams, Susan. *Savory Suppers and Fashionable Feasts*. New York: Pantheon Books, 1985.

Williams-Wood, Cyril. *English Transfer-Printed Pottery and Porcelain*. London, Boston: Faber and Faber, 1981.

Wood, Serry. *Hand-painted China*. Watkins Glen, New York: Century House, 1953.

Zemepisny Lexikon CR. Obce a sidla A-M, Stav k polvine 80.let. Zpracoval kolektiv autoru. Bozena Novakova, ed. Praha: Academia, 1991.

Zimmermann, Heinrich. 1990. *Porzellanfabriken in Böhmen, 1791–1945*. Edited by Anna Gnirs. München: Sudentendeutsches Archiv. Riess-Druck und Verlag Benediktbeuren, 1990.

Zühlsdorff, Dieter. *Markenlexikon, Porzellan und Keramik Report 1885 –1935*. Stuttgart: Arnoldsche, 1989.